Women in Society

INTERDISCIPLINARY ESSAYS

The Cambridge Women's Studies Group

Virago

Published by VIRAGO PRESS limited 1981
Ely House, 37 Dover Street, London W1X 4HS

Copyright (C) The Cambridge Women's Studies Group

Typeset by Colset Pte. Limited and printed in
Great Britain by The Anchor Press, Tiptree, Essex

British Library Cataloguing in Publication Data
Women in society.
    1. Women – Social conditions
    I. Cambridge Women's Studies Group
    305.2   HQ1121
ISBN 0-86068-083-5

HQ1121
.W89
1981

Contents

Introduction

This book is the product of a group of women who organise and teach a 'Women in Society' course in the University of Cambridge. The course was set up in 1973 by a group of feminists who had, as part of their aim, the confrontation of discriminatory practices against women in the University by making the analysis of sexual divisions a legitimate object of study. Although there has been some continuity in the membership of the collective, women join and leave each year, thereby changing the political views represented on it. Nevertheless we feel that, over the last seven years, we have managed to create a coherent and integrated course which is both interdisciplinary and politically relevant. This book is largely constructed out of work which initially formed part of teaching sessions on the course.

When the course first started, it consisted of a rather uncomfortable mixture of attempts to 'write women back' into various disciplines, and discussions on issues of immediate political concern to feminists, such as abortion or low pay. There are plenty of good reasons, both political and academic, for using the study of women and sexual divisions to reflect on traditional disciplinary boundaries. In the first place, the fact that women have been ignored as an object of study in many disciplines should lead to a more cautious approach to the received truth of such disciplines. In the second, making women 'visible' often changes the theories of a discipline. Thus the fact that many sociological studies assign women a class position on the basis of that of their husband or father not only casts considerable doubt on the usefulness of such studies, but calls into question the theories upon which they are based. Another example comes from anthropology, where much research, while not making women as 'invisible' as some other disciplines do, tends to cast ethnographic descriptions of society in terms of the views of their male members and concentrates on male activities and public life. The approach of 'writing women back' into different disciplines and areas of study — women and history; women and the law; women and psychology — is one adopted by many women's studies courses, but is, we feel, unsatisfactory if left at that.

The problem of this approach is that it follows the confines of traditional disciplinary boundaries; we have become increasingly convinced that the only way to move away from this towards a fresh analysis is to break down some of these confines. In practice, we found it difficult to forge a relation between this kind of analysis and the political aspects of feminism which were also a central concern. The difficulty here was that we had no unifying framework within which to place work on issues such as current abortion campaigns, changes in the legislation governing women's pay or discriminatory practices in schools, other than the notion of 'women's oppression'. This may be useful as a political slogan but will not do as a unifying explanation for the enormous diversity of social forms that sexual difference and division takes.

This difficulty with finding a unifying framework for the analysis of women's political struggles is mirrored by the difficulties involved in generating a theory which can 'explain' the diversities of the empirical material uncovered under the rubric of 'women's studies' in the last ten years. Attempts to produce theories using this knowledge have included 'explanations' of the position of women, either in some particular respect or universally, as the sex opposed and subordinated to men; this is a matter of trying to fit new material into some existing theoretical framework, be it psychoanalytic, Marxian, structuralist or whatever. Yet what defines 'woman' and 'man' changes from one social group to another and is often in contradiction within the same social group.

At first sight, it might seem as if concepts like male/female, man/woman, individual/family, are so self-evident that they have no need of 'decoding', but can simply be traced through various historical or social changes. These changes would, for example, give a seventeenth-century English woman a different social identity from a low-caste Indian woman of today, or would ascribe different functions to the family in industrial and pre-industrial societies. But the problem with both of these examples is that they leave the alleged subject of these changes (woman, the family) with an apparently coherent identity which is shuffled from century to century or from society to society as if it was something that already existed independent of particular circumstances. One purpose of this book, and of our course as it has gradually evolved, is to question that coherency: to show that it is constructed out of social givens which can themselves be subjected to similar questioning. This book, therefore, concentrates on themes that return to the social rather than to the individual sphere, emphasising the social construction of sexual difference.

We concentrate on themes that 'return to the social' not because we deny the individual experience of women but because the meaning and interpretation of this both for the women themselves and for the society of which they are a part, will not be found by taking the terms 'woman' and 'oppression' as pre-given. Nor, we feel, will it do to fall back on explanations of women's oppression in terms of, for instance, male coercion by physical force, or by conscious, rational, social control. Coercion, even naked physical coercion, succeeds or fails within an ideological context and a changing one at that. Thus violence against women cannot simply be equated across cultures or historical periods; it must be understood in terms of its specific emergence and repercussions at any one point. To give a concrete case, the possibilities open for action against wife-beating are very different now, when there is considerable ambiguity about whether such behaviour is permissible or not, from what they were when such practices were openly admitted as a normal and natural part of marriage. In fact, this book continually seeks to question definitions of 'women' which are framed in terms of 'the biological' or 'the natural'.

Our emphasis on redefining ideas of oppression and coercion is, therefore, not merely a matter of words, for it contains within it the seeds of an analysis which allows for change and thus, we feel, has political relevance. We know from our collective experience as feminists that the determinants of women's oppression are not all-powerful and static – they shift in substance and in emphasis.

A question that arises with any material of this kind, however conceived and wherever studied, is whether its subject-matter is somehow temporary and 'transitional'. Women's studies and feminist studies are still relatively new and exciting, but what is their future? The answer to this must surely be bound up with the question of whether a feminist movement will become dispensable at a certain stage of social development, when a combination of social, institutional and psychological changes might be argued to have guaranteed the place of women in relation to men. A basic question then, is whether any distinction between the sexes will always imply a power relation. Whatever the answer to this, we are convinced that, as long as the sexes are socially distinct, there will be a need for a critical examination of the social relations based on sex. There will always be an urgent need for feminist theoretical work, and, more important, for an active politics of feminism. The book reflects, we hope, these theoretical and political considerations. It attempts to show that facts are never 'self-evident', and thereby to counter the over-simplifications inherent in assertions both of women's 'natural inferiority' and of their 'oppression'.

This book is organised into four sections, each of which emphasises a particular theme or approach. The first section concentrates on the position of women under capitalism. It is impossible to understand the sexual division of labour in the paid labour force without an analysis which situates women in the reproductive cycle — in terms both of the economy, and of the ideology which goes to support lower wages, less job security, and no socialised childcare for women workers. We begin with a discussion of theories of women's position in the paid labour market; then we turn to psychological, historical and political theories about women as mothers, and in the family.

The second section is devoted to a number of topics which, when analysed together, turn out to be particularly revealing as consequences of the confining and repressive definitions of sex roles: mental illness, and the physical and mental violence practised against women. Here we face the problem of trying to locate and analyse the agencies by which women are controlled and coerced into conformity with sex-role expectations.

Section three describes and comments on past and present feminist campaigning around, and theoretical responses to, problems of sexuality and of sexual definitions and categories. Questions of both the technical and social grounds for the implementation of a more genuine choice in fertility control are raised. Here we are dealing directly with the intersections between an individual experience (of, for example, depression, or contraceptive use, or physical attack) and the external context of such experience: we attempt not only to understand the constraints on women, but also to locate possibilities for loosening them.

The fourth and last section examines two theoretical frameworks in which attempts have been made to present explanations for sexual divisions which cut across any particular form of social organisation. We analyse the uses that have been made of the terms 'nature' and 'culture', both in the identification of women as nearer to 'nature', and in the definition of certain things as 'natural' and thereby unchangeable — particularly those attributes or behaviours which are regarded as part of the biological make-up of one or the other sex. In conclusion, we look at recent attempts by feminists to account for the 'universal subordination of women' in terms of a theory of patriarchy.

Section 1

Women, the Family and Wage Labour under Capitalism

Chapter One

Work and the Family: who gets 'the best of both worlds'?[1]

JUDY WAJCMAN

The main aim of this article is to review sociological accounts of women as workers. Although women are an integral part of the British labour force, concern with women workers has never been among the major preoccupations of industrial sociology. Most studies of workers in industry still deal solely with men. Those that do feature women either fail to differentiate them from men or treat them as giving rise to special problems.[2] My argument here is that women's position in the labour market, as well as their experience of work, can only be understood in conjunction with an analysis of sexual divisions within the household. For both women and men, the experience of work is mediated by their place in the family. However, women and men, by virtue of their gender, occupy different social situations and this leads to diverging perceptions of work. The next chapter in this book examines theories about sexual divisions in the labour market. The focus of this chapter is the relationship between women's domestic labour and their wage labour.

I begin with a critique of some early sociological accounts of the problems posed by married women in employment. Although much of this literature has been superseded, it is still, as we shall see, influential as a model for analysing women's relation to wage labour. Next, I turn to studies which both deal with women's experience of work and examine this together with men's work experience. The third section will consider the body of literature known as the 'domestic labour debate'. Finally, I shall attempt to relate the domestic economy to the ideology of domesticity. It should be noted at the outset that this review is primarily concerned with *married* women workers.

Women's 'two roles'

Myrdal and Klein's book *Women's Two Roles* was first published in 1956. It established the intellectual parameters of subsequent sociological studies concerned with the position of women in post-war Britain.[3] These studies contain a number of common features: they are all responses to what was thought to be a recent and significant social development, namely, the increasing proportion of married women 'going out to work'. Writing in a period of post-war reconstruction, these authors tend to consider the increasing integration of married women into the work force as both a dramatic and a potentially disruptive social change. In Klein's words: 'In these circumstances it is of great importance to investigate how this potential labour reserve can be drawn upon without upsetting production techniques, existing labour relations, or the private lives of men, women, and children' (Klein, 1965, p.88). Their 'social problem' perspective, which emphasises the *novelty* of married women going out to work in this period, is concerned with how adjustments might be made to accommodate this trend.[4] There is an implicit assumption, however, that generally life is 'getting better' with industrialisation, and that this justifies the further assumption that, like everything else, women's position must also be improving. The effects of industrialisation cited as specifically affecting the position of women in employment are summarised by Jephcott, Seear and Smith (1962, p.135), in *Married Women Working*, as: smaller families, better health, improved services and lighter domestic chores. Although most of these books give a brief historical introduction, there is considerable ignorance of the exact nature of women's position before 'industrialisation', so that the significance of the supposedly crucial changes, such as the amount of domestic labour needed in the home, women's participation in production, and changes in sex roles and status, is difficult to assess.[5]

These studies assume that 'work' is inherently pleasant, so that all a woman needs to forsake the home and enter the labour market is the *opportunity* to do so. Thus there is no longer:

> the need for women to make a fatal decision between irreconcilable alternatives. The Gordian knot of a seemingly insoluble feminine dilemma has been cut. The technical and social developments of the last few decades have given women the opportunity to integrate their two interests in Home and Work. . . . No longer need women forego the pleasures of one sphere in order to enjoy the satisfactions of the other. The best of both worlds has come within their grasp, if only they reach out for it. (Myrdal and Klein, 1956, p.xvi)

From such statements the suspicion grows that this literature confronts not the problems of women *generally* but specifically those of middle-class *professional* women, who can enter the labour market for 'pleasure' and not out of financial necessity. This is not to say that working-class women do not feature in these studies, but that the discussion reflects a preoccupation with middle-class values. These values are concerned with choice, equal opportunities, pursuit of a career, the attainment of which is not within the grasp of the majority of either working-class or middle-class women. There is nothing new about women going out to work. During this century women have always constituted at least 30 per cent of the labour force. For most women, the choice to work is still really no choice at all; many more families would come near the 'poverty line' without the wife's income.[6] Working-class women have long been accustomed to 'enjoying the satisfactions' of work. It is clearly not possible to make generalisations about the reasons for women as a group entering and leaving the labour market in a capitalist society without first understanding the *class composition* of this female labour force.

Disregarding such class distinctions, the 'two roles' literature embarks on a consideration of women's greater motivation to go out to work today. Although it is assumed that any 'conflict' between women's two roles can be resolved by technology and social reforms, most of the writers would be in agreement with Klein (1965, p.76) when she concludes that: 'The outstanding impression gained from this survey is that women's lives, today as much as ever, are dominated by their role — actual or expected — as wives or mothers.' Thus women are seen as regarding their 'home' role as primary and waged work as secondary and, when they do go out to work, as having a lower commitment to it than men. My argument is that by concentrating on attitudes, this body of literature loses sight of the social context which imposes limits on women's behaviour. In order to understand the formation and significance of attitudes, we need first to examine the practical constraints which operate in the domestic sphere.

To take the first point: whether and in what proportion this 'natural' tendency of women to put the 'home' first is a question of need or pleasure is a moot point, and one not tackled by these studies. Does the 'conflict' between women's two roles just mean *too much* work, or does it mean that the two kinds of work are, in themselves, incompatible? These authors conceptualise this conflict in subjective terms, as an individual 'feminine dilemma', ignoring its social basis. Without a more precise understanding of the *different kinds* of constraint on women in different social positions to either 'want to go out to work' or to say 'my family must come first', we shall not know what such statements mean.

The second point, that of women's lower 'commitment' to work, raises somewhat different problems. Certainly we can get answers to the question: 'Do you think your family is more important than your work?' — but when it comes to *elucidating* the answers, in other words finding out what this relative 'importance' consists of, then we find that there is a whole host of further questions which are raised by this notion of 'commitment'. A woman may, for example, be 'committed' to housework either in the sense that she is house-proud, or in the sense that if she fails to do it her husband will beat her. To make such a vaguely defined attitude into a key variable in discussions of the problems faced by working-class women in the factory and in the home is to obscure more important and more practical questions. What is to be done, for example, if your child comes out of school at 4 p.m., and there is no employment available that will enable you to be outside the school at that time? There will be a number of *practical* constraints on the choice of solutions to such a problem. Given that women still bear primary responsibility for children, it is they who have to adjust their working lives to these obligations. Men do not have to make such adjustments; children's illness, for example, is not a legitimate or customary reason for men taking time off work. Does it follow from this that men are more committed to work? The notion of 'commitment' implies that the 'choices' made by married women — such as whether to work part-time or full-time — are a matter of will, rather than being largely determined by *structured* social arrangements.

Finally, a basic flaw in this literature results from its treating women workers in isolation, as a 'special study'. It is assumed that married women who work are problematic in a way that men are not. 'Married women are asked "why do you work?", a question whose equivalent in the study of men's work-attitudes is "why aren't you working?"' [7] This approach means that the scope for conducting studies which *compare* the motivation and behaviour of women and men in employment is severely diminished. While it is true to say that for women the family is still in certain respects the area of prime importance, the situation is not so very different amongst men. At the time that Myrdal and Klein were writing *Women's Two Roles*, Dubin (1956) was noting that almost 3/4 of American industrial workers did not see work as a central life interest. In Britain, Goldthorpe *et al.* (1969) 'discovered' a family centred life style as the norm among affluent male manual workers. More recently, in a survey of unqualified male manual workers in a wide variety of jobs, almost 90 per cent of married respondents rated a 'good family life at home' above enjoyment of their work life.[8] That men also put 'home' first is completely ignored by the 'two roles' literature, which is only about women.

Although working-class men and women have low expectations of work, and work is thus not a 'central life interest', this does not *mean* the same for men as for women. Some married women are in the position of being able to choose whether they take a job or not — no such choice is normally open to men. The expectation that men *have to have* a regular job and that women have to see that the children are cared for is reflected in social arrangements and becomes the basis of constraints. Furthermore, married men see themselves and are seen as the 'breadwinners', and to a large extent it is supporting their family which gives work meaning. Men's social identity within the family is shaped by this ideology of the 'male breadwinner'. For women, the work role as a source of social identity is largely replaced by the domestic roles of wife and mother. Now, the female role may be more rewarding, in that home life is more rewarding for both sexes, but it is linked with other inequalities which will emerge in the course of this article.

By focusing on women workers, the 'two roles' literature made a valuable break with male-oriented industrial sociology. It also provided some useful information, including the stages in the life cycle when women engage in paid work. More recently, Young and Willmott's *The Symmetrical Family* has perpetuated this optimism about women's changing role resulting from their entry into the work force. They argue that the effect of the increasing proportion of married women in paid employment is that marriage is becoming an egalitarian relationship. This increased marital symmetry, in the sense of a changed division of labour in the home, means that:

> Husbands also do a lot of work in the home, including many jobs which are not at all traditional men's ones. . . . There is now no sort of work in the home strictly reserved for 'the wives', even clothes-washing and bed-making, still ordinarily thought of as women's jobs, were frequently mentioned by husbands as things they did as well. The extent of the sharing is probably still increasing. (Young and Willmott, 1975, p.94)

However, they still maintained that most married women are less committed to their jobs: work means something different for women and does not reflect a weaker commitment to their domestic role. For Young and Willmott, the very fact of more married women working necessarily entails greater sharing of domestic labour between husbands and wives.

What Young and Willmott fail to see is that this 'lesser commitment' to their jobs may simply reflect women's acquisition of a paid work role *in addition* to their domestic one. In *The Sociology of Housework*, Oakley argues convincingly that while attitudes towards the sharing and organisation of housework have become more egalitarian, changes in behaviour have been much less marked. Husbands do not share domestic tasks equally with their wives. Rather, women remain *responsible* for housework and childcare, and husbands 'help' wives do their domestic work.

Furthermore, Young and Willmott completely ignore the fact that even when married women are employed, there is still an economic basis for marriage as a relationship of inequality. The majority of married women workers barely earn a subsistence wage. This leaves them dependent on their husband's wages for part of the living costs of themselves and their children. This lack of potential economic independence, even of employed women, is particularly important in perpetuating the domestic division of labour in its present form. Young and Willmott fail to make this connection because, as in the 'two roles' literature, they provide no analysis of sexual divisions in the labour market. Such an analysis would recognise the especially exploitative relationship between employers and their female employees — in particular, mothers who generally work part-time or as homeworkers. Ignoring the influence of discrimination in the labour market on women's experience of wage labour, Young and Willmott are left speculating on this problem in the conclusion to their chapter on 'The Work of Married Women': 'Many of the least psychologically rewarding jobs are reserved for women, as if to ensure that the competitive power of the home remains supreme' (1975, p.122).

Work and life cycle

An advance on the 'two roles' literature was provided by Lupton (1963), Cunnison (1966), and Beynon and Blackburn (1972), in their studies of the actual *work experience* of working-class women.[9] By studying women and men workers in the same factory, they were able to examine how sexual divisions in society produce *different* 'orientations to work' in women and men. For instance, rather than setting up simple alternatives of work or family 'roles' as being primary, Beynon and Blackburn argue that work experience and attitudes must be understood in the context of people's whole lives. The way in which the family provides the major meaning in life and work is evaluated in relation to family needs. Thus, their emphasis is on the way in which women's and men's orientations to work are filtered through their position within the family.

A particular attraction of this study, *Perceptions of Work*, is that it draws attention to the way in which women employees must be differentiated in terms of *life cycle* situation and experience, as well as the influence of the *labour market* on orientations.[10]

> It was their position within the labour market in combination with their position within the family which produced their particular and distinctive orientation toward the workplace. . . . This tendency for women to centre their lives around their position in the home has been reinforced by severe discrimination against them in the employment market. (Beynon and Blackburn, 1972, pp.159, 146)

Occupational segregation in the labour market means that few women are likely to be found in work situations identical to those of men. For working-class women all jobs are much the same, being essentially routine, low paid and lacking advancement possibilities, so that the attractions of work are substantially independent of the nature of the actual job. Recognition of the limited job opportunities available lowers women's involvement in work and reinforces 'commitment' to their domestic role.

I should like now to turn to the impact of life cycle changes on women's orientations to work.[11] Beynon and Blackburn (1972, pp.24–5) distinguish five stages in the life cycle in relation to work life. First, there is the time before marriage, when financial responsibilities are low; then there are the years of marriage before having children, followed by the period when the children are young and the wife is at home to care for them; as the children grow older, and make still greater demands on the parental income, the mother may return to work; finally the children grow up and become independent, after which the mother is free to work if she wishes, the financial pressures are eased and the next landmark is retirement. Other essays in this book discuss how women's oppression is also rooted in their reproductive role, but it is important to note here the far-reaching effects of this on the organisation of women's whole lives. The form that the life cycle takes is a cultural rather than a 'natural' one; there are social expectations for appropriate behaviour at each stage of the life cycle. What is needed is a careful elaboration of the developmental element of family life and its consequences for women's relation to employment.

Unfortunately, when Beynon and Blackburn come to discuss their data, for the most part they only really distinguish between two groups: single women and married women with children. The same can be said of Cunnison and Lupton. I would argue that further significant distinctions *within* the category of married women must be drawn. These three books all contain similar observations about the distinctive expectations of employment that the two groups of women have. To quote from Beynon and Blackburn's discussion of a group of women, the majority of whom were single and aged under 30:

> Most of the women who worked full-time did have to support themselves, however, so good pay and security were quite important to them. . . their interest in security lay between that of the part-time women and that of the men. . . . Their main attachment to their jobs lay in friendships with workmates. (1972, p.149)

They contrast this group with those who worked part-time, all of whom were married with children:

> They worked to supplement the family income but within the range open to them the actual amount was not so important. The other main reason for working was escape from the loneliness at home to the companionship of work. (1972, p.147)

The authors conclude that neither group had high expectations concerning the intrinsic nature of the job, but that the expectations of the full-time group were higher than those of the part-time group. For the married women, working hours that could be conveniently fitted in with their family commitments were their main concern; 'beyond this their expectations were very low'. In order to go beyond seeing differences in orientations of women employees simply in terms of whether they are single or married with children, it is necessary to treat the household economy seriously, by examining the distribution of labour and resources within it. Beynon and Blackburn fail to do this in their empirical work, so it is unclear what they mean when they write about women's 'position' within the life cycle. True, it is a more sophisticated notion than that of women's 'roles', but the specific connection between women's 'position' in the life cycle and their 'orientations' to work remains unexplained, except for identifying marriage as a point of differentiation, and a general reference to responsibility for childcare thereafter. An adequate analysis will have to be directed, in part, to distinguishing in this life cycle 'position' between components originating in the household economy (the domestic division of labour and women's management of the family budget), in psychological disposition (the ideology of domesticity/motherhood), and so on. Then childcare can be seen as just one part of women's work within the domestic division of labour.

Although these studies did emphasise the centrality of the family, their investigation of its significance for explanations of women's and men's orientations to work did not go far enough. There is, however, a body of literature which does attempt to analyse the family and the work that goes on within it. Initiated by feminists, the ensuing debate raised and explored the important question of domestic labour. This is the subject of the next section. But before embarking on this, it may be helpful to illustrate some of the points made above by turning briefly to my own study of working women.

Differentiating between married women

This study, conducted over the last three years, was of a women's co-operative factory in Fakenham. The work force there was divided into two shifts: the full time shift from 8.30 a.m. to 5 p.m. and the part time from 9 a.m. to 3.30 p.m. The full time shift comprised women who were single, or were married with grown-up children. The part-time workers were mainly women with school-age children, the age of the *youngest* child being the crucial determinant. Unlike the full time workers, they were in the stage of the life cycle when financial strain was greatest.

In the course of this study it emerged that the way in which the work force was polarised, over decision-making for example, often corres-ponded to the division between the two shifts. This division developed into a critical conflict over whether to accept a contract that entailed expansion of the full time shift at a time when the factory was des-perate for work. The part timers felt torn between their need for a part time job and the likelihood that the factory would have to close if they refused to work full time. For them, this factory was one of the few sources of employment that fitted in with school hours. They had experienced redundancy many times before and had little prospect of finding alternative employment. Despite this, and their need for the money, it was impossible for them to transfer from the part-time to the full-time shift. In the absence of any childcare provision after school and during school holidays, part-time employment represented for these women the only means of providing economic support for their families without sacrificing what they regarded as vital domestic commitments, especially to their children.

It was not just their attachment to a notion of maternity that res-tricted these women to part time work, but an accurate assessment of the repercussions for their children of a decision to work full-time. By contrast, having no childcare responsibilities around which to organise their employment, the women who worked full-time experienced no such conflict. For them the issue was clear — they would all lose their jobs if the part-timers refused to extend their hours. In this context they resented the part-time workers, while at the same time acknowledging that domestic responsibilities must come first. What this episode demonstrates is that the demands imposed by domestic responsibilities must be a central consideration in a full account of women's wage labour. It is women's stage in the life cycle that designates the precise nature of these responsibilities. By glossing over the significance of domestic labour, the theories outlined above could not embrace the complexities of home-work relations.

The domestic labour debate

The starting-point of what is known as the 'domestic labour debate' is the contention that sexual subordination flows from the sexual division of labour, which under capitalism takes the extreme form of separating the general economic process into domestic and industrial spheres, with women being relegated primarily to the domestic sphere.[12] Women are identified as domestic workers, responsible for the reproduction of the labour force; this involves maintenance and socialisation, as well as biological reproduction. With the development of commodity production, domestic work becomes separated from social production and takes the form of privatised, individual work. This division of labour is not neutral, but involves the denigration of housework, which disappears from the field of 'economic' activity. Although with the development of capitalism (in particular, the emergence of modern industry) the family becomes separated from the sphere of production, the labour performed within the family is essential for the reproduction of labour and of the social relations of capitalist production.

Different positions were taken in this debate as to how to conceptualise domestic work within the categories of Marx's labour theory of value. The contributors wanted to demonstrate that capital directly or indirectly appropriates the surplus labour of the housewife as surplus value. The questions which dominated the debate were: what part if any does domestic labour play in the creation of surplus value; and if surplus value is created by domestic labour, how is it appropriated by capital? The point of this was to show that not only do husbands benefit from the work of their wives, but capitalism also profits from unpaid domestic work. This, then, was said to be the explanation for the existence, persistence and even necessity of privatised domestic work under capitalism.

The value of the analysis of domestic labour was that it showed how women, working in the home without remuneration, and beyond the direct domination of capital, produce use-values for immediate consumption within the family. Whilst the most recent contributions to the debate have finally rejected the idea that domestic labour can create value or surplus value, the existence of the family and/or domestic labour is still ascribed to the functional requirements of capital.[13] Now it is one thing to say that the privatised toil of housewives persists because it raises the level of subsistence, but it is quite another to say that domestic labour is *necessary* for capitalism. This kind of functionalist economic reductionism prevented the contributors from seeing that it is on the basis of marriage and parenthood that the housewife's work is related to social labour. The marriage contract, and not the market, mediates this exchange; the marriage contract cannot be understood simply as an economic relation. It is precisely because of this — the relative autonomy of intra-familial relations — that substantial variation in the standards of domestic work and the time spent on it is possible.

The departure point of both the 'domestic labour debate' and of Oakley's *Sociology of Housework* (1974) is thus fundamentally misconceived. Both conceptualise housework as being analogous to wage labour, the former in terms of Marx's labour theory of value and the latter in terms of conventional industrial sociology. Yet domestic work is private and involves very different relations of production from wage work. In obscuring this, both attempts lose sight of what gives housework its distinctive character.

Further shortcomings flow from this framework. There is a tendency to assume that women are typically full-time housewives, and that all housewives do the same amount of housework. In this sense, the Marxist writing was a step back to the 'two roles' literature. Also, it failed to take into account the effects of variations in women's domestic workload over the course of the life cycle; these are attributable to women's responsibility for childcare, the most time-consuming element of their work. Ironically, a debate which set out to explore the relationship between women's paid and unpaid work became preoccupied with the identification of the two and ended up devoting exclusive attention to theorising the nature of housework, thus losing sight of its own original intention.

Moreover, this literature on the 'political economy of women' does not even provide a basis for understanding the household economy as a set of economic and labour relations within the family. As mentioned earlier, the degree of financial strain on the family fluctuates with the life cycle; these variations impinge significantly on married women, and in particular on whether they work from choice or necessity. This economic interdependence of wives and husbands is a crucial factor in the understanding of women's entry into and experience of wage labour. What urgently needs to be examined is the still unexplored area of the management and distribution of resources *within* the household. The concept of the household, with its concomitant image of all family members having equal call on a collective income, remains in current use amongst historians, economists and sociologists. This despite (or because of) the fact that little is known about the distribution of the family income *between* its members — a problem mentioned by Michael Young in 1952 that still persists.[14] From such work as has been done, it emerges that the differential distribution of tasks between wives and husbands is mirrored by a similarly unequal allocation of resources. The repercussions of this on women's relation to wage labour need to be elaborated.

The ideology of domesticity

The 'political economy of women' provides us with an account of domestic labour as the provision of a 'free' service not only to capital, but also to husbands. What remains to be explained is the origin and persistence of the *understanding* that domestic labour is *women's* work. At no point does the Marxian analysis of domestic labour address this issue. Rather, we find questions about the necessity of domestic labour under capitalism confused with questions about the ideological apparatus of female subordination. The ideology of domesticity is a distinctive factor in accounting for the different commitment of women and men to paid labour.

To appreciate the primacy that women themselves give to the domestic sphere, I turn briefly to Ann Oakley's characterisation of the feminine gender role.[15] In *Housewife*, she sets out to examine the emergence and nature of the 'modern housewife' role, through the exclusive allocation of housework and childcare to women. The essential constituents of femininity identified by Oakley are 'domesticity' and 'maternity'; the sense of 'being a housewife' is deeply rooted in self-identity as feminine. 'It is the interaction of the two which distinguishes the situation of the female (housewife-wife-mother) from that of the male (husband-father)' (Oakley, 1976a, p.78). Essentially, Oakley sees marriage as a relationship of inequality, in which the domestic oppression of women as unpaid labourers, housewives and childrearers is maintained and reproduced. She sees the relations of dominance and dependence structured by the institution of marriage as stemming from the sexual division of labour within the family. Bearing in mind that Oakley's work is limited to full-time housewives, this concept of the housewife role as an amalgam of domesticity and maternity nevertheless might contribute to an understanding of why women with a 'work role' should continue to be dominated by their 'home role'. Women in the labour force may be 'psychologically involved' with the housewife role in such a way that all experience, including that in the workplace, is filtered through a primarily domestic perspective.

Psychological identification with the domestic world is, then, one determinant of women's 'commitment' to housework, as well as of their 'motives' for entering paid employment. However, we must beware accepting explanations of, for example, women's low job expectations that are couched solely in psychological terms. These expectations must themselves be located in a materialist account of women's position in the family and in the labour market. In particular, married women's *experience* of severely limited job opportunities shapes their orientations to wage labour, irrespective of their attachment to the domestic-maternal role. It is the grounding of women's expectations of work in their actual experience both in paid employment and in the family that this paper has tried to emphasise.

The literature we have been considering here reveals, on close examination, a sad lack of sophistication. It is apparent that we have come almost full circle, back to the 'two roles' literature, which at least made an original contribution by focusing on women workers as women. But, whilst the 'two roles' literature made similar observations to Oakley's about women's attitudes towards their primary home roles, it viewed this as the 'natural' place for women. As a result of an ahistorical conception of the family and of women within it, roles were treated as given, ignoring the context in which they are socially defined and action is constrained. By contrast, Oakley tries to *explain* why *women* have these attitudes (such as feeling responsible for childcare) by examining the social construction of the housewife role. Further, she departs from the 'two roles' literature in seeing women's position in the family as one of subordination and dependence, both economic and psychological. However, as has already been pointed out, Oakley never looks beyond the family at the impact of housework on wage work.

Whilst I have concentrated on women workers in this article, I do not mean to leave the reader with the impression that the family impinges only on women's work. Life cycle changes are also of fundamental importance in *men's* relationship to their work, and for relations between women and men in the family. The way reproduction and childcare are currently organised means that the life cycle affects men largely in terms of financial strain, rather than imposing the necessity of part-time work to allow for childcare. No study of work experience is complete without a systematic examination of sexual divisions within the family.

Notes

1   This article was written as part of my doctoral research into a women's co-operative factory. I would like to thank past and present members of the women's paper teaching collective, especially Jenny Earle, Hilary Knight and Martha Macintyre for their continuing encouragement and helpful comments. I am also grateful to Bob Blackburn, Colin Filer, Tony Giddens, David Held and Michelle Stanworth.

2   Beynon and Blackburn (1972, pp.144–5) also make this point. For an excellent review of how women employees have been treated in industrial sociology, see Brown (1976).

3   The discussion in this section is based on the following books: Fogarty, Rapoport and Rapoport (1971); Jephcott, Seear and Smith (1962); Klein (1965); Myrdal and Klein (1956); Rapoport and Rapoport (1971); and Yudkin and Holme (1963).

4   Referring to these books, Brown (1976, p.27) makes the same point:
    The largest category of studies of women *qua* women as employees is that which regards the employment of women as in some way giving rise to problems — for the women themselves in combining their two roles; for the employer in coping with higher rates of absence and labour turnover, and demands for part-time work; for the social services in providing for the care of children of working mothers, or in coping with the supposed results of maternal neglect; for husbands and other kin in taking over part of the roles of wife and mother; and even for the sociologist in attempting to discern the 'motivation' of women in paid employment.

5   Reviewing this literature, Beechey (1978, p.169) says: 'It is inadequate to postulate industrialisation *per se* as an explanatory factor without specifying which elements of the development of industrial capitalism bring about particular changes, and without showing how these changes affect the demand for female labour.' This article has been published since my chapter was first written. It includes a useful review of the 'two roles' literature, although her critique is pitched at a more general conceptual level, largely in terms of its partial adoption of Parsons' functionalist framework.

6   See Land (1976, p.119):

Women's earnings are essential to many families. In 1970 the Department of Health and Social Security estimated that the number of poor two-parent families in which the father was in full-time work (poor being defined as having an income at or below the current supplementary benefit scale rates) would have nearly *trebled* if the father's earnings had not been supplemented by the mother's. Altogether an estimated 180,000 two-parent families had an income within £2 of the 'poverty line' and a quarter of a million more families would have been in this position if they had relied solely on the father's wages.

The essential contribution which married women's earnings make to the family income has now been well documented. For further references, see Hurstfield (1978, p.12).

7   Oakley (1974, p.19). Eighteen years earlier, Myrdal and Klein (1956, p.88) made a similar point about the attitude adopted in the case of women workers: 'It is characteristic that the numerous investigations into the motives of married women in accepting gainful employment are not matched by other studies examining the question of why married women, when they have no small children to look after, do *not* work outside their homes.'

8   Unpublished data supplied by the authors from the study Blackburn and Mann (1979).

9   Whereas most studies of women workers have tended to be of professional and white-collar employees, these studies look at the distinctive features of working-class women in the work situation.

10 This is not to deny the effect of the life cycle and the labour market in influencing men's 'orientations to work'. Again, we should beware of studying women in isolation. At the present time, however, life cycle changes must be considered to have more significance for women than for men.

11 In a footnote, Brown (1976) draws on much the same material as appears in this section. He also draws similar conclusions to some of those presented here, but I extend the analysis to a consideration of distinctions *within* the category of married women. The tradition of viewing women and men in terms of their life cycle has a long history in the discipline of anthropology (see Goody, 1971, for example). The problems of biological determinism have perhaps caused sociologists to shy away from any analysis which sees people's lives as structured in biology.

12 Gardiner (1975); Seccombe (1974); Himmelweit and Mohun (1977). The last of these contains a fuller bibliography on this debate.

13 See, for example, Gardiner, Himmelweit, and Mackintosh (1976).

14 Here Young provides some information about the uneven distribution of income between husbands and wives in working-class families, which operates to the economic disadvantage of wives and children. Oren (1974)

has more recently documented further evidence for Young's thesis. Unfortunately, both these articles are historical and only deal with families in which the wives do not go out to work. For a discussion of the limitations of official surveys, such as the *Family Expenditure Survey*, which take the household as the unit of analysis and, thus, fail to provide information about the distribution of income and wealth within the family, see the Equal Opportunities Commission's report based on evidence to The Royal Commission on Income Distribution and Wealth (1977).

15   Oakley (1976). I am leaving out of consideration the entire question of the differential psychological construction of the two sexes, both at the level of socialisation and at the level of psychic structuring. These areas are covered by other contributions in this book; see Lieven's chapters (12 and 15).

Further Reading

H. Wainwright, 'Women and the division of labour.' In P. Abrams (ed.) *Work, Urbanism and Inequality*. London: Weidenfeld & Nicolson, 1978. (For a description of the extent and nature of sexual inequality in the labour market.)

J. Hurstfield, *The Part-Time Trap*. Low Pay Unit Pamphlet 9. London: 1978 and Counter Information Services, 'Women Under Attack'. London: Counter Information Services. (For a good description of the conditions of work for part-time women workers.)

M. Snell, 'The Equal Pay and Sex Discrimination Acts: their impact in the workplace'. *Feminist Review*, 1979. (On the inefficiency of the Equal Pay Act and the Sex Discrimination Act.)

S. Garnsey, 'Women's work and theories of class stratification'. *Sociology* 12 (2), 1979. (For a positive critique of the analysis of women's work within theories of class stratification.)

M. Blaxall & B. Reagan (eds), special issue of *Signs*, Women and the Workplace: The Implications of Occupational Segregation, Signs 1 (No 3 & 2), 1976. (For a discussion of occupational segregation by sex from a variety of perspectives.)

The Bristol Women's Studies Group (ed.), *Half the Sky*: An *Introduction to Women's Studies*. London: Virago 1979.

E. Malos (ed.), *The Politics of Housework*, London: Allison & Busby, 1980. (This is a collection of historical and contemporary material on housework.)

Chapter Two

A Commentary on Theories of Female Wage Labour[1]

JANET SILTANEN

As a matter of fact

(1) The proportion of the labour force that is female increased from 30 per cent in 1911 to 40 per cent in 1974. This increase has two marked features. First, it has been mainly an increase in married working women. In 1974, 49 per cent of married women were working (10 per cent in 1911) and 62 per cent of women workers were married (43 per cent in 1951). Second, a greater proportion of women workers work part time. In 1975, approximately 23 per cent of women workers worked part time (13 per cent in 1951) (Wainwright, 1978).

(2) The increasing participation of women in wage labour has had little impact on the segregated nature of women's employment. In 1971, 61 per cent of all women workers were employed in ten census-classified occupations. In six of these ten occupations, women comprised at least 90 per cent of the total employed.[2]

(3) The occupations that employ a large number of women are low-status occupations and there are indications that this low-status concentration has increased over time. In 1966, 93 per cent of all professional women were in the minor professions (93 per cent in 1921); 72 per cent of all non-manual women were in routine grades (51 per cent in 1921); and 78 per cent of all manual women were in non-skilled jobs (64 per cent in 1921) (Westergaard and Resler, 1975).

(4) Although women's hourly earnings, as a percentage of men's hourly earnings, increased in the early 1970s, the gap is still

substantial and has widened recently. *EOC News* reports that while women's gross hourly earnings rose from 63 per cent of men's to 75 per cent from 1970 to 1976, they rose only 4 per cent in 1977 and have dropped back to 74 per cent in 1978.[3] Moreover, the size of this gap increases when other sources of income, such as overtime pay, are taken into account.

These are but a few factual statements about female wage labour. The question to be considered here is how we explain the sexual division and inequality in wage labour. The position and experience of women has been conspicuously invisible in the majority of analyses of wage labour. As Garnsey (1978) notes, women's work within mainstream stratification and class analysis is conceptually anomalous and methodologically inconvenient. This leads to women being either excluded from studies of work (literally and/or conceptually) or treated as a special problem.[4] However, women's position in wage labour is not a complete conceptual or methodological lacuna. My intent in this chapter is to provide a critical overview of three economic approaches to women's place in wage labour: human capital theory; labour market dualism; and finally, de-skilling and the reserve army of labour.[5]

Human capital theory

Can the sexual division and inequality in wage labour be explained by productivity factors? Are the different wages of men and women due to differences in education, skill, work experience? The main thrust of human capital theory is the explanation of wage differences by reference to productivity.[6] In general, the theory assumes that labour markets are perfectly competitive. Wages are a return to investments in human capital via the direct relationship between human capital and productivity. Individuals make investments in their potential productive capacity (their human capital) such as education, training courses, job experience and on-the-job training. These investments have costs such as the deferment of wages and tuition fees. They also have returns in that they increase productivity and hence wages. Wage differences between men and women, therefore, are due to differences in their stock of human capital and, ultimately, their productivity.

Human capital theorists argue that women's primary orientation to their childrearing role results in their stock of human capital being, in general, lower than men's. Women's role in the family affects their stock of human capital in two ways. First, on the assumption that they will be spending more time in the family versus in paid work, women will be less inclined to make human capital investments. Their time away from paid work reduces the return on their human capital investments and so they tend to invest less in the first place. Second, when women leave paid work to attend to childrearing tasks full time, there is a deterioration of their accumulated stock of human capital. Their skills may become rusty or obsolete, which puts them in a less competitive position when they return to paid work.

In short, human capital theory claims that, other things being equal, the economy is indifferent to gender. However, all else is not equal, owing to individual decisions about augmenting human capital. Human capital theorists claim that it is possible to 'understand poverty, underemployment and inequality by proceeding as if all workers and employers act rationally in pursuit of their individual self-interest and as if the outcomes were optimal outcomes in light of the existing organisation of work' (Gordon, 1972, p.42). For women, then, the choice between family and work priority and the consequent decisions not to work continuously and not to invest as heavily in human capital are rational and optimal decisions.

Is human capital theory a sufficient explanation of sexual divisions and inequalities in wage labour? To answer this question let's look at its empirical relevance, its assumptions concerning female wage labour and its blank spots. First, Bluestone (1977, pp.335—40) comments that by 'calling nearly everything that comprises worker productivity "human capital", these theorists were able, with a single semantic stroke, to explain all variance in employment status and wage rates in terms of the one parameter.' However, even though human capital has become an increasingly catch-all concept, most empirical analyses based on human capital theory do not completely succeed in the statistical explanation of all the variance in male and female incomes. For example, Suter and Miller (1973), controlling for occupational status, education, work experience and full- or part-time employment, statistically explain 62 per cent of the male/female wage difference. While this explained variance is quite high by social science standards, does it mean that human capital theory is correct or useful in the explanation of sexual divisions and inequality in wage labour? The answer to this question must be a qualified no. When analysing women's position in wage labour it is obviously important to consider the role played by their qualifications and experience in determining where they are employed and the wages they receive. However, even though human capital theory takes all these factors into account, there still remains a substantial wage difference between men and women that is unexplained by productivity variables.

Moreover, as Bluestone notes (1977, p.337) 'many of those who suffer from low wages and unemployment have a considerable amount of human capital'. This is particularly important with respect to women workers who tend to be underemployed. That is, women tend to have more educational qualifications than required for the jobs they do and, further, more education than men in the same job.[7] In addition, the empirical relationship between income and factors such as education, job tenure, occupational status and so on is by no means an empirical implication unique to human capital theory. This relationship is, in a sense, theoretically overdetermined, since there are a number of other theoretical perspectives with which it is consistent. It is consistent, for example, with certain analyses of social class, and yet the theoretical and political implications of this perspective are quite different from those of human capital theory.[8] Finally, a human capital approach has been used in conjunction with other perspectives of labour market processes. Dual labour market theory, for example, suggests that a human capital model operates in the primary labour market but not the secondary labour market. Studies of discrimination in the labour market often use a human capital approach as an aid to determining the extent of discrimination. Wage differences that are unexplained by productivity factors are then assumed to be explained by discriminatory practices.[9]

Second, by assuming that women will choose working at home to working for pay, human capital theory gives full credence to the adage that women work for pin money. One of the most enduring conceptions of women and work is that women have the luxury of a choice between working for a wage and working for husband and children. While this choice may, in fact, be a real one for some women, the growing necessity of two wages in double-parent families and the increasing incidence of families solely dependent on the female wage makes this 'choice' an illusory one for many working women.[10] An 'explanation' of female wage labour based on the assumption of women's wages as pin money is clearly inadequate.

Third, human capital theory does not admit the structural constraints on individual choice. The achievement principle is assumed to operate in full force. This has two consequences. First, any inequality in wage labour is a problem of individual choice. Processes that structure access to education and vocational training are not considered. Second, the theory emphasises factors in the quality of labour supply. Thus, changes in the demand for labour and the general nature of the economic structure itself are not dealt with. Both are crucial factors relating to women's position in wage labour. For example, human capital analysis, by emphasising wage differences, introduces differences in where men and women are employed as an explanatory factor. Yet, in an analysis of female wage labour, women's concentration in low-status, low-paying jobs is precisely what we want to explain. Some of these issues are considered in the analysis of labour market dualism.

Labour market dualism

As we have seen, wage and employment inequality between men and women is not satisfactorily accounted for in the productivity approach. Indeed, the inadequacies in the conventional framework of economic theory were first remarked upon by researchers primarily interested in racial differences in poverty, underemployment and inequality in the United States. The question posed in this case was why is it that in some cases traditional productivity characteristics, such as education and training, are not related to job allocation and wages? Theories of segmented, 'balkanised' and internal labour markets developed out of this problem. Two of the most prominent analyses have been Doeringer and Piore's (1971) dual labour market theory and Gordon's (1972) radical version.

An internal labour market operates within an administrative unit, for example a manufacturing plant, and involves the governing of wages and job allocation 'by a set of administrative rules and procedures' (Doeringer and Piore, 1971, p.2). Certain jobs act as ports of entry to the internal labour market and the hiring for these jobs is based on competitive forces in the external market. However, once access has been made to an internal market, external market forces do not apply and promotion and wages are determined by the structure of the internal market. There are areas of employment which do not have an internal structure of promotion and wage determination. Dual labour market theory addresses itself to the schism between a primary labour market with an internal labour market structure, and a secondary labour market which either lacks an internal labour market structure or has a very undeveloped one. In Doeringer and Piore (1971) and Piore (1970) a number of arguments are put forward concerning the creation and maintenance of a dual labour market structure. Some of the main points are summarised below.

(1) The primary market is characterised by the skill specificity in jobs and the importance of on-the-job training. Since training costs are borne by employers, they will attempt to maximise their long-range investment in labour power. It will, therefore, be in their

interest to reduce labour turnover in these jobs and employment stability becomes a key differentiating variable between primary and secondary markets.

(2) The schism between the two markets is less oriented to technology and more a result of custom and practice. Many kinds of work could be performed within either sector. It is the influence of trade union organisation and managerial control in the codification of work rules relating to pay and promotion that fosters a schism between primary jobs and secondary jobs.

(3) Workers may be confined to secondary employment not because they do not have the requisite skills or qualifications but because they have, or are assumed to have, an unstable work pattern. While 'pure' discrimination may confine certain workers to the secondary market, statistical discrimination is an important factor in the assignment of workers to primary or secondary employment. Dual labour market theorists argue that, since the assessment of future employment stability is problematic, employers will rely on highly visible characteristics (such as race and sex) in hiring for the primary and secondary market, on the assumption that particular versions of these characteristics are associated with employment stability. It is argued, for example, that the intermittent employment pattern of women earmarks them for the secondary sector. Statistical discrimination would take place if an individual woman was hired for a secondary sector job on the assumption that women in general were unstable employees.

(4) The incentive to employers of a dual market structure involves both maximising the return on training investment and trade cycle flexibility. In the latter case, the secondary sector acts as a buffer for the primary sector. For example, when product demand is low, a firm can shed labour from the secondary sector and rehire in that sector when product demand picks up.

(5) Differentiation between the primary and secondary sector is reinforced by the interaction between characteristics of jobs and characteristics of workers. Jobs in the primary market are characterised by:

high wages, good working conditions, employment stability, chances of advancement, equity and due process in the administration of work rules. Jobs in the secondary market, in contrast, tend to have low wages and fringe benefits, poor working conditions, high labour turnover, little chance of advancement, and often arbitrary and capricious supervision (Doeringer and Piore, 1971, p.165).

The characteristics of workers are also different in the two sectors. For example, workers in the secondary sector tend to have a higher turnover, greater absenteeism and higher rates of lateness than workers in the primary sector. This, however, is not a static match between workers and jobs, for dual labour market theory suggests that once within the primary or secondary sector, workers will tend to develop the employment traits of that sector. So, for example, the instability of secondary jobs encourages the instability of secondary job workers which, in turn, encourages their confinement to the secondary sector.

The radical version of dual labour market theory basically differs in terms of the incentive to create and maintain a balkanised labour force. Contrary to the economic flexibility incentive proposed by Doeringer and Piore, Gordon emphasises the incentive of control over the labour force. He maintains that by encouraging a 'fetish for hierarchy' and status achievement, employers can effectively divide and rule the labour force. The use of racism and sexism aids the divide and rule strategy, pitting groups of workers against one another and hindering the development of class consciousness.

Dual labour market theory involves some important implications for the analysis of female wage labour. This is particularly true with respect to the relationship between employment patterns and orientations to work and the jobs people do. Female wage labour is often characterised as more capricious and less committed than male wage labour. While it is true that on average there is higher turnover in female wage labour than male wage labour, it is also true that this difference is work as well as gender related. Indeed, there is some evidence to suggest that when we control for the type of job, male/female differences in turnover disappear.[11] Low commitment to work, low promotion initiative and intermittent employment are familiar characteristics attributed to female wage labourers. These orientations to work are often considered to be explained by women's priority of home over waged employment. Dual labour market theory suggests that these orientations can just as well be attributed to women's confinement to secondary sector employment. The implication of drawing the distinction between the characteristics of work and workers and analysing the relationship between them is that women's decisions to leave paid employment may be less a reflection of a moral choice between family and work and more a reflection of the reality of their position as wage labourers.[12]

A convincing empirical analysis of women as a secondary labour force has yet to be put forward. Bosanquet and Doeringer (1973) mention clothing, textiles, laundries, distribution and catering as industries in Britain with secondary labour market conditions. They are also industries which employ a large number of women. Barron and Norris (1976) specifically address the relationship between sexual divisions and the dual labour market. They list five main attributes likely to identify a source of secondary workers: dispensability, clearly visible social difference, little interest in acquiring training, low interest in wages and lack of solidarity. They argue (on rather shaky evidence) that these characteristics differentiate female from male wage labour — excluding old, young and black males. The most cogent point made by dual labour market theory, however, is the necessity of differentiating job structure and orientations to work and analysing the relationship between them. To give a convincing analysis of the existence and operation of dualism in the British labour market and its relation to sexual divisions, one would have to examine both job characteristics and the characteristics of workers as well as the relationship between the two. But although Barron and Norris recognise this, they fall back on their characterisation of female wage labour as evidence for women's secondary sector employment. As a result, they cite evidence of women's disadvantaged position (such as their under-representation in areas of higher education and in occupational training schemes) as reasons for their disadvantaged position in the economy. As Beechey (1978) points out, their explanation approaches a tautology.

Considering dual labour market theory in general, three critical comments can be made with respect to its adequacy in the explanation of sexual divisions and inequality in wage labour. First, once created, job structures are viewed in fairly static terms. For example, Piore (1970) argues that once jobs become rooted in one sector or the other, the difficulty and expense in shifting the distribution of jobs between sectors makes this movement unlikely. This position conflicts with a de-skilling approach which would suggest that skill specificity is on the decline and, consequently, more secondary sector types of jobs are being created. This approach will be discussed in the following section. Second, while dual labour market theory can possibly account for very general male/female differences, it does not address the differences in male and female wage labour within the secondary (or primary) sector. The radical version does address these differences somewhat but relies on 'sexism' as an explanation. We do not, however, get an explanation of what sexism is or of how it is legitimated within the social practices of wage labour. Third, while trade unions are argued to have a hand in the creation and maintenance of labour market segmentation, the major onus for this rests on employers. A more detailed analysis of women's relation to trade unions and of trade union practices generally is important in the explanation of women's position in the secondary labour market.

There are alternative views on structured or internal labour markets which address the above points. Bonachich (1972) discusses the notion of split labour markets in relation to ethnicity. The focus in this analysis is the importance of power relations geared to the threat of wage undercutting as the key to the creation and maintenance of segregated jobs. Rubery (1978) stresses the inadequacy of dual labour market theory when faced with the phenomena of de-skilling and worker organisation. She argues that worker organisations are central to the maintenance of structured labour markets and that the existence of such markets has yielded gains for the working class. She does not mention, however, that these gains have been, for the most part, gains of the male working class. Let us turn to an approach that offers a more dynamic conception of women's wage labour.

De-skilling and the reserve army of labour

This section will concentrate on Braverman (1974), whose analysis of the degradation of work in monopoly capitalism provides the major reference point for discussions of women's relation to de-skilling and the reserve army of labour.[13] In his celebrated analysis of the effects of transitions in the labour process on the composition and conditions of the working class, Braverman struck at least a publicity blow for female wage labour in Marxist analysis by claiming that it is central to the understanding of contemporary capitalism. Braverman's work concerns three coterminous processes in the accumulation of capital in monopoly capitalism: the increase in the relative surplus value in industry via the mechanisation and scientific management of production, the growth of labour-intensive, working-class occupations, and the growth of the reserve army of labour.[14] I shall discuss these within a general discussion of the accounting of value, clerical labour and the composition of the working class.

Braverman argues that as capitalism moves into its monopoly stage, the accounting of value becomes more complex. The distance between the production of a commodity and its consumption becomes increasingly wider to the extent that labour involved in the accounting of value (following and recording its movements and changes of form) begins to overtake the labour involved in the production of value. For a very crude example, it may take a number of people to manufacture a book but it also takes a number of people to record the movement and changes of form of that book — someone will record that the book has been produced, someone will record that it has been transported to Coventry, someone will record that it has arrived at the Coventry book store, someone will sell the book, someone will record that the book has been sold and yet another someone will record that the person now reading the book is in debt to the Coventry book store for three quid, and so on. Braverman argues that the growth in working-class occupations has been in the area of the accounting of value such as clerical, service and retail occupations. These tend to be labour-intensive and female-dominated occupations. However, not all of these accounting occupations have escaped mechanisation — clerical work is a case in point.

Compared to its previous position of relatively high pay, job autonomy and skill, clerical work today is highly mechanised, highly supervised, highly routinised and de-skilled. Two other fundamental changes in clerical work are evident — pay has sunk below the level of factory work, and it has become a female job. It is an open question whether the coincidence of de-skilling and feminisation in clerical work is a general phenomenon. Discussion of this relationship is still at a very preliminary stage (Beechey, 1977; Revolutionary Communist Group, 1976) and requires further theoretical and empirical work.

The rationalisation of the work process and its mechanisation not only de-skills labour but discards it as well. As workers are discarded from industrial production, they move to labour-intensive jobs not as yet, or unlikely to be, mechanised, or they join the ranks of the unemployed. Braverman identifies the excess labour from industry and female labour drawn from the home as the two major sources of the industrial reserve army of labour. It is important to recognise that Braverman, following Marx, discusses the reserve army of labour in two contexts. First, it is discussed in relation to the general law of capital accumulation, which suggests that the reserve army of labour is a precondition and a consequence of the development of wealth on a capitalist basis. Second, it is discussed in the context of its concrete forms. There are basically three concrete forms discussed by Braverman, again following Marx, although the latter noted that the reserve army of labour exists in many forms. The 'floating' reserve is constituted by workers repelled from and attracted to industry. According to Marx, many of the workers repelled from industry remain unemployed because their skills are specific to a particular branch of industry. Braverman re-casts the floating reserve as that which is highly mobile — both across jobs due to de-skilling, and geographically. The source of the 'latent' reserve is agricultural labourers thrown off the land because of the capitalisation of agriculture. The 'stagnant' reserve is the casually and irregularly employed. Marx claims domestic industry is its exemplar form. Speaking of the growth of the reserve army of labour, Braverman states that among 'male workers it takes the form of a sloughing off into the ranks of the so-called nonparticipants in the labour force, or in other words an increase of the "stagnant" portion'. On the other hand, among female workers 'it takes the form of a growing body of female labour which is drawn from the mass of women who previously did not work, and hence represents an enlargement of the "floating" and "stagnant" reserve army of labour' (Braverman, 1974, p.391).

Before I pass on to an alternative conceptualisation of women as a reserve army of labour, I would like to make some comments concerning Braverman's analysis of female wage labour. While Braverman certainly publicised the importance of understanding female wage labour in contemporary capitalism, he *arrived* at this conclusion. Does his contribution advance the task of explaining the sexual division and inequality in wage labour for those who take this as a point of departure? The relationship between the proletarianisation of jobs (or more specifically de-skilling) and the feminisation of jobs is a potential contribution, but one that needs more theoretical specification and empirical support. Why has de-skilling in industry not resulted in a replacement of male by female labour? Again, we must consider the importance of trade unions and women's relation to them. As Beechey (1977) notes, Braverman minimises the importance of working-class resistance to the dilution of skill. The degree to which working-class resistance to skill dilution is also a resistance of male against female workers is an important theoretical and political question. Equally important, in this respect, is the relationship between the entry of women into an occupation and the depression of wages. Beechey (1977) equates this relationship with de-skilling, which seems to be too liberal an application of the concept. However, some conception of the feminisation of jobs may, if adequately elaborated to include not only its economic but also its cultural aspects, be helpful in the explanation of incidents like that at the Stockport factories of Roberts Arundel, 'where in 1966 fifty-one men earning twenty pounds a week were replaced by fifty-one women working the same machines for ten pounds a week' (Sullerot, 1971, p.131).

Another series of questions arises out of Braverman's characterisation of women as a reserve army of labour. Cutler (1978) criticises this point, arguing that this characterisation violates the basis of the creation of a reserve army — the changing organic composition of capital (i.e. the proportion of labour to machinery in production). Cutler emphasises that a reserve army of labour is created by the greater use of machinery, relative to labour, in the production process. Thus, the concept applies to an already existing working population. Women's influx into employment, he continues, mainly relates to the extension of the boundaries of a working population and not to the increase in the reserve army of labour. This criticism raises an important point. Why characterise women's entry into paid labour as swelling the ranks of the reserve army of labour? Why do women not enter wage labour as members of the active working class? Is it true that all women undertake wage labour on a 'casual' and 'irregular' basis and, therefore, as a segment of the stagnant reserve? With respect to this last question, our response must be the same response we give to the statement that women work for pin money. In short, no. However, I think it would be most helpful if we re-cast the content of the stagnant reserve to include part-time work. Working part time is a particular form of the reserve army in contemporary capitalism and it is a form that is predominated by female wage labour. I also do not consider it unreasonable to characterise women in the home as a form of the latent reserve. This suggestion does not violate the important theoretical basis to the creation of the reserve army. Domestic labour is continually being capitalised. Not only is the nature of domestic labour itself more machine-oriented, but it is whittled away by the capitalistic production of use-values previously produced in the home. This capitalisation of domestic labour has been an important factor in 'setting free' female labour in the home for its use in capitalist pro-duction. While the concept of the reserve army may be a useful one in explaining certain aspects of female wage labour, I think its utility will be determined by the degree to which we are able to re-think the contemporary character of its concrete forms as well as the relation-ship between the contemporary reserve army and the active working class.

An interesting attempt to re-think the concrete forms of the reserve army is presented by Bland *et al.* of the Birmingham Women's Studies Group (1978). They attempt to restructure the content of the concrete forms of the reserve army in terms of the relationship between the relations of production and the relations of reproduction. They mention that women 'do not rest easily' with Marx's description of the concrete determinations of the reserve army. While they accept his typology of its form, they relate women's position *as women* to the content of those forms. Thus, women are a source of the floating reserve 'voluntarily' shifting in and out of paid work in concert with their reproductive life cycle and with little cost to employers or the State when they are 'voluntarily' unemployed. The situation of women set free from childcare responsibilities is argued to be analogous to the position of agricultural workers set free from their work on the land. Women in this position, then, are a source of the latent reserve. As a source of the stagnant reserve, married and unmarried mothers with children who work where and when they can are pointed to, and Black, West Indian and Asian women specifically mentioned. Finally, the 'pauperism' sector of the reserve army is mentioned, particularly in relation to women who make up the stagnant reserve but who are likely to be precariously near destitution, such as unmarried mothers, widows and prostitutes. The Birmingham group make the important point that 'women as a reserve army' are not a homogenous lot. They are differentiated within themselves in terms of their dependence on an income other than their own, their reproductive life cycle and the types of work they form a reserve for.[15] With respect to this latter factor, they argue, for example, that the floating reserve, which tends to be women employed before they leave paid employment to raise children, also tends to be women employed in jobs where their sexual attractiveness is an integral part of their job. While this is an interesting conceptualisation of women within the reserve army of labour, we cannot leave the analysis here. The analysis of women as a reserve army of labour in relation to the relations of reproduction and production appropriates the concept of the reserve army solely for this analysis. Further work is needed to relate the conceptualisation of women's position in the reserve army to the position of men in the reserve army and to the general law of capital accumulation.

As a matter of explanation

In closing, I would like to make some general remarks concerning the explanation of women's position as wage labourers.

Most people would agree that the division of labour in contemporary capitalism, both between domestic and wage labour and within wage labour, is structured by sex and gender. Yet, as the discussion in this chapter illustrates, there is disagreement as to whether the sexual division in the labour market is incidental or integral to the social relations of capitalist production. However, there is a sense in which sexual divisions are incidental to all of the three main economic approaches discussed. That is, they were all initially conceptualised with something other than sexual divisions in mind. This necessarily affects the adequacy with which sexual divisions in the labour market are conceptualised. Moreover, taking female wage labour, or more generally the sexual division and inequality in wage labour, as our analytical problem can itself be a problem if female wage labour is considered solely as an 'economic' entity or divorced from female domestic labour.

A consistent comment in any discussion of female wage labour is the importance of women's position in the home in relation to their position in the labour market. There is a danger in separating women's work in the family and women's waged work. It can lead to a very one-sided understanding of women's position in society and, ultimately, to a circularity of explanations. Often the sexual division of labour within the family and the dictates of the family under capitalism are relied upon to explain the sexual division in wage labour. Equally often, the sexual division in wage labour and the dictates of the capitalist workplace are relied upon to explain the sexual division of labour in the family. Recent attempts to 'get behind' the supposed separation of family and work to analyse women's relation to the family-production relationship (Beechey, 1977; Bland *et al.*, 1978) start us off in an important direction toward the explanation of the sexual division of labour in contemporary capitalism. The previous chapter is also a step in this direction.

Notes

1   My thanks to Cathie Marsh, Sandy Stewart and members of the Book Collective for their helpful comments and suggestions as to the organisation and substance of this paper.

2   These six occupations are: hand and machine sewers and embroiderers, textile and light leather products; typists, shorthand writers, secretaries; canteen assistants, counterhands; maids, valets and related service workers; charwomen, office cleaners, window cleaners, chimney sweeps; nurses (from the Department of Employment, *Women and Work* 1974, Table 26). The additional four include the following: clerks and cashiers; shop sales staff and assistants; primary and secondary school teachers; proprietors and managers, (sales). Clerks and cashiers constituted 17.5 per cent of all working women in 1971 (from Equal Opportunities Commission, *Second Annual Report 1977*, 1978, Table 3.2).

3   *EOC News*, 'Women's Pay Takes Knock', December 1978. The reported figures have been rounded to the nearest whole number.

4   Several articles have been written on the male bias in the theory and

research practice of stratification analysis, class analysis and the sociology of work, generally. See, for example, Acker (1973), Brown (1976), and Middleton (1974) as well as Garnsey (1978).

5 This overview is necessarily selective. I have chosen those approaches that seem to be currently in vogue. What is in vogue is, of course, politically heterogeneous. An important aspect of Cambridge Women's Studies is the provision of intellectual weaponry for women to battle against academic theories that implicitly or explicitly condone women's present position in society.

6 Some of the main references include Becker (1964), Mincer and Polachek (1974) and Sandell and Shapiro (1977). Chiplin and Sloane (1976) attempt to determine the amount of 'pure' discrimination against women in the British occupational structure by first accounting for male/female wage differences by human capital factors. For a feminist critique of Chiplin and Sloane, see Breugel (1978). For a review and critique of human capital theory see Bluestone (1977) and Gordon (1972). For an interesting critique of the 'achievement principle' in contemporary organisations of work from a general perspective, see Offe (1976).

7 For references, see Hartnett (1978).

8 See, for example, Giddens' (1973) discussion of market capacity and the new middle class and also Wright and Perrone (1977) who analyse the relationship between income and education by class, race and sex.

9 I decided not to include discrimination theories for two reasons. First, the economics involved is quite complicated and mathematically sophisticated. Second, there seem to be two major approaches to the analysis of sex discrimination neither of which is very helpful for the explanation of sex discrimination itself. Either discrimination is assumed and its economic effects analysed, or discrimination is considered a residual process as in Chiplin and Sloane's (1976) analysis. The language of economics is in some cases (unintentionally) absurd. For example, economists use the term 'comparative advantage' in the context of the competitive position of commodity producers stemming from differential, including natural resources and expertise. Chiplin and Sloane claim that the complete equality between men and women in the labour market is likely to be constrained by the comparative advantage of women in childbearing and rearing !!! See Madden (1973) for at least a more sympathetic analysis.

10 For a discussion of the importance of women's income to the maintenance of both themselves and their families see Counter Information Services (1976), Equal Opportunities Commission (1978) and Land (1976).

11 For references see Hartnett (1978) and Stevenson (1978).

12 I think we should be somewhat mistrustful of official statistics relating to women's reasons for leaving employment. To what extent, for example, do women use pregnancy as an excuse for quitting work? In interviews with working women, I have been told of a number of cases where women were reluctant to tell their employers that intolerable working conditions and

low pay were the reasons they were leaving their jobs. These women were even more reluctant to tell their employers that they had been hired for a new job elsewhere. They did, however, consider pregnancy to be a much more legitimate reason for leaving their jobs. Although factually untrue, pregnancy appeared on the employer's termination of employment form and this 'fact' no doubt contributed to the annual statistics of female wage labour.

13 There is another version of women as a reserve army of labour which uses the term in relation to employment fluctuations in female wage labour according to economic conditions. The main argument is that women are a reserve for the dominant male labour force. The movement of women in and out of wage labour is under the sway of ideology — women's place is in the labour force when the economy is buoyant and their place is in the home when they are no longer needed in the economy. See, for example, Benston (1969). Milkman (1976) argues against women as a reserve army making the point that occupational segregation by sex creates an inflexibility in the labour market which does not allow the direct replacement of men for women (and vice versa) in jobs.

14 The terminology of Marxist theory may be new to some people. For a crash course see Fine (1975). There is also a glossary in Mandel (1975).

15 Readers interested in the possible effects of the dependent position of married women on the value of labour power should read Beechey (1977). In this article, Beechey puts forward a thesis on the 'semi-proletarianised' status of married women workers. She argues that the employment of married women is advantageous to capital since they are not totally responsible for the reproduction of their own labour power. Beechey's discussion raises some complicated issues and there are internal difficulties with her arguments but she takes an important step by attempting to problematise the family-production *relationship* as a key to understanding the position of female wage labour. The importance of this has been discussed in chapter 1 by Wajcman.

Chapter Three

The History of the Family

L.J. JORDANOVA

Introduction

Studying the history of the family raises some important, and difficult, questions for feminists. It has been a central tenet of European ideology for at least two hundred years that families are built on the female role of wife and mother, and that the well-being of the family unit therefore depends in an essential way on the woman. **Women** *are* **the family.** The identification of women with the family has not been confined to those who govern or generate social policy and dominant ideologies. In reality, women very often did bear special burdens in the raising of children, and also experienced their own lives as determined by the family situation. As a result, understanding the history of women can only come by confronting the history of the family. The role of a historical perspective in providing a sense of process, of how things change, is already familiar in feminist writings. The continual emphasis on the flexibility of social life and on the inadequacy of seeing established patterns of behaviour as natural and inevitable are valuable contributions which historical study can make to feminist thought. However, not all history of women and the family helps in these ways. It is therefore important that feminist historians both establish their own sets of questions and priorities, and that they become fully aware of the shortcomings of existing work in the field. A critical history of the family, therefore, has an important role to play in developing a feminist perspective on contemporary family life, by revealing the ways in which categories and roles are actually constructed and struggled over.

A historical approach suggests that we must see social phenomena in relational terms — there is no history of women which does not take account of how women are placed relative to men and to children, how middle-class experience relates to that of the working and upper classes, how employer and employee, master/mistress and servant are historically related.

The current burgeoning of interest in the historical sociology of the family has come from a contemporary crisis in the family, or rather, from the widespread belief that we are in the process of such a crisis. Many people believe that the past can help explain the present. There is heated debate among those who study the family as to how it should be envisaged; as a retreat from society and the pressures of modern life, as a place where socialisation in the interests of capitalism takes place, as a convenient place to keep surplus female labour, or as an 'affective unit', the locus of love (Lasch, 1977; Laslett, 1965; Macfarlane, 1978; Shorter, 1975; Stone, 1977).

One of the major problems we encounter in studying the history of the family is that mythologies have been created about the past which simply aren't true. An excellent example is the myth of the extended family of the past giving way to the nuclear family of the present with an associated loss of sense of community. In fact, the nuclear family, that is a group comprising parents and children alone, has been in existence for a very long time. Such beliefs draw on prevailing assumptions about the correct form of family life from which we need to rid ourselves. But we need to be careful not to put new myths in place of the old ones. Stereotypes about the nuclear family, the extended family, the role of housewife, need to be demystified and destroyed. The same applies to the past in general, which was neither a 'golden age' we have lost, nor the 'bad old days' before the sexual revolution and modern capitalism made us free.[1]

In recovering the past we discover traditions of women's activities and women's struggles which have been forgotten. In particular, the idea of woman as housewife, whose only sphere of operation is the privacy of her home, can be put in its proper context as a creation of the mid-nineteenth century, i.e. the product of a particular point in time and a particular economic context. As a result, 'the ideology of domesticity' can be subjected to analysis and its socio-economic meaning sought.[2] The *public* inactivity of women is not a historical constant, neither is the emphasis on the cult of homemaking as the paradigmatic female occupation.

Until relatively recently, the exact period depending on class and geographical location, many occupations were family ones in which all members, including women and children, took part (LePlay,

1855). This was the case with weaving families, those running small businesses at home such as washing laundry, and those working on the land. Especially in peasant cultures, and in families living at subsistence level, the *economic* participation of women and children was taken for granted (Hufton, 1975-6). A wife or husband would therefore be chosen with such practicalities in mind, and a woman's skills, proven work capacity, hard-earned dowry, even her proven fertility if labour were needed, were all important assets. These remarks apply to cases where factories had not yet become the dominant form of organised work, where most activities took place in or around the family home, in other words, where the members of the family exerted a significant degree of control over their labouring and leisure activities. In Britain the development of factories was well advanced by the end of the eighteenth century, while in many parts of France peasant organisation persisted and, to some extent, survives to this day. The pattern of families living and working together as a unit is generally referred to as the family economy.

Women's position in the family only makes sense in the context of the family's location in the broader social sphere, and in particular its economic features. Patterns of childcare, working arrangements such as mode of payment, place of work, laws regulating female and child labour, the wages each member of the family commanded, and cultural factors such as leisure, the possibility of family limitation, are among the most important variables which shaped a woman's life. The reason for emphasising the real economic struggles of family life is that too often exclusive attention has been paid to middle- and upper-class families who had few basic survival problems. Yet such people formed a minute, and probably atypical, proportion of the population. If we want to understand the lives of the vast majority of women we must look at those families whose existence was more precarious and could be seriously theatened by a bad harvest, an epidemic or the death or desertion of an adult member. Most families were poor families, using all their available resources to survive, and it has been argued that in this strategy to overcome hardship and destitution it was the woman and her capacity to do flexible work which was crucial (Hufton, 1974). Such people, by definition, left few remnants of their existence, and this poses inevitable problems for the historian who attempts to reconstruct their lives and to uncover those of women in particular.

Approaches and methods

Considerable difficulties are posed by a historical study of the family, and there is at present no consensus as to how the task should be carried out. There are obvious problems with sources and the use of evidence, but determining the most appropriate theoretical and analytical tools is also far from easy. There are two principal schools of thought on the correct method for historical analysis of the family; the quantitative approach used by demographers, and the reliance on the history of ideas by historians of '*mentalité*'. I shall discuss each of these in turn and then mention two theoretical perspectives — modernisation theory and psychohistory — which have informed recent writings on the history of the family. It is worth stating quite baldly that in each case different assumptions are made concerning what a family is and the role a woman plays in it. It is important that such assumptions be subjected to feminist scrutiny.

Initially we need to be clear that there are many different ways of defining what a family is. Demographers have tended to study households, that is, those living under one roof. Although this solves many of the practical difficulties which might otherwise stand in the way of quantitative analysis, it does not express the full complexity of the term 'the family'. Family is also, of course, a normative notion and carries with it connotations of ideal, stable, social units. Many groups carry out the tasks of caring for children and sustaining the needs of adults which are not traditionally considered to be 'families'. On these criteria one-parent families, communal households and gay couples all qualify. So it is important to ask what a family is and how it may best be defined. In fact, taking these questions seriously is basic to any historical or sociological work. No single criterion such as blood relationships, marriage ties or membership of a household is adequate. 'The family' is a relative term, whose meaning can change with time and place, with class and sex, with whether the speaker is part of the group being described, or an outsider. Particular care is needed with the use of terms like 'extended family',[3] which has no meaning when divorced from its social and cultural context. To be more precise:

> The extended family of the proletariat primarily functioned as a private institution to redistribute the poverty of the nuclear family by way of the kinship system. The extended family of the peasant, on the other hand, served as an instrument for the conservation of property and the caring for the older members of a family. (Medick, 1976, p.295)

For the most part, historians concerned with the material conditions of the family have employed quantitative data in their attempts to provide a more complete picture of the lives of the mass of the population. Using such sources as birth and death certificates, parish registers, taxation documents, wills, legal and administrative records, bills of mortality and so on, demographers have amassed vast amounts of data. Such information is hard to use for a number of reasons. First of all, it may not be reliable enough for statistical treatment nor representative enough for general conclusions to be drawn. Second, there are inherent limitations in such data, vital statistics tell us little about the quality of life, about how birth, death and marriage are experienced. Since the numbers alone tell us nothing, the way they are interpreted becomes of paramount importance.

An excellent example of the fierce debates generated by quantitative work is the analysis of the rising illegitimacy ratios of the late eighteenth and early nineteenth centuries. Edward Shorter (1975) argued that more illegitimate babies were born because working women of the period were expressing new desires for sexual freedom, and for romantic love attachments, with inevitable, undesirable consequences. In reply, Joan Scott and Louise Tilly (1975) argued that rising illegitimacy resulted from changing patterns of work, which led young men and women to leave their homes and seek work in the city where they had neither the financial resources nor the social pressures to marry and set up their own households. They further argue that women were particularly vulnerable to abandonment, so that more illegitimate births indicate the persistence of traditional patterns of behaviour in new circumstances rather than an attitudinal revolution as Shorter suggested. Both these interpretations rely, however, on assumptions about modernisation, a point to which I shall return later. There is obviously a problem in extrapolating from bare facts to an explanation of changing attitudes. To some extent this has been overcome for France by using the accounts unwed mothers-to-be were forced to give which describe, often in great detail, the circumstances of conception, and these survive in large numbers in some archives. It is on the basis of such documents that Fairchilds (1978) has been able to show the inadequacy of Shorter's view. Other interpretations of the data on illegitimacy are of course possible. One suggestion is that the tightening up of common law marriage arrangements in Britain at the end of the eighteenth century meant that many who before would have been considered married no longer were, making their children illegitimate.

Although the new quantitative demographic work has received enormous acclaim, many people have reservations about the extent to which it can usefully be applied to a wide range of historical problems. It is, for example, extremely difficult to gain much insight into the texture of women's lives in their most intimate relationships through a numerical index. Attempts to remedy this have been made using sources which are both quantifiable and contain other information. Shorter (1977) has recently attempted to do this using information on the gynaecological diseases of women as a basis for determining the nature of their sexual relationships, but this is far from satisfactory. In its ruthless search for quantifiable data, demographic work has failed to tackle the questions feminist historians attach greatest importance to — the social relations of the family from the perspective of its female members.

Among the principal conclusions of the demographic onslaught are the discovery that the distinctive patterns of the Western European family preceded the industrial revolution by several centuries. This pattern was a household comprising mostly parents and children, rather than an extended family of more distant kin, although sometimes servants might live in. Marriage typically took place when people were in their mid- or late twenties, with the partners being close together in age. This is a familiar pattern to us, and it suggests that there have been more important continuities of behaviour over long periods of time than was previously thought. This finding appears to cast doubt on the contention that there have been fundamental changes of social structure associated with industrial and monopoly capitalism in the last two hundred years.

We can thus safely say that the criterion of household size, that is, an assessment of the *quantity* of kin, is an unreliable index of the *quality* of relationships and of their social meaning. None the less, demographic data may be useful, especially where other evidence is lacking, if they can be integrated into a broader perspective. One of the most perplexing fields from this point of view is that of infant mortality.

Infant mortality began to decline in Britain from the 1870s on, at a time when family size was also decreasing.[4] These two changes probably had dramatic effects on the day-to-day lives of ordinary women. They had fewer pregnancies, and experienced the death of a child more rarely. But what conclusions can we draw from long-term demographic trends? It has been suggested that babies had a better chance of survival following changes in the attitudes of mothers. Hence, greater maternal love and desire for intimacy with children resulted in better parenting and so in better chances of survival for babies. On the other hand, it has also been suggested that parents, especially mothers, could only allow themselves to become emotionally involved with their children once they knew they stood a better chance of living to be adults. Either way the claim is hard to prove.[5] However, these two explanations make different assumptions about human relationships, and so interpret mortality statistics in different ways. Both, however, acknowledge that understanding the attitudes and beliefs of the past are an essential part of the history of the family.

The approach which looks at beliefs and ideas is usually referred to as *histoire des mentalités*, there being no English equivalent of *mentalité*. Among the most influential books using this approach is *Centuries of Childhood* by Philippe Ariès (1973), first published in 1960. Although his work was concerned with the place of the child in society and with the discovery of childhood as a special state of being, the thesis Aries put forward contains some important interpretations of the history of women and the family. He argues that childhood was a new idea which entered Western culture in various forms between the sixteenth and eighteenth centuries. In the nineteenth century another stage, adolescence, was interposed between infancy and adulthood. These stages were seen as ones in which the child was vulnerable and needing the continued guardianship of the mother. Consequently, children who had previously been apprenticed very young were increasingly seen as unsuitable for work, needing to stay at home with their mothers instead. As a result, the family would lose the incomes of two of its members and come to depend more on the father's wage. There may indeed be an association between beliefs in childhood innocence and vulnerability and the withdrawal of children from the workforce. What remains problematic is exactly how an abstract idea affects concrete material life. It seems more plausible to suppose that an ideology of childhood and motherhood was used to support economic changes which were part of a larger overall shift in work patterns.

Aries associates the growing importance of childhood with the rise of a bourgeoisie which became increasingly private in its habits, so that, by the nineteenth century, and in some cases much earlier, children were cared for at home by a very small group of adults. This withdrawal from the broader social sphere means to Ariès that 'sociability and the concept of the family are incompatible' (Ariès, 1973, p.393). His approach is most successful in its analysis of attitudes to boys, and of middle-class customs in general, which withdrew the family out of public view and so inevitably increased the vulnerability and isolation of women and children through their estrangement from other people.[6] Ariès used a variety of evidence from paintings, architecture, educational theories and practices, diaries and writings of all kinds. A severe limitation of his method is, in addition to its almost exclusive attention on the male child, its inability to say much about the family lives of the majority of the population who did not leave cultural monuments which revealed their private lives as the middle and upper classes did.

Here again there is a problem of evidence. The methods which Aries used, like those of Laurence Stone (1977) in his recent book on the history of the family, rely heavily on the testimony of family members writing about their experiences. Like fiction and prescriptive treatises, diaries, letters and memoirs cannot be taken at face value. But even allowing for distortion, interpreting such material still raises the question of the psychodynamics of the family. Psychohistory, that is the use of psychoanalytic perspectives in historical research, is not a new area of study, but there has been a recent flowering of its use with respect to the family, particularly methods of upbringing.[7] The idea is to show how patterns within families give rise to broader cultural movements. Although this is sometimes done by applying psycho-analytic theory in a rather rigid way, all historians who consider family relationships make assumptions about the psychology of intimate relationships whether they are aware of it or not.

The most serious shortcoming of the psychohistory of the family seems to be its tendency to divorce the family from its social, political and ideological context. This results from the genuine difficulty of connecting facets of private, intimate life with large-scale processes and changes. The attempts to make such connections often turn out to be superficial and unconvincing. Historians are, however, accustomed to using another theoretical perspective which sanctions the positing of such connections — modernisation theory.[8] Modernisation theory explains the evolution from traditional to modern life in terms of urbanisation and industrialisation, and the values associated with such social processes. Two forms of society are assumed, the traditional and the modern, and for each form there is an ensemble of beliefs, organisations and ways of behaving which are typical. Women and the family are central to the modernisation approach. Because it attempts to explain all aspects of a society by reference to a single para-meter, its degree of modernity, this perspective envisages family life and personal life as part of a larger pattern. One of the most pervasive notions of modern society is that people become increasingly indi-vidualistic, and families become more isolated. In other words, family behaviour and the position of women become convenient indicators of the extent to which a society is modern. And this belief is based on the determining influence of economic changes such as the development of factories taking men away from the home and isolating women and children, and the growth of towns forcing geographical mobility, so breaking up communities.[9] Recently, modernisation theory has come under heavy fire, principally because it assumes ideal types of societies which never existed and thus becomes a vehicle for contemporary stereotypes which feminist approaches to the history of the family seek to break down.

I have argued that recent work on the history of the family has concentrated either on its demographic aspects or on the experience of family members. Those who have tried to avoid the two extremes of quantitative history or psychohistory have tended to rely on modernisation theory to hold the different pieces of evidence together. The reliance on measurement distorted the real complexity of material conditions, while an emphasis on ideas and beliefs ignored the fact that families exist within real contexts which have to be taken account of.

Women and work

Perhaps the most important lesson which recent research on the social history of the family has taught us is the need to see work and home as closely related, rather than inherently opposed aspects of women's lives. Women's daily existence was closely bound up with the need to survive, this in turn meant work for the vast majority of them (Tilly and Scott, 1978). Work brought them into relationships with employers, fellow workers, with the marketplace as both producers and consumers, and with employees, for many women ran their own businesses and workshops.

The dynamic interplay between public and private which is crucial in understanding family life is particularly clearly seen in periods of transition and perceived social change. Special importance has therefore been attributed to the stages of early industrialisation (sometimes called proto-industrialisation) where remnants of an agrarian peasant economy and of cottage industries still existed (Medick, 1976). Here the family economy and capitalism existed side by side, and the extraordinary variety of possible forms of work and family life are being brought to our attention. What such work does not specify is the political status of women. We must therefore be on our guard against assuming an identity between economic activity and political rights. Formal equality before the law does not eradicate the particular economic vulnerabilites of women, and neither does the full economic participation of women give them a political voice. Although women were active in popular protests in the early modern period, and participated in bread riots and counter-revolutionary demonstrations during the French revolution (Hufton, 1971; Duhet, 1971), political theorists of the eighteenth century uniformly accorded women a passive role in public life, which they were allowed to affect through their family responsibilities, rather than directly as full citizens.

The development of an industrial mode of production in nineteenth-century Europe saw little change in the percentage of women in the labour force, but increasingly working women tended to be young and unmarried (Tilly and Scott, 1978, pp.70, 83, 85). Women also tended to work in jobs where the labour force was exclusively female. Women were paid low wages when compared with men, and it was often observed that it was extremely difficult for a woman to be self-supporting.[10] At an ideological level, the dependence of women on male earning capacity was encouraged. This dependence was by no means a feature of life for working-class and peasant cultures, where women simply had to contribute to the economy of the family as a whole, even if the work was done at home. The economic dependence of women seems to have been a middle-class phenomenon originally, in the sense that it was put forward as an ideal for and by the bourgeoisie long before it was in any sense a general feature of middle-class life as it was actually lived. However, many nineteenth-century writers painted a romanticised picture of the leisured and supported wife and advocated it an ideal to which all classes should aspire. This cult of domesticity was prominent in both Europe and the United States in the Victorian period; it was an ideology which explicitly sanctioned women staying at home and not entering the paid labour market, and correspondingly glorified the role of the strong support and control only a father and husband could give. It is much less easy to explain why these ideas should have arisen and been promulgated with such force at this particular time. They certainly had the effect of obscuring the real need for many women to work, and of supporting a long-standing conviction, still alive today, that men have greater rights to a job than women.

Earlier I stressed the importance of putting women's work in the context of the family economy, where each member contributed to earnings as far as they were able. The family functioned as a unit, often working together, sometimes drawing a wage as a family, and taking decisions which took into account the situation of the family as a whole.[11] My point was to emphasise that, far from being dependent and passive, women were not just economically active but frequently orchestrated the survival strategy in times of crisis, for instance by organising children to go begging or indulging in a bit of smuggling (Hufton, 1974). But it does not follow from what has been said that there was no sexual division of labour in such situations. It seems that men and women performed different but complementary tasks, and that women's jobs tended to be more closely associated with the home, care of the family, and the production and preparation of food. These involved heavy physical work, and in many areas women performed burdensome agricultural tasks. In cottage industries where families worked together the women and children usually did some jobs while men did others. There thus appears to have been a division of labour based on *custom* which was inevitably subject to marked geographical variation. The question remains whether there was a *hierarchical* relationship between male and female labour, with one sex being consistently seen as performing more valuable jobs which were more demanding and prestigious, and requiring more skill, than the other. Scott and Tilly (1975) argue that a hierarchical division of labour within the family emerged only during the nineteenth century, with the growth of an industrial wage economy which deliberately measured and set the skills each job required, and so put a value on it which was expressed by money. By contrast the married woman who bore and cared for children had no 'objective' value placed on her work.

To mention the word 'family' is to conjure up an extraordinary range of meanings and associations. The history of the family includes a similar diversity of approaches depending on whether vital statistics, lived experience, ideology, psychopathology or childrearing is the dominant concern. However its historical study is construed, looking at the family over long periods of time can teach us two simple, but important, lessons. First, women were inexorably bound up with a complex web of relationships both within and outside the family. They depended upon the actions of other members of their families, just as they frequently depended on her for their capacity to survive. In these intricate sets of interdependencies, attitudes and social policy towards the family are equally decisive. Second, the history of European society over the last three hundred years shows the extraordinary variety of possible familial arrangements. What remains an open question is the extent to which they manifested deep similarities.[12]

Notes

1 The latter assumptions dominate Edward Shorter's book (1975), which has been trenchantly criticised by Scott (1977). For an equally firm attack on

Laurence Stone (1977) see Thomas (1977).

2   The ideology of domesticity has come under scrutiny recently by both
    sociologists and historians, for example, Welter (1966); Oakley (1976a);
    Davidoff *et al.* (1976). It has been discussed from the point of view of
    psychohistory, by Robertson (1976). It was particularly clearly exemplified
    in nineteenth-century medical writings which have been discussed by
    Duffin (1978), and Haller and Haller (1974). A contemporary version is
    Leach (1979).

3   The term 'extended family' is now in common use to refer to households
    which include relatives more distant than parents and children such as
    aunts, uncles and grandparents. Anthropological work concerned with
    kinship has shown the immense variety that is subsumed under the term
    which renders it meaningless if used without qualification. The term is
    made even more problematic because it has also acquired a romanticised
    meaning in referring back to an unspecified time when people lived in
    large groups with a greater sense of community than they do now. For
    these, and other reasons, household size has become an important issue in
    historical demography (see Vogel, 1978, esp. p.54).

4   Some primitive statistics may be found in Sillitoe (1973, tables 18−19,
    32−3). For a discussion of late nineteenth-century debates on infant mor-
    tality and the ways they were used against working women, see Dyhouse
    (1978).

5   Both Shorter (1975), and Ariès (1973), stress the importance of attitudinal
    changes towards greater emphasis on love and intimacy between family
    members, and date the shift as being well under way by the end of the
    eighteenth century. Burguiere (1976), on the other hand, stresses the
    desire to control family size for basically economic, prudent reasons, and
    he locates this shift to deliberate control during the eighteenth and early
    nineteenth centuries. Of course, there were many different ways a family
    could control its size without birth control, some temporary, others per-
    manent, such as infanticide, abandonment, sending children into chari-
    table institutions or other people's homes as apprentices.

6   A different approach which looks at popular childrearing customs may be
    found in Loux (1978).

7   See the journals *History of Childhood Quarterly* and *Psychohistory
    Review*. A useful overview is Poster (1978).

8   The apologia for modernisation theory by Hareven (1976), a prominent
    historian of the family, is illuminating. For a general discussion of
    modernisation theory, see Appleby (1978).

9   The notion of community has been debated by Macfarlane (1977a and b)
    and Calhoun (1978). See also Macfarlane (1978).)

10 The point about the low wages of industrial women workers was eloquently
    made by the historian Jules Michelet (1860, p.xx). Although he con-
    demned the exploitation of female labour, he nonetheless believed that

women should be financially dependent on their husbands. For an account of the British situation see Hewitt (1958). Hartmann (1976), is a feminist perspective on 'job segregation by sex'.

11 In considering the family as a unit it is important to recognise that it has a life cycle, and that the ages of its constituent members play a decisive role in its ability to survive in times of hardship. On family cycles a general survey is Boocock (1978).

12 I would like to thank Leonore Davidoff for her advice and help on this subject.

Further reading

General works on women, family and work:

S. Alexander, 'Women's work in nineteenth-century London: a study of the years 1820—50.' In J. Mitchell and A. Oakley (eds), *The Rights and Wrongs of Women*. Harmondsworth: Penguin, 1976.

S. Burman (ed.), *Fit Work for Women*. London: Croom Helm, 1979.

N.Z.Davis, *Society and Culture in Early Modern France*. London: Duckworth, 1975.

O. Hufton, *The Poor of Eighteenth-century France*. Oxford: Oxford University Press, 1974.

M. Poster, *Critical Theory of the Family*. London: Pluto Press, 1978.

E. Power, *Medieval Women*. Cambridge: Cambridge University Press, 1975.

L. Tilly and J. Scott, *Women, Work and Family*. New York: Holt, Rinehart & Winston, 1978. (Good bibliography.)

A. Wohl (ed.), *The Victorian Family*. London: Croom Helm, 1978.

Popular working-class culture and the family:

P. Burke, *Popular Culture in Early Modern France*. London: Maurice Temple Smith, 1978.

J.M. Phayer, *Sexual Liberation and Religion in Nineteenth-century Europe*. London: Croom Helm, 1977.

Authority within the family:

J.M. Mogey, 'A century of declining paternal authority.' *Journal of Marriage and the Family*, 19, 1957.

D. Roberts, 'The Paterfamilias of the Victorian governing classes.' In A. Wohl (ed.), *The Victorian Family*. London: Croom Helm, 1978.

Children and education:

W. Minge-Kalman, 'The industrial revolution and the European family: the institutionalisation of "childhood" as a market for family labor'. *Comparative Studies in Society and History*, 20, 1978.

J. Murphy, *The Education Act 1870: Text and Commentary*. Newton Abbot: David & Charles, 1972.

G. Sutherland, *Elementary Education in the Nineteenth Century*. London: Historical Association, 1971.

Control of the family by experts and the State:

J. Donzelot, *La police des familles*. Paris: Les editions de minuit, 1977.

B. Ehrenreich and D. English, *For Her Own Good: 150 Years of the Experts' Advice to Women*. London: Pluto Press, 1979.

J. Hodges and A. Hussain, Review article: Jacques Donzelot, *La Police des familles. Ideology and Consciousness*, 5, 1979.

Control of individuals and families through work:

E. Thompson, 'Time, work-discipline, and industrial capitalism.' *Past and Present*, 38, 1967.

L. Vogel, 'The contested domain: a note on the family in the transition to capitalism.' *Marxist Perspectives*, 1, 1978.

Divorce and family violence:

R. Phillips, 'Women and family breakdown in eighteenth-century France: Rouen 1780–1800.' *Social History*, 2, 1976.

Chapter Four

Motherhood and Mothering[1]

BARBIE ANTONIS

This chapter takes as a basic premise that giving birth to and nurturing children are experiences central to the lives of many women, regardless of class or culture. While patterns of childbearing and rearing have varied with different periods of history, it remains that these processes have universal significance. In focusing on contemporary Western culture (especially Britain) I shall consider whether the experiences of mothering actually correspond to the commonly held beliefs (ideologies) about motherhood. It is central to this critique that we challenge the assumptions about why, how, when and where women bear children.

The re-examination of women's contribution to production in the home and beyond, in particular their role as mothers, is an urgent and important task. It is a task with consequences for the lives of women, men, children and the structure of society. Chodorow (1978), in her analysis of the reproduction of mothering, and Dinnerstein (1978) have begun this task, and both authors use psychoanalytic concepts critically to understand the meaning of women's mothering to the development of human personality and behaviour. Woman, by her capacity to bear children (her creative potential) is simultaneously powerful and envied and also vulnerable and denigrated. Or so theory has it.[2]

The inclination towards, preparation for, management of and involvement in mothering and motherhood constitute a process laden with ambiguities and contradictions.[3] This is especially marked if one analyses motherhood as an institution, governed by overt and covert rules, which in turn generate models of the relative positions of women to others (men, children, doctors, judges) in society. Men, as potential and actual fathers, also experience the pressures of cultural expectations. Some of these, both for women and men, may be specific to industrialised modes of capitalist production. It has been argued, however (Zaretsky, 1976), that it is not capitalism which produces these conditions, but patriarchy, a system which predates capitalism and survives under socialism.

I have chosen to consider four broad aspects of motherhood and mothering: inclinations toward or against bearing a child; psychological preparation for parenthood; management of pregnancy and childbirth; and, finally, involvement in childcare. These aspects should be understood not as separate stages in the motherhood career but as interrelating contributions to the politics and experience of motherhood.

In recent years there has been a noticeable increase in media coverage about pregnancy, childbirth and childcare. Academic writing (some feminist, some not) about women as mothers has also increased. This burgeoning of academic and popular publications is, I think, a direct response to public interest. The late 1960s counter-culture attitudes, especially in the United States, concerned with the importance of deep, human relationships rather than materialism, may be a root of the more recent interest, but this itself is a debatable point.[4] Legal developments such as the Equal Pay and Sex Discrimination Acts, which entail changes in maternity leave and allowances, and the more recent Child Benefit legislation, reflect this public concern. They have also illuminated (if nothing else) the economic and social position of women. The effect of the women's liberation movement and consumer pressure in raising public consciousness about the personal and political realities of childbearing and childcare is difficult to assess.

My own concerns have moved away from the study of sex differences in children's behaviour to the experience and medical management of pregnancy and childbirth, and they now centre on the realities of trying to combine motherhood, a career and health. The focus on early sex differences, so popular in the 1960s and early 1970s, has been replaced by an enquiry into the development of gender identity in the context of different ideologies of childrearing. Emphasis on the effects of technological advances in obstetrics is still prevalent in both psychological and sociological research, but has been extended to question the meaning of childbirth as an important life event for women and men.[5] The problems adults encounter when trying to combine childcare with work in the paid labour force now provide socially relevant and academically respectable questions, where once they were relegated to the arena of private concerns (Women in Employment Conference, Brunel 1976). 1979 saw the first conference in Britain on the role and experience of men in the bearing and rearing of children (BSA, Warwick 1979). The literature on fathers and their relationships with children and mothers is growing rapidly (Lamb, 1977; Richards, forthcoming) and this too will have implications for the politics and experience of motherhood and mothering.

This article aims to highlight some of these approaches but does not claim to have covered the field. The essential question with which I begin and end is 'Why do people enjoy having and rearing children, – or do they?'

Inclination toward or against motherhood

Dare I suggest that the most compelling pressure towards conceiving, bearing and nurturing another generation, is not 'Society' or 'Culture' or 'the Media' – or even Mother! It is Nature itself that drives us to reproduce the species. Of course we are not mindless. Maybe some of us have some measure of choice, and instinct is not so strong in some as others. . . . Many would confirm that they could debate the matter disinterestedly, until they found themselves 'mated' and with some emotional security . then almost in spite of oneself comes the nest building and broody feeling. (Letter to the Editor, *Observer*, Dec. 1978)

After conception, gestation and childbirth are exclusively female functions. A distinction should, however, be drawn between these quintessentially female processes, and mothering, which is nurturing and caring for others.[6] The mothering function is not intrinsically limited to the female sex, it can be and is in certain cultures (e.g. the Arapesh; the Mbuti) shared by men. Some authors (Rapoport, 1977) talk of the 'parenting' function and this is slightly more satisfactory, but only if 'parenting' is extended to adults who are not necessarily *biological* parents.

It is important to ask where the use of the phrase 'maternal instinct' originated, how it was used, where the term has currency and whether it is useful. Attempts to answer these questions may illustrate how quasi-biological concepts (which themselves are not politically neutral) have been used and may indicate how readily explanation termed scientific, and taken to be objective, is absorbed as truth and given credence.

In the eighteenth century the idea of a maternal instinct was used by the natural scientist and author Goldsmith (1774)[7] to describe a female *animal's* behaviour with her young, and a century later Lamarck and Darwin used the concept to refer to behaviour in the lower species which was thought to be unlearned or innate. 'The very essence of an instinct is that it is followed independently of reason' (Darwin, 1871). The 'maternal instinct theory' of behaviour became the perfect explanatory tool for nineteenth-century scientists in their evaluations of female nature. It appeared to explain so much; women's limited intellect, their emotionality and why they were less variable and more childlike in physical form than men. Interestingly, in Victorian society some instincts were acceptable, while others were not. The maternal instinct to bear children was not to be thwarted, but sexual instincts of women and children were considered dangerous and had to be suppressed.

In 1915, in an essay entitled 'Instincts and their Vicissitudes', Freud opens with the statement that 'instinct' is a 'borrowed concept on which psychoanalysis . . . has to lean but which can be regarded as no more than a convention'. This point, made by Freud, should be heeded. The use of the word as an explanatory concept or principle is very limited. The popularity of the concept of maternal instinct has been fostered more recently by animal and human ethologists. Their method, of naturalistic observations and descriptive studies of behaviour, with its links to 'instinct theory' has failed to consider sociocultural effects and variations. When the term 'maternal instinct' is used, a rigid interpretation is offered of what is a very complex and variable phenomenon.

Is the argument for a maternal instinct not tautologous, seemingly explaining those characteristics which serve as the rationale for its existence? And does the perpetuation of the concept, by social scientists, doctors and others influenced by ethology, popular natural history and psychoanalytic theory reflect and reinforce their own acceptance of the status quo (Wortis, 1971; Shields, 1978)? What requires further analysis is the way that biology is socially constructed and how this in turn involves the devaluation of female 'biology'.

When the expression maternal instinct is used now, it usually refers to the individualistic desire for childbearing, and also describes the social and psychological aspects of mothering behaviour. Significantly, the physiological reflexes involved in pregnancy, childbirth and lactation are susceptible to disturbance (emotional upset) on the social and psychological level. This in turn illustrates the interrelatedness of all human reactions and behaviour. Furthermore, any dualism posited between the 'social' and the 'biological' implies that some factors or scientific concepts could conceivably be 'non-social'.

The presence of an infant does often stimulate nurturant or caregiving behaviour on the part of most mothers, and also from people who are not biological parents. However, a woman who has not previously handled, fed or cared for an infant may have great difficulty in the first days of a baby's life in establishing feeding (whether by breast or bottle). New mothers may be helped by being shown how to hold the baby, wind, bathe and dress it. With experience most women succeed very well and become very skilled with time and involvement. Men, on the whole, have very little exposure to babies and consequently are thought to be (and may be) very inept. Mothering is not the manifestation of an innate mechanism, it is a skill which develops through learning (which begins in mother-daughter relationships where women are the primary care-givers) and experience with children.

From another viewpoint, one can ask why, if wanting and bearing children were instinctive, are the efforts to socialise girls into wanting babies so pervasive and persuasive. The aim of this section is to stress that motherhood and mothering are influenced in many ways. In asking how maternity and childcare affect women's lives, and how remaining childless affects women, it is very difficult to separate these factors.

The ideological framework in which reproduction occurs in our society not only 'equates being a woman with motherhood' (Gavron, 1966) but also assumes that for normal individuals parenthood is universal. There are strong negative sanctions against both illegitimacy and voluntary childlessness. The true victim of the latter was, and to a large extent still is, seen to be society. If cheated of its most important 'product' further evolution was impossible! Hence the surfeit, in the nineteenth century, of 'tracts disparaging the higher education of women and glorifying woman as the angel of the home' (Shields, 1978, p.753). Busfield (1974, p.14) argues that 'On the one hand it is expected and regarded as desirable that those who marry will have children; and on the other . . . that those who want to have children will marry.' These stereotypes are supported by much of the research on reproduction which uses as its yardstick the nuclear family. Sex, marriage and reproduction are linked together in a way implying that each explains and necessitates the other.[8] As Macintyre (1974, p.5) points out: 'We still need to enquire into the meanings attributed and processes leading to marriage and reproduction among differently situated social groups or individuals.'

Any discussion of the process and meaning of childbearing must consider both the form and availability of childrearing practices and provisions and the conditions of the availability of contraception, abortion and sterilisation. How, when, and to whom these services are provided illustrates the mechanism by which medical practice, public morality and the State promote or limit fertility and influence women's notions of their own sexuality and reproductive role. Macintyre (1974) has shown that when a woman is seeking to terminate her pregnancy, a different outcome is likely according to whether she is married or single. Two theories exist among the medical and helping professions regarding the nature of the maternal instinct, and Macintyre's work illustrates elegantly the pressures of reproductive ideology and the politics of the family. The assumptions that Macintyre describes are:

For married women

(1) Pregnancy and childbearing are normal and desirable and conversely a desire not to have children aberrant and in need of explanation.

(2) Pregnancy and childbearing are not problematic and to treat them as such indicates that something is wrong.

(3) Legitimate children with a living parent should not be surrendered for adoption, as this would occasion too much distress for the mother. A married woman who wants to get rid of her children is by definition aberrant.

(4) If a couple is childless it is clinically advisable that they receive diagnostic attention and, if necessary, treatment for infertility.

(5) It is clinically advisable on occasion to advise a woman to have a child.

(6) The loss of a baby by miscarriage, stillbirth or neo-natal death occasions instinctive deep distress and grief.

For single women

(1) Pregnancy and childbearing are abnormal and undesirable and conversely the desire to have a child is aberrant, selfish and in need of explanation.

(2) Pregnancy and childbearing are problematic and to not treat them as such indicates that something is wrong.

(3) Illegitimate children should be surrendered for adoption and a mother who wants to keep her child is unrealistic and selfish.

(4) Diagnostic attention and treatment for infertility is not clinically advisable or relevant — unless the woman is about to get married. It is not proper for her to adopt a child.

(5) It would be inadvisable and inappropriate clinically to advise a single woman to have a child.

(6) The loss of a baby by miscarriage, stillbirth or neo-natal death should not occasion too much grief or distress and may even produce relief.

(7) In summary: one solution for the problems of a single, pregnant woman is to get married. If she is going to get married, she will want the baby, if not, she will not want it.

So, MATERNAL INSTINCT (as a good thing) IS ASCRIBED TO MARRIED WOMEN ONLY!

Discussion of the possible existence of a maternal instinct is often very emotive. Many women refer to their own 'maternal instincts' to explain why they 'feel broody', 'are very good with children' and why in fact they love their children. In their relationships with men, who may not want children, women may reduce their wish to bear children to their maternal instincts. Some women may also feel obliged to explain their positive and negative feelings about children. In other words, there is a contradiction between feeling that mothering comes naturally and feeling that one's emotions as a mother have to be justified. This paradox exists at a time when a positive 'politics of the family' has yet to be developed; such a positive politics would consider the various non-traditional ways that the family may be reconstituted (single parent, communal parents, lesbian parents). The issue, therefore, of women's inclination to bear children or not, is one that should be situated within evolving ideologies of the family and reproduction.

Preparation and priming for motherhood

Motherhood is the chief occupation for which females are reared. It is central to the feminine gender role that a female child learns this from her parents, peers, school, books, television advertisements; i.e. from society. There are different interpretations of this complex learning process by which females get geared up for maternity. It is the case that sex-stereotypic expectations exist even before the birth of a baby (probably before conception). These are manifested in parental attitudes towards the child. Expectant parents have reasons they would prefer a boy or a girl and these relate to characteristics they see as being male or female.

> I suppose it's the family thing of having a son and also to please Derek. He says he doesn't mind but he really wants a son. He wants a boy, I think, because he thinks girls are more fragile.
>
> Boys are fussier — I mean they cry much more and get dirtier but girls are quieter and usually good.[9]

Research by Smith and Lloyd (1978) shows that adult men and women attribute entirely different characteristics and behaviour to the same child, according to whether the child is said to be a boy or a girl. Their work is an excellent illustration of sex-stereotypic ascriptions in operation. These ascriptions may be related to how men and women feel about their own sexual image and their relationships with either a son or a daughter. Several women interviewed in a London study (Antonis, 1975, unpublished) thought that they would find it easier to identify with a female child:

> As a female perhaps I'll know better what to do with another one.
>
> I think I know why I want a girl. I think one tends to keep a daughter whereas one loses a son, in many respects. I don't particularly want a daughter because I can dress her up.[10]

I would contend that what influences and informs the handling of any particular child by his/her caregivers is the *meaning* of that child to the adults. Meaning, that is, in terms of how the adults perceive their roles and sexuality, the sex and parity of the child, and their own relationship which changes with the birth of a child. I include the child's sex here because of the conscious and unconscious preferences that the caregivers may have, and the pleasure and disappointments which often accompany these feelings.

The ways in which girls are socialised toward notions of femininity and for motherhood, in our culture, are dominated by popularised psychoanalytic theory. It has contributed many pervasive and tenacious ideas about women and their sexuality. It supports the synonymity between female sexuality and reproduction suggested by earlier evolutionary theory. Freud's own theories of female sexuality have been adopted and modified (for better and worse) by later psychoanalysts. Erikson (1965), in characterising women as 'the bearer of the ova and maternal powers', represents a fairly reductive view, but most psychoanalytic writers agree in placing motherhood at the centre of woman's psycho-emotional development. An assumption here is that the woman who has a stable sexual identity perceives no conflict between her sexuality and her reproductive role. The corollary is that a 'woman will reveal her maturity through her desire for children, her stable sexual identity and the selflessness with which she approaches maternity' (Rosser, 1978). Lidz and Deutsch, among other psychoanalysts, see motherhood as crucial to the meaning of femininity and the apex of the female experience. Deutsch speaks of pregnancy as the 'direct fulfilment of the most powerful wish of women'. Lidz has also asserted that:

> if the expectant mother has come to terms with being a woman, which includes some lingering regrets at not having been born a man, she feels that her pregnancy is fulfilling her fate, completing her life as a woman and she knows a creativity that compensates for past restrictions and limitations. (Lidz, 1968, p.93)

The traditional Freudian viewpoint holds that a young girl experiences her lack of a penis as 'castration', and that to become a woman she must substitute pregnancy and a baby for the missing male organ. Therefore, motherhood is seen as the practical resolution of penis-envy. Women are led to think of themselves as mothers, to want to be mothers while the actual process of becoming a mother and the concomitant changes physically, in role and status, are suppressed. This situation is confirmed in much psychoanalytic literature which, in concentrating on the pathology and disturbance of pregnancy and mothering, locates the problem within the individual woman's psyche and not within the external cultural pressures she experiences.

Bibring (1961) does attempt to dispel the myths of a glorified pregnancy and motherhood. However, even Bibring's innovative approach has not gone far enough in situating the reasons for, meaning and experience of pregnancy and mothering within woman's social context. On the one hand pregnancy is seen as the norm for young women, while on the other it is perceived as a maturational hurdle to be overcome, after which normality will return.

More recently, work by Breen (1978/24) shows a view of pregnancy as an active, creative and initiating process. This perception contrasts with the traditional equation of passivity and helplessness with femininity. But she also stresses 'the deeper psychobiological aspect of a woman's wish to confirm the goodness of her body, the healthy functioning of her female organs and her wish to come closer to, in a concrete way, her femaleness' (p.24). This emphasis suggests to me her acceptance of the main thrust of psychoanalytic understanding of the importance of motherhood to women, and an inadequate evaluation of the power of ideologies of sex and reproduction.[11] With the assertion of both her sexuality and reproductive role, a woman enters into a new relationship; that with her baby — a relationship which can be unconditionally loving and very rewarding but which is susceptible to stresses often induced by unnecessary medical intervention and insensitive medical care.

A contradiction exists between the notion that bearing a child is the highest goal a woman can achieve, and the low, marginal status in which she finds herself when pregnant and as a mother. The ambivalence this contradiction generates is illustrated by Rosser's work

(1978). She suggests that anxiety and ambivalence about the process of motherhood and the capacity to mother, are inevitable. When bearing children women feel they are following their natural course but also 'sealing their fate as second-class citizens' since motherhood is an undervalued, under-rewarded occupation and mothering an undervalued skill. This conflict highlights a double-bind with which women have to cope. They should do their duty (for husbands, their parents, society and themselves) and bear a child (or preferably 2.4 children) but once this is done their role in society is appreciated primarily in relation to that child, because it is he/she who now becomes the valued person.

Whether motherhood is an occupation in the usual sense of the word is itself a valid question. It is not an occupation which is 'chosen' in the usual sense of the word or from which one can earn a living wage, come home, or even have a holiday. But it *is* time-consuming work with emotional commitment. It is work which deserves to be recognised and financially rewarded. We have to be wary of those policy makers who suggest that it is an occupation only for the selected group, adequately trained in the skill of parenting, and who then meet the criteria of 'good parents'.[12]

Management of motherhood and mothering

There is ample evidence that women are often unprepared for the physical, emotional and social demands of motherhood (Oakley, 1980; Rich, 1977; Breen, 1978). This section will ask why women are so unprepared for the realities they encounter; and illustrate that these realities are continuously variable.

Maternity as a career is fostered by commercial interests (such as special, costly accessories!) and public and private rules. A pregnant woman is channelled into new relationships with other women (knowledgeable mothers), the health services and the State. Pregnancy is not only enshrined on its own medical pedestal (obstetrics) but also has its niche in psychiatry. Of the terms used by the psychiatric profession to characterise mental disturbance after childbirth only 'post-natal depression' or 'the blues' is commonly used and expected by pregnant women (Oakley, 1979). In recent literature concerned with mental illness in pregnancy and soon afterwards (Sandler, 1978), only one chapter is devoted entirely to socio-cultural determinants and another one to possible psychological influences. The main thrust of the work concerns supposed 'biological' correlates of mental illness and illustrates the narrowness and inadequacy of hormonal theories of puerperal mental disturbance.

The relationship between women and the medical profession is particularly and peculiarly complex. From the day she informs the GP or hospital (or is informed by the GP) that she is pregnant, the expectant mother is faced with a variety of expectations. These expectations and prescriptions are fostered by folk beliefs, mass media, the law and medical, psychological and sociological research. Early in pregnancy questions are asked of the woman for which she is often unready: 'Is the birth to be in hospital?' (First births are rarely allowed to be at home anymore.) 'Will you breast or bottle feed?' 'Will the baby's father be at the birth?' More important than the mistiming of these questions is the insufficiency of clear, accurate information that is offered to her. What is more, even the most recent studies of the organisation and satisfaction with antenatal care show that the opportunities for expectant mothers to ask their own questions and to develop some familiarity with the people who will attend the birth, are severely limited (Graham, 1978; Cartwright, 1979; Cambridge Community Health Council, 1979).

The literature on pregnancy and motherhood promotes two rather distinct images of pregnancy: that of passive, dreamy women who are quite at the mercy of their hormones; and at the other extreme the unemotional, practical, active women of the washing powder commercials. Neither of these images is realistic or helpful, as they may only reflect some women's experiences, some of the time. The paradox, which this dichotomy reveals, is amplified by those doctors and others in the paramedical professions who often do not treat women as individuals during their antenatal care. Rather, a task-oriented ritual is operated where urine, blood-pressure, weight are the concerns. Many professionals do not (dare) credit women with the intelligence to understand what pregnancy and labour are about and, moreover, see pregnancy as a time of 'illness'. So, within the management of pregnancy and childbirth, there is a clear split between the importance attributed to physiology, with its objective, quantifiable variables and the human emotions which accompany the process. The latter are dismissed as irrational and unquantifiable and therefore not worthy of serious consideration. It is evident in the medical literature that pregnancy and childbirth are only considered normal in retrospect, that is, after a normal delivery.

The explicit and implicit management of pregnancy and childbirth as pathological states has several consequences. These consequences which have personal and political dimensions, have been termed the 'medicalisation'[13] of motherhood (Oakley, 1975). This medicalisation has altered not only the autonomy and control that women have over their bodies and their health, but also the location of that control. The roots of these changes probably lie in the *rise of science* which Oakley does not discuss in her arguments about the 'transfer of power' from midwives to gynaecologists. Scientific thought and practice not only gave rise to its own brand of professionalism which empowered its practitioners to 'treat' the ill, but, in effect, took over medicine. Those who became 'scientists' were generally men, and herein lies the basis for the shift of control from the midwives to the male obstetricians. The result of this 'transfer of power' is seen to result in women feeling alienated from their own reproductive functions. There is evidence of this result in the accounts of women's experiences during childbirth, but there may be many causes.

The evidence for this process of medicalisation comes from the dramatic increase in hospitalisation for childbirth (in Great Britain, in 1972, 91.2 per cent of all births took place in hospital). The latter has encouraged the adoption of new drugs and technology. The argument which stresses the importance of hospital-located childbirth, for the safety of mother and child, is based on 'scientific data': perinatal mortality and morbidity statistics. However, the associations between hospital confinements and lowered maternal and perinatal mortality rates do not necessarily amount to cause-and-effect. In Holland there is a home-confinement rate of about 50 per cent, but there is also a comparatively low rate of infant mortality (17 : 1,000 compared with 22:1,000 in England; Kitzinger, 1978). Present-day obstetric techniques may have their benefits but the widespread use of induction and acceleration of labour, epidurals, the increased use of instrumental delivery (forceps) and Caesarian section can also have detrimental effects on the mother and the baby (Chard and Richards, 1977).

To challenge the authority of the doctor, and moreover that of purported scientific evidence, is difficult enough. To do so at a time when you are busy with other concerns, and anyway considered to be far from rational, is all but impossible. Asking questions of the doctors and nurses takes time and by doing so the expectant woman is aware of 'holding everyone else up'. These are the difficulties that many pregnant women encounter.

An analysis of the problems that women experience between this medical and specifically obstetric ideology shows a concentration of research (in many disciplines) on childbirth as the critical moment for mother and child. Childbirth is only an end-point if so defined. It is in fact part of a much wider, larger experience. One might ask why there has been such a convergence of interest in 'labour' in Western society. Part of the reason for women's and patients' groups (such as the Association for the Improvement of Maternity Services) may well be genuine concern that parents and children be spared the unnecessary technological innovations which our society so readily adopts. Moreover, large numbers of *healthy* people experience hospitalisation for childbirth and are perhaps more able than the 'ill' to be critical of the care they receive. Also, attacks on medical practice are fashionable now, however well-deserved they may be. The results of some of the research, which warns against the use of insufficient or 'loose' criteria for inductions, episiotomies, epidurals and even the admission of small-for-dates babies into special care nurseries, are slowly filtering through into hospital practice. It is interesting, however, that when women themselves complain against these practices, their voices are not heard (Riley, 1977).

There is also a tendency in obstetric research to look for the relationship between certain maternal characteristics during pregnancy and those of the subsequent child. This trend implies a search for maternal factors which will predict future problems, and especially a situation where mother and baby may be 'at risk'. The implicit burden of this research concerns not medical factors, but psychological and sociological ones. Recent work (Chisholm *et al.*, 1978) supports the notion that 'anxious' pregnant women have more difficult, irritable babies by showing a positive correlation between maternal blood pressure and these infant characteristics. The danger inherent in interpreting such a correlation is twofold: first, it assumes that a variety of experiences can be reduced to a physical measure (blood pressure); and second, it confuses many levels of analysis. It may indeed be wise to recommend rest to reduce blood pressure and resting is what many pregnant women know about, but being able to rest is not the same as having all the family, economic and personal difficulties removed. In addition, the 'admission' of these difficulties may serve as an indicator for social workers, health visitors and doctors that the woman is a 'problem case' and suitable material for the 'risk register'.[14] This is the junction at which legal and medical ideologies meet. At the time of her 'peak of femininity', her pregnancy and early post-partum period, a woman is, in law, also potentially insane. According to the Infanticide Act (1938) a woman who kills her child before he/she is a year old, or while she is breastfeeding, may be liable not to the charge of murder but to that of manslaughter — to a verdict of guilty, but insane.

Prescriptions concerning childcare and infant feeding, in the past and now, seem so rigid as to induce confusion, anxiety and perhaps even feelings of madness. Trends in the promotion (or not) of breast-feeding are historically well-documented as this activity provides a visible arena for public pronouncement, the influence of childcare 'theorists' and changing fashions. Gomm (1976) makes the point that the 'facts' on which medical, hygienic and nutritional indications for breastfeeding are based, were equally knowable and true when doctors, midwives and health visitors were promoting bottle-feeding. Currently, in Britain, there is a positive breastfeeding policy in most hospitals and breastfeeding has become one of the criteria for 'good mothering'.[15].

Discussion of the way that ideologies exercise an effect on people's behaviour, by holding up prescriptions which they are meant to meet, should question the notion of 'social control' which is currently in use. The notion, in relation to images and rules for pregnancy and mother-ing, may imply

(a) that there was a time when such rules did not exist,
(b) that women have no voice with which to counter them, and
(c) that women are merely the 'passive substratum' which absorbs these rules.

The historical evidence is that while there is a tradition of folklore concerning the 'do's and dont's' relating to childbearing, this know-ledge was accessible to women because it was transmitted by women to women. Second, there is contemporary evidence that reports of consumer satisfaction are only now gaining acceptance as valid data. Finally, perhaps, women have, to some extent, 'played the game' and conformed to those stereotypes which are supposed to be part of their 'natural' repertoire. It may often seem easier to collude with the system, even unconsciously, than risk the label of deviant.

Involvement in mothering and childcare

The passage to parenthood is instant, ferocious and irrefutable; it comes on you like being winded. . . . This is not to say that it is love alone. The new world inspires rage and fear as well. The exhaustion of the first few weeks is hallucinatory. (Marina Warner 'New-born mother' *Guardian*, Jan. 1977)

It is not disputed nor surprising that mothers and mothering have consequences for children and that there is a reciprocal effect from the children. Mothering also has effects on those doing it and these do not always match the prevailing ideal of the contented woman, secure in her role, satisfied with the rewarding task of childrearing, comforted by the knowledge that she is doing what only she can do.

The first few months living with and caring for a new baby present a learning period for the mother as intense as at any time in her life. This intensity is brought about not only by the novelty of the situation and the responsibility which it engenders but also by the personal and social context in which mothers learn to mother. Questions concerning women's sense of their own 'competence and confidence' to mother and the way external agencies both measure and determine this are important to an analysis of the relationships between women, their reproductive role and family and economic structure. Most women in Britain cease working in the paid labour market with the birth of their first child and often cannot become wage earners again until the child is at school. With the birth of a child most women become financially dependent. While there are sectors of women for whom this is an acceptable circumstance, there are others for whom it is unsatisfactory. Moreover, there are women for whom financial support is unavailable or at best minimal. The welfare system explicitly encourages the traditional nuclear family by reducing and sometimes withholding social security benefits to women and men who are not married but are seen to be cohabiting (Wilson, 1976b). This is very clear in relation to men, too. Men who are looking after children on their own are assumed by the welfare system to be, and to want to be, in paid employment.

Financial dependence is, however, only one feature typical of a mother's status. As important is the fact that the day-to-day care of young children, in addition to all the other invisible work that women do, such as shopping, cleaning, fetching and carrying, is often isolating and generates a sense of low self-esteem and worth. Post-natal trauma, depression and exhaustion are common and female admissions to psychiatric wards are raised due to 'neuroses and psychoses' following childbirth.

Though few new mothers in Britain have much practical experience of caring for infants before their own are born, it is the case that many have highly developed ideas of what is expected of a mother and what babies are like. But, there is often a disparity between a mother's expectations of 'ideal mothering' and the 'ideal baby' with the experience of herself as a mother and her real baby. The baby may cry a great deal, need frequent feeding in the early months, wake regularly at night and continue to do so for months. The mother may experience frightening feelings of anger and frustration in herself. These things may in fact be exacerbated in our culture where the social routines (breakfast at 8 a.m. and tea at 5.30 p.m.) are inflexible and there is inadequate leisure time for all members of 'the family' to be together.

The mis-match between experience and expectations is important for several reasons. One of these relates to the high value placed in our society on knowledge produced and distributed by 'experts'. Because of this rise of professionalism in the area of childcare and development, 'the business of childrearing is often felt to be problematic and is anxiety-provoking' (Richards, 1976). Moreover, not only is anxiety aroused but confidence with one's own competence is severely diminished since there is an implied 'right way of doing things' known only to the 'experts'. Another significant reason concerns the incidence of child abuse; 'the battered-baby syndrome' and depression in women and children (Brown and Harris, 1978; Swan *et al.*, 1978; Richman, 1976). The growing enquiry into these problems has directed more attention to the social position and context of women. Some of this work points to the disjunction between women's actual role and work as mothers and their powerless economic position. Mothers carry a heavy responsibility in being accountable for their children's health, their intelligence and performance at school, the clothes they wear and their general development. It is also understated that there are many different ways of being a good parent. We know much more about what can 'go wrong' with 'parenting' than the *different* ways of being right.

One of the most influential theories to shape recent ideas about child development and 'good parenting' is Bowlby's Attachment Theory (1951; 1969). His theory's most provocative feature is its focus on the mother-child relationship as an adaptive mechanism selected in the course of evolution because it promotes infant survival. The implication often drawn from this that has received most criticism, is that infants are predisposed to establish a relationship with a single, consistent caregiver (mother) and that deviations from this pattern will be detrimental to the infant's development. Historically, Attachment Theory developed as a response to, and as an attempt to explain, the often catastrophic consequences for children of institutionalisation or 'maternal deprivation', especially during the Second World War. Bowlby's theory, which relied heavily on evidence from separation experiments with animals (arguments about which still persist), has had the positive effect of altering the material and psychological conditions of children's institutions and the emphases in paediatric practice. At the negative extreme, the implications of the theory have made maternal deprivation a 'crime' which children potentially suffer at their mothers' hands; a 'crime' which mothers fear committing. No one with any concern for people, children and adults alike, would disagree that we all suffer because of separations, that we all 'cry' when separated from someone we love. But it is the quality of care between individuals which counts, not the quantity.

With the acceptance of the main theme of Attachment Theory, that *mothers* should look after their children with constant, loving care, the wish women have to continue working when the children are young is turned into an indicator of selfishness, irresponsibility and even immaturity. Even mothers who carry the main burden of childcare feel guilty when they want a little time to themselves. The question of maternal deprivation, which now focuses on psychological not material deprivation, has been analysed by many (Rutter, 1972) including feminists (Wortis, 1971; Humpty Dumpty, 1978). The concept of deprivation must not be restricted to the child; it should be extended to include parents (biological and social). A realistic analysis of the relationships between parents and children can illuminate the ways these relationships are grounded in psychological and social processes.

Women with very young children *do* go out to work. They do so, often not to earn 'pin money' but to contribute to the family income, frequently out of necessity and to sustain some link with the 'real' world and their sanity. The work they opt for is often part time, for which wages are notoriously low and for which accompanying benefits such as sick leave, holidays and pensions are often lacking. In the 1971 Census, 19 per cent of mothers with pre-school children were working; now the figure is closer to 26 per cent. About 800,000 small children require day-time care. The realistic options for this care are limited: playgroups, private nurseries and local authority nursery schools are inadequate because their hours bear no relation to those the mother actually works. There has been a steady run-down of State nurseries since the war (Riley, 1979) and numbers have fallen by two-thirds to 23,000 places. Only those in severe social need get places. Factories', universities' and other educational establishments' creches are few. The backbone of the care is provided by childminders. Childminding is cheap, considering the responsibility and decision-making involved, for several reasons. Childminders have marginal status in the work-force and have little power as a result. Also childminders know how little mothers can afford — about £17 per week is the average for five full days work and that includes the child's meals. In a recent EOC document this service was, however, almost condemned because childminders 'lack equipment', 'are unsupervised', 'exploited' and 'not expert'. Owen (1978) characterises the problem of childcare as 'sorting out how women, and men, can sneak five years off for being human out of 50 on someone's production line, without being shut out of all prospect of human achievement for the rest of one's days.'

There are various schemes abroad aimed at achieving this. In Sweden, expectant mothers and fathers can take more than a year's maternity and paternity leave, with pay, and there is also the option for part-time work for both parents. 'Flexi-time', which allows re-arrangement of the hours worked to suit women's needs, exists in Switzerland and covers 60 per cent of female employment there. Job-twinning is another possibility where parents can work in alternate cycles. The EOC report mentioned above does not encourage exploring these options in Britain, except for that of flexible hours. The emphasis in Britain is still very much on the mother's respon-sibility for childcare. There is insufficient acknowledgement of and demand for the involvement of fathers and others who may not be biological parents, in the care of small children. That concepts of paternity leave, job-sharing and collective responsibility for child-rearing are unsupported in this country indicates further the problems for women. Women who work all day are isolated from the company of other mothers with their children and may even resent this. Women spending most of their time with their children may have some support from other mothers in a similar situation but envy these women who work. There is as yet *no* satisfactory appreciation of the treble task that many women manage; work in paid labour, unpaid work in the home and the job of rearing the children. Altering the availability and conditions of paid employment might be a partial solution for women and men caring for children. Until society faces these issues directly, the context and experience of women's lives will remain harshly circumscribed. It is a sad reflection on the priorities of our society that those conditions likely to provoke such a reappraisal are the emergency need for women in the labour force (as in war) or intoler-able pressures on inadequate welfare services.

Mothering and motherhood are central to women's lives. These pro-cesses have important human consequences, individually and socially. I have tried to show that throughout the passage into motherhood there are instances where ideologies fail to meet experience. It is important for women to understand the biology of their sexual and reproductive capacities, the reasons behind the devaluation of their biology and to share this knowledge amongst themselves. Shared understanding developed in this way may enable women to create images of themselves compatible with their actual experience.

Notes

1 I would like to thank Robin Crighton, Martin Richards and Shelley Day for their helpful criticism of this paper.

2 For interesting elaborations of the theories of women's power and vulnerability and denigration as potential or actual mothers see Chodorow (1978), Dinnerstein (1978) and Rich (1977).

3 These contradictions and ambiguities may not be experienced by all women and for some may be balanced by pleasures and satisfactions. However, they are inherent within the ideologies of gender and reproduction and the latter are increasingly becoming the concern of women's groups, patients' associations, radical midwife and radical science groups.

4 See Lasch, C. 'Life in the Therapeutic State' for his analysis of the historical roots of the political changes in the 1960s.

5 Ann Oakley's book *Women Confined* (1980) is a good illustration of this. Also Shelley Day's work on post-natal depression and the politics of reproductive care.

6 Chodorow (1978) elaborates the need for this distinction pp.16, 205.

7 Oliver Goldsmith in *An History of the Earth and Animated Nature* (1774) gives the following description: 'At this time the female is instinctively taught that her young ones want relief.'

8 See Lasch, C. again for an historical analysis of these ties.

9 This statement comes from interviews with pregnant women taking part in a study exploring attitudes to the first baby: Antonis (unpublished; Bedford College, London University, supported by the Social Science Research Council).

10 Rich (1977), Chodorow (1978), Dinnerstein (1978) and Oakley (1980) all describe the particular ambivalence in mother-daughter relationships, though many women may anticipate that the identification will be easier. Oakley also finds that mothers in her study are 'less satisfied' with daughters.

11 Both Chodorow and Dinnerstein offer very interesting analyses of the failure of psychoanalytic theories to account for the reproduction of mothering.

12 See Zoë Fairbairns' book *Benefits* (1979) for a chilling elaboration of this theme.

13 'Medicalisation' is a term coined by Ivan Illich referring to the medical control of health and illness. *Medical Nemesis* 1975 and *Limits to Medicine* (1977).

14 The 'risk register' is now formally called the Central Child Abuse Register (BASW, 1978). One of the criteria for placing a child's name on the register is as follows: All newborns whose parental and perinatal histories suggest a high risk of abuse. This will include the small group of children

whose parents clearly show many of the predictive factors acknowledged to indicate a strong potential for child abuse.

15 See Cromer (1978) for a discussion of the effect of the Truby King regime in the 1930s and 1940s and the ambiguous influence of Spock too.

Further Reading

N. Chodorow, *The Reproduction of Mothering*. California: University of California, 1978.

D. Dinnerstein, *The Rocking of the Cradle and the Ruling of the World*. London: Souvenir Press, 1978.

A. Philips and J. Rakusen (eds), *Our Bodies Ourselves*. Harmondsworth: Penguin, 1978.

A. Oakley, *Becoming a Mother*. London: Martin Robertson, 1979.

A. Oakley, *Women Confined*. London: Martin Robertson, 1980.

A. Rich, *Of Woman Born*. London: Virago, 1977.

Chapter Five

Left critiques of the family

DENISE RILEY

'Abolition of the family! Even the most radical flare up at this infamous proposal of the Communists.' Thus Marx and Engels in their *Manifesto of the Communist Party* in 1848 introduce a vigorous and exhortatory attack on the bourgeois family. I want to start by discussing the elements of this attack, and then later place them in the context of other critical socialist analyses of the family. For what Marx and Engels have to say in this deliberately summary and programmatic text will serve well enough as a classical instance of one dominant nineteenth-century socialist critique, of which some elements are reiterated in twentieth-century critical theorisings on the family. My aim, however, is not the impossibly large task of summarising a 'history of ideas' of the family throughout Marxist and libertarian thought. Instead I want to pick out the more politically conspicuous Left theoretical treatments of the family, comment on their moral and futurological elements, and, finally, to suggest both the necessity and the originality of various points of entry of Left feminism into this area.

In its treatment of the family, the *Communist Manifesto* fights largely, though not entirely, on moral territory. This morality is not an effect of the text's status as a manifesto alone. For its moral terms are both defensive and critical in ways which characterise large amounts of socialist anti-family polemic of the late nineteenth century. Bourgeois morality, it insists, is in practice bourgeois hypocrisy. And bourgeois attacks on communist principles are best refuted by examining the behaviour of these guardians of official morality themselves. 'But you Communists would introduce a community of women, screams the whole bourgeoisie in chorus. The bourgeois sees in his wife a mere instrument of production. . . . He has not even a suspicion that the real point aimed at is to do away with the status of women as mere instruments of production.' Prostitution is a practice decidedly illustrative of the hypocrisy of a class which itself ascribes to communism the aim of unchecked sexual libertarianism. The 'virtuous indignation' of the bourgeoisie is enshrined in the true immorality of its own practices. The necessity and inevitability of prostitution under capitalism was widely argued by socialists refuting the standard charges of licentiousness against their own movements, or asserting the spiritual superiority of socialist domestic reforms. Writers as diverse as, for instance, Robert Owen and August Bebel argue from this point.[1] For Marx and Engels in 1848, prostitution was one effect of the reduction of 'the family relation to a mere money relation' – 'the bourgeoisie has torn away from the family its sentimental veil'. The specificity, as they saw it, of the bourgeois family 'in its completely developed form' to capitalism 'finds its complement in the practical absence of the family among the proletarians, and in public prostitution'. With the abolition of the capitalist mode of production would go 'the abolition of the community of women springing from that system'. (Marx and Engels, 1968)

Thus at this point Marx and Engels' critique of the family is based on its bourgeois manifestation as an institution which embodies or entails socially and morally damaging practices. Both these practices and that family spring from a system of capitalist economics, and with that system they will stand or fall. This analysis appears and reappears, with variations, in many subsequent Left critiques of the family. As an analysis, it was by no means uniquely originated by Marx and Engels; early nineteenth-century socialists and communitarians including Owen, Fourier and Saint-Simon had bitterly criticised the conjunctures of love and economics which characterised marriage. Owen's *Book of the New Moral World* of 1844 attacked the links between the family as institution and the perpetuation of private property and class difference. His 1835 *Lectures on the Marriages of the Priesthood of the Old Immoral World* opposed the 'irrationality' of single, separately dwelling families and indissoluble marriages, which he described as 'this most unnatural mal-arrangement of society'. The groupings of Owenite followers in the earlier 1840s had included socialist feminists who were passionately critical of the moral and economic implications of marriage for the status of women (Taylor, 1978).

Marx and Engels' critiques of 'utopian' socialism[2] as marked by eclecticism and a lack of scientific understanding were nevertheless later accompanied by full acknowledgement of Fourier's 'criticism of the bourgeois form of relations between the sexes'. Like other socialists, they independently reiterated his point that the degree of women's emancipation, in the broadest sense, acts as an index of the general level of humanity and civilisedness of any one society. Similarly, Owen's co-operative innovations and practical reforms were both criticised and credited by Marx and Engels from different aspects. There are, however, conspicuously shared moral and humanitarian elements in the objections to the family in its conventional form advanced by Owen and other 'utopians' and by Marx, particularly the 'early' Marx, and Engels. These moral elements are indicative of the broad history of socialist theorising of the family and of sexual relations. In the case of Marx in particular, his treatment of Hegel's societal philosophy feeds into this broad history as a sharp, if sometimes distorting, polemical attack. For Hegel's *Philosophy of Right* discusses marriage as, in ideal terms, the concrete embodiment of the highest moral principle; and his *Phenomenology of the Spirit* posits a congruence of the family and the State as potential forms of the ethical ideal. Marx's 1843 *Critique on Hegel's Philosophy of Right* sets out to undercut idealism by pointing to 'reality'; the land-propertied family, he argues, instead lives only 'spiritless family life, the illusion of family life'. For 'in its highest form of development, the principle of private property contradicts the principle of the family' and instead of congruence there is 'the barbarism of private property against family life'. And, alleges Marx in his *Critique*, Hegel has no analysis of the ways in which the family, civil society, and the State 'fit'; 'what is not clarified is the way in which familial and civil sentiment, the institution of the family and those of society, as such, stand related to the political sentiment and cohere with it.'

Marx did not undertake any such sustained clarifying work of analysis himself (although the first volume of *Capital* is full of asides and observations about the effects of women's labour, in a period of rapid industrialisation, on the working-class family). The writing which occupies the status of Marxist classic 'on the family' is of course Engels' *The Origin of the Family, Private Property, and the State*, of 1884. As such it has attracted much socialist, and especially socialist feminist, attention — particularly in the last few years.[3] Since this is so, I'll only give a quick mention to its salient points for immediate purposes here. This will mean ignoring its problematic aspects like its use of the concepts of a 'natural' and 'sexual' division of labour, or the more easily grasped datedness of some of its anthropological assumptions. But from the point of view of theories of the future development of the family, what's most significant about *The Origin of the Family* is that it assumes that once economic shackles are removed through a socialist economic revolution, then 'personal relationships' will spontaneously attain some ideal state. Thus 'the predominance of the man in marriage is simply a consequence of his economic predominance and will vanish with it automatically'. And 'full freedom' in marriage is possible only with the ending of capitalist production, and its property relations whose results 'still exact so powerful an influence on the choice of a partner'. A future of what Engels calls 'individual sex love' will come into its own 'after the impending effacement of capitalist production'.

That is, Engels' critique of the family characterises the 'modern' family as specific to capitalism, and as liable to fall with the fall of that economic order. And − again by no means uniquely − he asserts that the disappearance of economic constraints in marriage will call into being a new, spiritually superior form of sexual behaviour. Men will be levelled up to women in matters of spiritual-sexual conduct once a socialist revolution has been achieved. 'Prostitution disappears; monogamy, instead of declining, finally becomes a reality − for the men as well.' The assertion of the moral superiority of women as a sex, that is, wasn't confined to bourgeois feminism of the later nineteenth century. Anthropology advanced a form of psychic evolutionism which characterised monogamy as a pinnacle of human relations; in particular, Lewis Morgan, the American anthropologist whose work is used by Engels in *The Origin of the Family*, held that monogamy and greater sexual equality for women were interdependent.[4] Engels argued a distinction between false, economically determined capitalist monogamy, shored up by legislation, and true, unconstrainedly chosen monogamy of kindred spirits under socialism. 'Since sex love is by its very nature exclusive − although this exclusiveness is fully realised today only in the woman − then marriage based on sex love is by its very nature monogamy.' Although, he adds, the only truly moral marriages are those 'in which love continues'; separations should therefore be procedurally straightforward. Engels is, in this respect, solidly within the terms of moral socialist and utopian-socialist family futurology. It might be objected that to look at a materialist writer's inevitably uncertain visions of the new family is beside the point. But I think that the limits revealed here are not just fortuitous but are significant enough as marking the edges of the 'classical Marxist' work on the family, as well as the edges of non-Marxist work. This is all the more striking when the importance of *The Origin of the Family* is given full credit as an extended and painstaking attempt to demonstrate the historical specificity and the interrelatedness of forms of social organisation like the family and forms of production.

When one adds Engels' famous pronouncement on women's liberation to his supposition that love and economics stand in a roughly superstructure-to-base relationship, then the limits and strengths of his position are clear.

> The emancipation of women and their equality with men are impossible, and must remain so, as long as women are excluded from socially productive work and restricted to housework, which is private. The emancipation of women becomes possible only when women are enabled to take part in production on a large, social scale and when domestic duties require attention only to a minor degree. (Engels, 1968)

From Engels' perspective in 1884, this was a possibility brought about 'only as a result of modern large-scale industry, which not only permits the participation of women in production in large numbers, but actually calls for it, and, moreover, strives to convert private domestic work into a public industry.' To point to the terms that are missing in this characterisation is not to diminish Engels' recognition of the crucial importance of women's involvement in the labour process. But there are huge absences from the classic Marxist-Engelsian critique of the family which posits the modern family as specific to the capitalist mode of production and which continues the socialist vision of a new and happy heterosexuality arising from the base of a socialist economic transformation. A critique, moreover, whose moral stance is in good part reactive — in that it inverts the ascriptions made by bourgeois morality to communism, and throws them back again at bourgeois morality. There are, of course, excellent polemical grounds for doing just that. And the notions of a spiritual evolutionary process culminating in a new moral order is by no means restricted to early Marxism. Visions of 'new forms' of relations between the sexes are common, as has been mentioned, to many socialisms, to socialist feminism and to bourgeois feminism. Olive Schreiner's *Woman and Labour*, for instance, published in 1911 and called 'the Bible of the women's movement', leans on a psychic evolutionism, in which the pre-condition for a true sexual-spiritual equality is the participation of women in all forms of work.[5]

The historical specificity of family forms, on which Engels usefully insists in *The Origin of the Family*, is nevertheless an argument which may serve to retain orthodox conceptions of 'the family'. In itself it does not contain any challenge to the idea of the family as a directly cellular unit of the body politic, a microcosm of society. The historicisation of the family, if left at that, may indeed confirm the treatment of the family as an unanalysed entity. This is especially so if the mode of exposition takes the form of demonstrating that the entity is squeezed hither and thither by the forces of changing modes of production. A first-stage historicisation of the family lends itself towards an essentialism of the family. And − although this is not an inevitable theoretical progression − 'the family' thought of as an undifferentiated unit can then take on a privileged status as the arena for the imposition and inculcation of norms of society or the State, in an undifferentiated way.

One vivid instance of the effects of operating with a holistic version of 'the family', as opposed to specifying the separate interests of its members, is afforded by certain treatments of the idea of repression, sexual repression in particular. Some Leftist critical theories of the family have emphasised it as the site of repressive sexual misery. That the family, the bourgeois or 'nuclear' family especially, does produce its own unhappiness despite its self-portrayal is a venerable and widely proposed ground of socialist attack. The suppression of female sexuality was apparently debated by socialist feminists and 'sexual radicals' in the 1850s, although the succeeding feminist arguments for a superior female morality were couched in terms which displaced any polemical concentration on ideas like women's 'sexual fulfilment'.[6] That is, general ideas of sexual liberation and sexual oppression as elements in socialist critiques of the family do have a pre-Reichian existence, as it were, and aren't merely effects of a popularised Freudianism.

I want to mention certain Left critiques of the family which stress it as the site of specifically sexual oppression. To trace in detail the vicissitudes of ideas of the family as an agent of sexual misery would be a huge task. I'll only discuss aspects of Wilhelm Reich's influential work here. Reich's writings have affected theories of sexual liberation and oppression which are of immediate contemporary socialist and feminist concern, although their terms are rightly under constant critical reformulation. In particular, Reich's version of sexual oppression within the family is especially congruent with the view of the family as main agent for inducing a political as well as a moral conservatism in women − a failure of class-consciousness at a critically influential point. Reich, writing in Germany, initially as a Communist Party member in the late 1920s, was obviously under tremendous pressure to account for the rise of fascism and the apparent success of the Nazi approach to the family. 'The development of the ideology of the family in Germany today deserves the greatest attention,' he wrote in *What is Class Consciousness?* in 1933. This text is in part a demand for socialist attention to issues affecting women which would otherwise be colonised unopposed by fascism — issues including contraception, abortion, sexuality, economic dependence on men. Reich insisted that the German Communist Party could only write off psychoanalysis as a bourgeois science if it was willing to remain in a politically fatal ignorance of the ideological effects of the capitalist family. This is argued theoretically in *Dialectical Materialism and Psychoanalysis* (1929) in particular. *The Sexual Struggle of Youth* (1931) is also concerned with the political imperative of 'winning over' women and girls to communism, and argues that such a conversion can only be brought about by means of a full acknowledgement of their needs in and out of the family. The stifling effect of the latter on children and adolescents, and the obscurantist powers of religious youth organisations, are given a privileged position in Reich's account of the ideological apparatus of Nazism. The bourgeois family is credited with facilitating the rise of fascism through its inculcation of authoritarian masculinity and submissive femininity. 'The limiting of the freedom of imaginative and critical activity by sexual repression is one of the most important motivations of the bourgeois sexual order.' At the same time, Reich wrote, it was necessary to understand the function of the family as a protective institution, in so far as it constituted a form of economic shelter for women and children who would otherwise be at the mercy of the labour market.[7]

The Mass Psychology of Fascism (1934) which Reich described as 'thought out during the German crisis years, 1930–33', characterises the authoritarian family as the key institution for the reproduction of the authoritarian State. Not as its sociological basis, but as a main ideological support — 'political reaction's germ cell, the most important centre for the production of reactionary men and women'. This book, by no means a purely theoretical-political production, but rather part of an immediate war of propaganda, continues the plea for more effective socialist propaganda in the area of what Reich called sexual politics. He describes the Nazi portrayal of bolshevism (communism) as demanding the 'communalisation' of women (compare the *Communist Manifesto* here) and as thus working on the anxieties and conservatism of women. This conservatism is produced by domestic confinement and sexual repression in the family. His own ranks had 'failed to comprehend and to allay women's fear of sexual health', whereas 'sexual reaction . . . exploited the sexual anxiety in women and girls, and to this it owes its success'. My point here isn't to comment on such ideas of 'health' but to emphasise that Reich locates the family as the special site of women's political undereducation. Thus, analysing State propaganda about the family, Reich saw a 'desexualising' of motherhood as important to fascist social policies, 'the setting-up of an antithesis between woman as childbearer and woman as sexual being'. Whereas 'sexually awakened women, affirmed and recognised as such, would mean the complete collapse of the authoritarian ideology.' This, because the consequent demands of such women for contraception and abortion facilities, and their refusal of domestic passivity and confinement, would not be tolerated by the authoritarian State and its key institution, the repressive family. The task, it followed, for a genuinely revolutionary politics would be not only to point to the 'objective basis of the authoritarian family' as a State support, but also to appeal to people's frustrated 'yearning for happiness in both life and love'. Allowing for the fact that *The Mass Psychology of Fascism* is largely an emergency appeal for a better socialist understanding of and propaganda against fascism at a specific moment, rather than a fully reflected theoretical presentation, it's still the case that Reich's gradually developed insistence on the primacy of a *sexual* revolution for any societal revolution is based on a simplified theory of sexuality. This sexuality is conceived in such a way that it effectively displaces any detailed analysis of what 'the family' is in relation to the State. While he correctly points to the political failure of communism to speak to 'human needs' and its abandonment of that area to conservative thought and fascist interventions, Reich's insistence that the bourgeois family is the microcosm of the State makes the question of the necessary analysis of the separate spheres of the members of that family less visible. Or the visibility is restricted to a narrowed and reductive version of the sexual. While the inclusion of demands for fertility control, for adequate housing, and so on are rightly placed by him at the end of the 1920s and early 1930s as crucial to a socialist programme, the idea of 'sexuality' which he comes to use is more and more pre-Freudian and energetic. So that the problem of the construction of sexual differentiation, for instance, which is necessary for an understanding of the familial placing of women, becomes unaskable. Reich came to rely ultimately on a depiction of sexuality as a central instinctual pool, a biological reserve of energy. To make this comment is, of course, to collapse a series of politically and conceptually interesting shifts; Reich's work on the family and subsequent concerns have received detailed critical attention in recent years, including feminist attention (Mitchell, 1974).

The need to account for the rise of Nazism is also the moral and political imperative for other Leftist accounts of the 'authoritarian family'. Family typologies have tended to degenerate into reductionist psycho-sociological accounts of the 'personality theory' genre, as in some American cross-cultural work of the 1930s and 1940s. The positions taken earlier, however, by Frankfurt School theorists of the family are instructive — those of Horkheimer in particular. Instructive, that is, as instances of attempts to analyse the 'patriarchal' family from a Leftist position; and, in the case of Horkheimer, for the terms of the subsequent backtracking. The ambiguity traceable throughout the latter's work lies in the status of paternal authority in his account, and whether the dissolution of such authority would predispose to a healthy critical rebelliousness, or instead to a conforming helplessness in the face of the advances of monopoly capitalism.[8] This argument is constructed around the notion of the 'internalisation' of authority as happening within the family. But the family still appears as in part a preserve of moral, humane resistance to a generalised social dehumanisation, despite what Horkheimer takes as the fact that 'the family in crisis produces the attitudes which predispose men for blind submission'. His 1936 *Studien uber Authorität und Familie*,[9] originally intended to include empirical material on the mentality of workers in the Weimar Republic, and situated in the psycho-sociological tradition established by the Frankfurt School investigations,[10] argues the conservatising function of the bourgeois family.

> The family, as one of the most important formative agencies, sees to it that the kind of human character emerges which social life requires, and gives this human being in great measure the indispensable adaptability for a specific authority-oriented conduct on which the existence of the bourgeois order depends. . . . the bad conscience that is developed in the family absorbs more energies than can be counted, which might otherwise be directed against the social circumstances that play a role in the individual's failure. The outcome of such paternal education is men who without ado seek the fault in themselves. (Horkheimer, 1972)

As in Reich's analysis, the economic dependence of women in the family plays into its conservatising force; and monogamy causes the inhibition of 'important psychic energies'. The family, to Horkheimer in 1936, 'is becoming a simple problem of technological manipulation by government'; its function as a 'refuge' was less significant than its 'role in the authoritarian structure of capitalist society'.

Despite the political distance between authoritarian personality work and classical Marxism, the dominant critical theories of the family of the late 1930s shared a moral and holistic approach to the family. This is clearly evidenced in the shifting analyses of it as a conservatising or a potentially radicalising institution, but anyway as a cornerstone of the State. The political and historical circumstances of the production of Reich's and Horkheimer's earlier work must be remembered in any assessment of them. Later writings which claimed some kinship or influence were more diluted; the 1940s 'basic personality type' work drew on ego-psychoanalytic thought, like that of Fromm, to reduce comparative studies of the family to cross-cultural work on childrearing. The specific theme of the family as privileged agent of sexual repressiveness and hence political conservatism resurfaced, in a modified form, only with the second-generation Frankfurt School's reworking of the forms of capitalist psychic oppression theories. It's arguable that Marcuse, despite his own criticisms of the limited nature of Reich's ideas of sexuality, does himself ultimately rely on an image of a pre-Freudian naturalised sexuality which is instrumentally repressed by a bourgeois order fearing the force of 'derepressed' energies.

That 'sexual liberation' is in many respects a doubtful theory on which to mount a critique of the family of any incisive power is now largely recognised by feminists, along with the uncertainties of any simple theory of 'sexual fulfilment'. The recuperability, or incorporation-prone nature of sexual liberation — that it may be advantageously tolerated or even encouraged by contemporary capitalism — was also proposed at length in Reimut Reiche's *Sexuality and Class Struggle*.[11] This rests on a theory of manipulation by the State of 'sexual need' and its partial satisfaction, as in Marcuse's idea of 'repressive desublimation'; the licensed slackening of the more severe prohibitions — as with the introduction of the free distribution of contraception, say — only produces a quiescence which leads to the tolerance of capitalist social relations. But once more, the idea of a *true* sexual liberation, which will come into being under socialism, seems to underly Reiche's critique of the false sexual liberation advanced by Western European capitalism of the late 1960s. This supposition, as I've tried to indicate, has a venerable pedigree in most Marxist and socialist consideration of the family. It is a supposition based on a largely undifferentiated notion of both 'sexuality' and 'the family', one which tends to take the family as a self-contained arena of oppression which is filtered down from the State above.

The effect of all this is to obscure the fact that the family is crisscrossed by other definitions and practices (including those in legal, medical and welfare spheres). In effect, insufficient distance is taken on the ideological portrayal of 'the family' as a self-contained material-spiritual unit. The vagaries of various socialist accounts of the family include its depiction as a rebellion-inducing force, conservatising force, a place of retreat from a heartless world outside,[12] or in itself a hell,[13] as a court of explanatory appeal for moments of political retrenchment, as a bastion of working-class resistance,[14] or as an institution whose erosion acts as an index of capitalist de-humanisation.[15] All these share a tendency to conceive of the family as a genuinely unitary entity in itself, irrespective of its historicisation. The great advantage, it seems to me, of socialist feminist critiques of the family which can depart from the essentially moral terms of classical Marxism and their historical context, is their capacity to break the theoretical edges of 'the family'. And to take the separate questions of women in the family in relation to reproduction, to sexuality, to entry into or exclusion from the labour market, in such a way as to undo the idea of the family as an all-purpose guarantor of women's oppression inside it. To say this isn't to deny the polemical usefulness of the sociological work on the family, including that produced by feminism in the early 1970s and before, which concentrates on the paralytically depressive effects of being shut up at home 'in the family', as experienced in particular by mothers of young children.[16] But it's necessary to distinguish between described experience and political analysis, and not read the one off directly from the other.

I want to turn now to some concrete instances of points at which Marxist theories of the family and of appropriate socialist morality have come up against other formulations of socialist policies and practices. I'll take the shifts in pronouncements on the family, women, morality and reproduction, made in revolutionary and post-revolutionary Russia, though any mention will be in a heavily abbreviated form.[17] The work of Alexandra Kollontai has been translated and republished in recent years as part of the fresh interest in the history of Marxist-feminist debates and politics, and her career, especially as the Bolshevik Commissar for social welfare, has been traced.[18] In *Sexual Relations and the Class Struggle* of 1919, (Kollontai, 1978) she writes about the contemporary 'sexual crisis' affecting all classes, and the need for a 'radical re-education of the human psyche' on the basis of a social-economic transformation. But, in this text at least, she objects to the supposition that an economic revolution automatically brings in its wake a progressive emotionality.

> As if the ideology of a certain class is formed only when the breakdown in the socio-economic relationship. . . has been completed! All the experience of history teaches us that a social group works out its ideology and

consequently its sexual morality in the process of its struggle with hostile social forces.

She advocates the development of 'a code of sexual morality that is in harmony with the problems of the working class', leading to 'new relationships between the sexes that are deeper and more joyful'. This quite orthodox and classic Marxist view of the superior spirituality of heterosexuality under communism − at most, a serial monogamy is advocated − gives the lie to the later representations of Kollontai as an absolute libertarian. She was falsely represented as a proponent of 'free love' and a defender of the 'glass of water theory', according to which the satisfaction of sexual needs should be as easy and straightforward as drinking water.

The sophistication of Kollontai's discussion of sexual morality, including her treatment of prostitution, and her refusal to entertain simple superstructural accounts of it, none the less mark her off from both her conservative contemporary and Stalinist detractors and from Engels' treatment of 'individual sex love'. Her *Communism and the Family* (1920) insists on the economic inevitability of the destruction of old social forms; this is an explanatory and exhortatory text which tries to assure women of the emancipating force of the collectivisation of domestic labour. With the introduction of public restaurants, laundries, creches − 'the dawn of collective housekeeping' − a new form of marriage would arise; 'a union of two equal persons of the communist society, both of them free, both of them independent, both of them workers.' Soviet marriage would constitute 'a free and honest union of men and women who are lovers and comrades'. The decently easy availability of divorce accompanied rather than undercut the relative orthodoxy of the depiction of marriage and childrearing under the new communism; it is the stress on the collectivisation of childcare and housework which is new. Alexandra Kollontai emphasises the mutual responsibility of the mother and the community in a pro-natalist vein; childbearing is to be seen as 'social' in nature, and special attention paid to 'the protection of maternity'. Her 'critique of the feminist movement' from the 1923 text, *Women's Labour in Economic Development*, attacks what she terms the naiveté of bourgeois 'equal rights' feminism and its indifference to the needs of women with children. Continuing her emphasis on the social and economic merits of the collectivising of private housework, she ascribes the shortcomings of the social revolution to the prevailing poverty and lack of goods in Russia then. 'Once we follow up the line of development of our economy, it becomes clear that the workers' collective will gradually swallow up and assimilate the bourgeois family.'

It's obviously essential to read Alexandra Kollontai's work against the background of its political and material surroundings — including the course of Bolshevik and later debates on family policy and the provision of abortion, the elevation of 'the Soviet family' in the 1930s and 1940s, and the continuing pressures of war and poverty. My present purpose is only to point to the combination of her adherence to a well-established if visionary socialist tradition of the future of the family and the 'new morality', and her practical stress on the special needs of women and mothers in revolutionary Russia. The fragmented nature of this combination, given her rather isolated political position and the theoretical resources available to her, is hardly surprising. None the less, her determined coupling of a moral-theoretical attack on the bourgeois family with immediate and sustained measures to organise and provide for the collectivisation of family functions, material scarcity or not, marks her off from other Marxist commentators on the family.

For the moral level at which communist objections to the family were standardly pitched facilitated the reduction of the debate to the 'bourgeois' or 'revolutionary' nature of shifts in sexual morality. The sectional relegation of 'women's issues' to a separate and secondary sphere was an outcome of the failure to analyse the family in terms which overtook Engels' work, although clearly there was a political rationale for such a relegation. The extent to which the Bolshevik party was, in fact, genuinely committed to the fight for women's emancipation is an interesting question, for which our evidence is probably incomplete.[19] Lenin's own discussion of 'free love' in his exchanges with Inessa Armand (Lenin, 1972) rightly attacked the vagueness of the term, but continues a parodic characterisation of it as a 'bourgeois not a proletarian demand'. This characterisation is extended by Lenin to include desires for 'freedom from childbirth' or 'freedom to commit adultery', all of which are alien to the 'proletarian civic marriage with love' and which could only be articulated by bourgeois feminism. This illustrates the superficiality of attempts to assess conflicts in the areas of reproduction and morality as inherently pro-or anti-capitalist. Such attempts decisively mark the 1930s debates on communist morality, but are by no means confined to them. A case in point is Clara Zetkin's recollections of her conversation with Lenin in 1920 (Lenin, 1972).

Taking to task those German communists who were organising discussions on sex and marriage with working women for potentially dulling their class-consciousness and detracting from the main struggle, Lenin cites Engels approvingly. For the latter had pointed out 'in his *Origins* how significant it was that the common sexual relations had developed into individual sex love, and thus become purer'. Further debates on morality were bourgeois and diversionary, and represented a lapse in political judgement on the part of the German women comrades. The philistinism and short-sightedness of Lenin's comments are, admittedly, accompanied by a tirade against the spirit-shrinking nature of housework, as well as against the deficiencies of a merely emancipatory feminism. Of the original Bolsheviks, apart from Alexandra Kollontai, it was Trotsky who was able to pay some imaginative attention to the problems of the social transformation of women's position. He, too, recognised the imperative of the collectiv-isation of domestic labour and the advantages of communally run housing, although he urged a tactical caution in the introduction of such innovations. He described motherhood as the question of all questions:

> The depth of the question of the mother is expressed in the fact that she is, in essence, a living point where all the decisive strands of economic and cultural work intersect. The question of motherhood is above all a question of an apartment, running water, a kitchen, a laundry room, a dining room. But it is just as much a question of a school, of books, of a place for recreation.

Providing public facilities would succeed 'only if the social organi-sation learns to satisfy the most primary demands better than the family. Special attention must be paid now to the questions of quality' (Trotsky, 1973).

Analysing, from the viewpoint of 1936, the failure of the Bolshevik social revolution, and bitterly critical of the Stalinist elevation of the family as 'the sacred nucleus of triumphant socialism', Trotsky's *The Revolution Betrayed* ascribes that failure to economic lack. It occurred 'not because the family was so firmly rooted in men's hearts' but because

> society proved too poor and too little cultured. The real resources of the State did not correspond to the plans and intentions of the Communist Party. You cannot 'abolish' the family; you have to replace it. The actual liberation of women is unrealisable on a basis of generalised want. Experi-ence soon proved this austere truth which Marx had formulated eighty years ago. (Trotsky, 1972)

Yet, in fact, what Trotsky actually does is to analyse a political and ideological failure too, a lack of imaginative planning which had its effects over and above the given material scarcity.

Trotsky's analysis, except for the space it gives to a sympathetic assessment of women's needs, remains within the classic Marxist inheritance in so far as it struggles for a definition of 'the genuinely socialist family' in which love will be freed from economic shackles. And in so far, too, as it restricts its analysis of reproduction to questions of the practical problems of the collectivisation of childcare and housework. 'The family' is regarded as unproblematic in itself. And, in general, Left critiques of the family which submerge the critical elements of reproduction and sexual differentiation into a blanket anti-familial stance, or conversely a defence of 'the working-class family', thereby make impossible an understanding of what 'the family' is. 'The family' cannot be criticised on or in its own terms, as if it always possessed a real unity to which it ideologically lays claim, or may possess experientially. (Examining the history of critical-socialist ideas of extra-familial 'deviations' like illegitimacy and homosexuality would be interesting − if only as instances of revealing absences.)

I've suggested that the furthest reaches of the Marxist-Engelsian treatment of the family in its emancipatory vision comprise the socialisation of domestic labour, the entry of women into the workforce, and a monogamous or serially monogamous happy and spiritually elevated heterosexuality. Despite the merits of this family futurology, such a combination of a moral-philosophic stance, the historicisation of the family, and a pragmatic approach is disjointed. The necessity of a socialist feminist analysis for any critique of the family lies in its potential to break with the conceptual autonomy, the closed edges of 'the family'. This would leave the established grounds of a purely moral or a purely economistic debate, and make a fresh point of critical entry − the examination of the structures of reproduction, of sexuality and sexual categorisation, of domestic and waged work, of fertility control, of childrearing − which are both in and outside the conventionally given edges of 'the family'.

Notes

1   See, for example, Bebel's *Die Frau und der Sozialismus*, (Berlin, 1922), which is translated in an American edition only as *Women Under Socialism* (1972), or Robert Owen, *Lectures on the Marriages of Priesthood of the Old Immoral World, delivered in the year 1835, before the Passing of the New Marriage Act* (1835).

2   In the *Communist Manifesto*, ch.III, and in *Socialism, Utopian and Scientific* by Engels.

3   For instance, Rosalind Delmar's 'Looking Again at Engel's *Origin of the*

Family'. And Beverley Brown's '*The Natural and Social Division of Labour — Engels and the Domestic Labour Debate*' in *m/f* 1, 1978.

4   See 'The Sexual Politics of Victorian Social Anthropology' by Liz Fee.

5   Thus Olive Schreiner writes on feminism as an aspect of 'the great movement of the sexes towards each other', the latter being the pinnacle of psychic progress for the human race.

6   This is elaborated in the introduction by Jeffrey Weeks and Sheila Rowbotham to *Socialism and the New Life*.

7   Protection, that is, from the rigours of extra-familial economic survival; a double-edged protection whose variants can be traced in versions of the 'family as refuge' position; see note 12.

8   Changed positions in Horkheimer's work on paternal authority are discussed in Jessica Benjamin's 'Authority and the Family Revisited; or, A World without Fathers?' in *New German Critique*, 13.

9   The essay 'Authority and the Family' is translated in the collection of Horkheimer's writings published as *Critical Theory* (1972) and was originally in the *Studien Über Autorität und Familie*.

10 An example of attempts to demonstrate changes in family relationships in the American Depression, in paternal status particularly, is afforded by Mirra Komarovsky's *The Unemployed Man and His Family* (1940).

11 The German original was written in 1968 but it was not published in English until 1974, by New Left Books. There is a useful discussion of this book in Ros Coward's ' "Sexual Liberation" and "The Family" ' in *m/f*, 1, 1978.

12 See discussion in Christopher Lasch's *Haven in a Heartless World* (1977).

13 For one influential example, see the work of R.D. Laing; and the commentary by Andrew Collier in his book on Laing (1977), especially his ch.4, 'The Contradictions of the Family'.

14 An economy-based version of this is afforded by Jane Humphries' paper 'Class Struggle and the Persistence of the Working-Class Family'.

15 See, for example, Engels' *Condition of the Working Class in England*.

16 Such work includes Hannah Gavron's *The Captive Wife* (1966) and George Brown and Tirril Harris's *Social Origins of Depression* (1978).

17 One useful documentary and critical source for this area is Rudolf Schlesinger's *The Family in the USSR* (1949), which includes reprints of changing laws and family policy statements.

18 The most recent collection is pretty comprehensive and has a good commentary and bibliography; Alix Holt's *Selected Writings of Alexandra Kollontai* (1978).

19 The books footnoted above by Schlesinger and Holt are very helpful as critical documentation here and both point to further sources. See also the remarks on Soviet population policies and changes in abortion legislation in the chapter in section 4 below on 'Feminist Thought and Reproductive Control; the State and the Right to Choose'.

Further reading

Mark Poster's *Critical Theory of the Family* (London; Pluto Press, 1978) has appeared since this chapter was written.

Section II

Definition and Coercion

professionals who have the social sanctions to deal with them. Implicit in this is the assumption that the professional classes, as agents of the ruling class and of the State, have succeeded in their bid for power over the most private and intimate parts of women's lives. There is doubtless some truth in this, but it is too one-sided; it neglects the processes by which people come to see themselves, and those around them see them, as mentally ill. To insist on this second point is really to stress the subjective dimension of our study. For example, it is true that a woman's sense of self may be constructed in the context of continual bombardment by the media which portray femininity as synonymous with weakness, dependence and incapacity for autonomous action. But at this obvious ideological level, the same message has been purveyed for at least two hundred years, during which time the precise forms of female mental illness have changed dramatically.

The construction of a female consciousness takes place at so many different levels, that to isolate one for exclusive emphasis inevitably leads to distortion, and, for this reason, the mental illnesses of women must be seen in the broader context of forms of emotional expression of *both* sexes. That's why I take a different approach from the other authors in this section, both of whom deal with the more obviously asymmetrical power relations seen in violence against women. Very few men suffer physical violence from women, but they do suffer from mental illnesses. My premise does not require that women actually have more mental problems than men, but that they suffer them in specific and distinct ways. What I intend to focus on are those definitions of mental health which have been applied specifically to women, such as 'depression'. What I'm after is the *covert* manipulation which is always harder to perceive than physical oppression, especially when it is harnessed to the claimed value-neutrality of medicine and science which reconstruct social relationships as reified diseases.

Approaches to mental illness

The literature on women and mental illness falls into five main groups; that produced (1) by the women's movement, (2) by sociology, (3) by medicine and psychiatry, (4) by psychoanalysis, and (5) by historical and critical traditions. In this section I want to describe these major orientations briefly.

The women's movement gives pride of place to the lived experience of mental illness, its connections with female construction of self, and to specific feminist therapies such as women's consciousness raising groups. Sharing private suffering as a route to healing is the basis of such self-help groups. The idea of shared lived experience is important in individual feminist therapy too, since it is crucial that both therapists and patients be women committed to political struggle. It is not easy to give a definition of feminist therapy, indeed it would be worthwhile to study the diverse theories and practices employed under its rubric.[3]

The sociological literature gives less importance to subjective aspects of mental problems, and is mostly based on empirical studies using social survey techniques. It therefore emphasises the study of large samples of women, and the analysis of parameters which are quantifiable. A good deal of attention has been paid to the methodological difficulties of such work and to developing techniques which, if not exactly 'objective', attempt to be independent of 'interviewer bias'. Such research relies heavily on clinical judgement of individual cases and seeks to discover the specific aetiological factors in pre-given clinical entities. By definition, such work cannot ask why doctors employ the diagnostic categories they do, nor analyse the implicit assumptions behind the ways in which female mental illness is medically constructed. Such surveys are frequently conducted by those who consider themselves humane, liberal and sensitive to the women's movement. But their emphasis is not on the social *construction* of illness, but in the *correlations* between quantifiable variables (Brown and Harris, 1978; Tuckett, 1976).

So far, critics of contemporary definitions of mental illness have paid most attention to the medical and psychiatric literature and to the 'medical model' which provides its conceptual framework.[4] Medical science has come to see illness as pathology, be it physical or psychological, with a traceable aetiology (set of causes), uncovered by scientific theories and methods. The stress on causal explanations means that psychic disturbances traced to hormone levels, for example, can, within the medical model, be logically and legitimately treated by artificially readjusting the hormone balance. The presumed cause of the illness and the therapy given are therefore very closely related. In fact there is in medicine a general adherence to physico-chemical explanations and treatments, which stems from the predominantly reductionist orientation of the contemporary life sciences. For this reason, drugs and physical treatments, such as electric shock therapy, are widely used, despite the fact that their exact mode of working may not have been elucidated. These are seen to be preferable to psychotherapy, which is regarded as speculative and of unproven efficacy. This whole approach is based on the assumption that illnesses which involve physical changes are best treated physically, and the question of how social factors might be related to those physical changes is left unexplored. Even though these putative pathological signs may mediate or express much more complex, non-mechanistic processes, the power of pharmacological intervention is undisputed. A corollary of this position is, of course, that illnesses become defined in terms of recognisable pathological characters, so that illnesses which do not at first sight possess them have to be redefined in those terms. Thus kleptomania — a fairly common female 'disease' — has been treated by drugs which affect specific centres of the brain, although it could equally plausibly be argued that it has nothing to do with pharmacology and everything to do with boredom, a sense of inadequacy, low evaluation of self and so on.

The experience which clinicians have of mental illness also structures their perceptions. Roughly speaking, patients fall into two classes: cases where a crisis has led to hospitalisation, such as suicide attempts, anorexia, or a dramatic psychotic episode, and those cases of low key undramatic unhappiness which come to out-patient clinics and GPs' offices. The second group, of predominantly female patients, who are anxious, depressed or both, are treated with drugs like Valium over long periods of time. Unlike those suddenly hospitalised, these depressed women can cope with an apparently 'normal' life, their needs aren't dramatic but most often relate to long-term dissatisfactions and a sense of hopelessness. In all kinds of psychiatric treatment drugs play a major role.

Like the medical and psychiatric approach, psychoanalysis also seeks causal chains which have led to the illness. Invisible, internal, subjective signs of illness are as important as the objective, bodily signs and symptoms to which scientific medicine pays exclusive attention. It is this sense of internal conflict and suffering which will bring an individual woman into psychoanalysis. At the moment, traditional psychoanalysis emphasises long-term treatments which commonly take a number of years. During this time getting better through self-knowledge and understanding is important. In this sense, the 'cure' is quite unlike the 'cause' of the illness, and consists precisely in bringing to the conscious level things which were previously unconscious. Psychoanalysis has not always emphasised long, verbal treatments, but has also used physical ones like massage, baths, hypnosis, and so on.[5] The broad church has included an immense variety of perspectives, and it would be seriously misleading to present psychoanalysis as if it was a single orthodoxy.

Bearing in mind our desire to give most emphasis to the sex-specificity of mental diseases, psychoanalysis does present a coherent perspective on the importance of sexuality in development. It thus provides a handle for examining the association between being a woman and having certain kinds of mental illness, a possibility which has indeed been taken up. But it should also be emphasised that many feminists have been critical of the particular ways in which psychoanalysis has conceptualised the nature of femininity — most obviously penis-envy, and the emphasis on motherhood as a necessary sexual maturation. Indeed, a substantial part of contemporary feminist scholarship is devoted to the critique and refinement of psychoanalysis.[6]

It would also be mistaken to believe that all psychotherapy emphasises the indvidual and therefore makes no contact with the social and political level to which much feminist literature addresses itself. An important development over the last few years is the rise of a holistic approach in group, and in family, therapy. This is significant as far as women are concerned because it places them in the actual context of many of their everyday struggles, such as division of labour with other members of the family, the different roles mothers and fathers assume, and the lack of supportiveness from other members of the household.[7] Doubtless therapists differ considerably in whether they take a basically adjustment position by urging a woman to come to terms with her situation where certain elements are held to be unchangeable, or whether their primary interest is in the open-ended development and growth of each person, regardless of the changes they bring.

Psychoanalysis has also been widely used as an analytical tool for the study of groups as well as of individuals. The best known examples are literary criticism and psychohistory which may examine women as a psychoanalytically defined group, and aspects of social life where early experiences, especially sexual ones, were decisive in later developments.[8] It should not be thought that such a methodology is unproblematic. The difficulties are particularly acute in cross-cultural work. In what sense, for example, can we speak of psychological structures being shared by women in very different social and cultural environments? It seems to me to be more important to trace the common elements of female psychology for a very specific time and place, in terms of the culture itself, and not of any putatively universal categories.

It is often said that psychoanalytic therapy has a conservative impact by encouraging individual accomodation rather than radical structural change. This presents a caricatured set of alternatives. It would be as simplistic to suppose that women's mental problems could be solved by universal free nurseries as it would be to suggest they would all be happier if they had access to therapy. The point is that private and public struggles go together.

Like Western scientific medicine, psychoanalysis is built on a relatively coherent theoretical position. Unlike medicine, it has continually reviewed its own practice and theory in a self-critical way. The ways in which women and children are conceptualised are changing and can be continually refined.[9] This difference stems from the fact that much theory in scientific medicine, especially as far as sexuality is concerned, remains implicit and, therefore, not acknowledged as such by most practitioners. As a consequence it cannot be discussed and reformulated at an explicit level. This is not the case with psychoanalysis.

It is in the resolution of these difficulties of giving full weight to individual and to social experience that historical and critical traditions have been most successful, although they have not been extensively applied to women. Critics of contemporary treatment of the mentally ill have sought to make 'madness' a relative category which has a different meaning in each time and place. This tradition, which includes some of the best known critics of modern society such as Szasz (1963; 1965; 1970a and b; 1972), Goffman (1961; 1968) and Foucault (1965; 1976; 1978), has also emphasised the importance of historical processes in understanding the present situation. This has led to attempts to find the specific conditions under which definitions of sanity and insanity were formulated and diagnostic categories elaborated. Such work has displaced exclusive interest in patients, and has analysed the *environment* of illness and deviance instead. One extreme example of this is labelling theory, where the act of defining a person as mad, ill or abnormal is seen as the crucial step. The interest in the environment of illness led to a number of studies of institutions such as hospitals, prisons, asylums, poor law institutions and so on.[10] Such detailed study of the social setting of mental illness has undercut the idea that it is a 'natural' event, and has emphasised its social construction. It is remarkable, however, that so little attention has been paid to home and work environments where similar questions about the social construction of pathology could be asked. To some extent this is a consequence of methodological difficulties for historians in retrieving appropriate materials. Recent historical work has also emphasised the notion of role conflict in arguing that female insanity was the only form of escape from a complex set of contradictions and expectations which proved imcompatible with the individual woman's needs. It has further been claimed (Smith-Rosenberg, 1972) that women were socially defined in such a way as to be prone to mental disorder, so that actually being an adequate woman presented the danger of insanity. This is probably an incomplete picture which reproduces medical ideology, rather than describing the actual conditions of women's lives.

Historical and critical traditions have two major deficiencies. First, they have been rather insensitive to the different experiences of men and women, and have in fact placed very little emphasis on a range of socially significant groups that patients belonged to. Class has been taken to be a more primary division than sex, and we need to refine our knowledge of the relationship between them. The second deficiency is the tendency to rely on notions of 'social control', and so to imply the passivity of the patient, indeed of women as a group.[11] As a result, the need to study the lived experience of mental illness, with all the struggles and contradictions it contains, is minimised. The historical critical literature has played a significant role in liberating people from medical ideology, especially the oppressiveness of making diseases out of social relations, and it has opened up new possibilities for critical analysis. But it often falls into the traps set by presuppositions, like social control, which seem 'natural'. We must fight all forms of simplistic, uni-dimensional and one-sided assumptions about power and oppression.

The nature of mental illness

Every approach to the study of mental illness contains assumptions about what constitutes deviance, the aetiology of mental 'disease', the therapy deemed appropriate, and the meaning of mental illness. Here I shall examine some of the ways in which these features of mental illness are conceptualised.

Since Parsons (1951), it has been common to see illness as deviance, and deviance may be theorised so as to assign responsibility for the dislocation to a variety of agencies. For instance, deviance can be seen as a consequence of, and a reaction to, oppression. The very state of being a woman, it has been argued, contains so many contradictions and so much suffering that what appears as deviant behaviour is, in fact, an unwillingness or an inability to fit the oppressive stereotype of health. This argument is part of a broader approach, where deviance is essentially caused by factors outside the patient, whether it be high-rise blocks of flats, patriarchy, or the labelling act of a doctor. Labelling theory, particularly prominent in the 1960s, essentially argued that people are deviant in so far as they have been called so. Among the best known examples of the approach is the work of Laing and his associates on schizophrenia, which stressed the family's role in defining and generating this particular form of madness in one of its members.[12] This model of deviance is consistent with the emphasis on the social control of passive, powerless groups. It is far from obvious what form of therapy would relieve suffering according to this view, although discovering their own rights and rationality as a route to gaining power to defy the labellers would be possible for the victims.

The model of deviance conventionally employed by medicine and psychiatry leads to very specific treatments designed to act directly on the physiological mechanism putatively responsible for mental illness. Deviation and norm, after all, suggest a simple, quantitative relationship between abstract variables. Here, illness as deviance is a pathology – an organic malfunction. In the treatment of women for depression associated with childbirth or the menopause, for instance, hormones act as the physical mediators between social and biological functions, and serve to emphasise the ways in which unacceptable behaviour may be rooted in 'real' physical causes. This is a notion of deviance which is at heart mechanical; it stops when a biochemical 'explanation' has been found, and fails to look beyond that to social causes. The patient as an individual is also dismissed from the analysis, not just because it relieves her/him of guilt and responsibility, which may in fact be humane, but because the event of being depressed, for instance, is not given any special significance or meaning in the life of the sufferer. The complex range of emotions a woman experiences following the birth of a child is a good example where reducing it to a question of hormone levels negates the experience by claiming that the turmoil, uncertainty or downright terror she may feel are really just chemical phenomena. Attempts have been made to broaden this perspective by analysing 'life events' as aetiological agents.[13] In this case, the mechanical processes of the disease remain untouched, although it may be seen as partially caused by crisis, loss or other traumatic events.

In what is commonly called the medical model, mental illness is not taken as a form of communication, but merely as symptomatic of pathologies, even if those pathologies are not understood. The form the illness takes (depression, neurosis, psychosis, etc.) does not count as evidence of what significance the suffering has for the patient. The so-called illness is emptied of its content. Thus the patient is a passive repository of physiological events; she endures these, since they are outside her control. Her own agency in expressing her feelings and defining her mental universe is ignored. In fact, the bio-medical sciences have not found a language which is capable of expressing the individual and collective significance of disease. In my view, it is among the most important features of psychoanalysis that it is based on the premise that illnesses are forms of communication, and so have a content that needs to be understood.

The idea of deviance or madness assumed in psychoanalysis is not reductionist in orientation. It is built on the content and subjective experience of mental illness and receives it as a communication, with meaning and significance. The patient learns how to read the meanings she is unconsciously expressing, and how to grow again in a healthy way. Here, deviance could not be seen to be caused by a single agent, but an enormous variety of factors which contribute to the suffering, many of which go back to the subject's very early experience. Psychoanalysis conceptualises deviance in terms of human relationships, their quality, even their absence.[14]

Social scientists have seen deviance as a product of more abstract features of social structure. Men's and women's mental illnesses are both determined by social features, although different aspects of society affect them in different ways. This approach is designed less to assign responsibility or blame, than to elucidate the specific social conditions which lead particular groups to manifest deviance. Successful historical and political critiques analyse the social construction of illness in this way, but it is very difficult, using this model, to explain why and how one individual becomes insane rather than another.

On the issue of the causes and mechanisms of mental illness, there are two basic approaches. The first is based on a clearly traceable aetiology, and this applies both to psychoanalysis and to the biomedical sciences. Causal, linear explanations are traced, and through this process the appropriate therapy becomes clear.. The remedies prescribed vary enormously, as do the range of explanations given for mental illness. It is worth noting that this is to some extent true of antipsychiatry, as well as of other more conventional modes of treatment. What these approaches have in common is the belief in *causal* chains which can be systematically elucidated in each individual. Environmentally caused illnesses, on the other hand, are much harder to trace, so that the second category of aetiologies which attribute a major causative role to social factors, offers few specific explanations. Using such an approach, it is hard to understand why similar individuals react differently to the same social conditions. Because the causal links are more difficult to elucidate, suggesting specific remedies is also more problematic. One way would be to recommend that the patients change their life style, and Minuchin, in his family therapy, tries to instruct them in completely new ways of interacting. More generally, those who see mental illness as caused by social and environmental conditions may call for the reform of social institutions, such as alternatives to the family, decarceration and so on.

In fact, it is all too easy if one believes in the social origins of mental illness, to be distracted into utopian discussions about the propriety of building high-rise blocks of flats. The danger of this is that it offers no concrete help to the people, principally women, who suffer as a result of housing conditions. It may in theory alleviate future distress by affecting planning policy, but this is rather remote and abstract when compared with present-day pain. In this context, self-help and consciousness-raising groups may help women to improve their lives and their environment. For example, if George Brown and his co-workers (1978) are right about the large numbers of depressed women with pre-school children, then agitation for nursery and other facilities for children would be better than Valium.

None of this helps those women who experience a crisis which makes them unable to cope with their day-to-day existence. It's no consolation to them to be told by a sociologist, who uses elaborate statistics to support his case, that their illness is part of broader social problems and that most other women in their situation also feel terrible. This is obviously a caricature, but it highlights the immediacy of the problem for women, and the need to think in terms of immediate action, not just the distant solutions implied in abstract analysis.

The importance of specific therapies offered to individuals is that they go further in acknowledging the suffering actually being experienced, and they may offer solutions, albeit imperfect ones. Therapies are not just treatments which fit in with aetiological models. They are part of the social processes surrounding ill-health, and must be analysed as such. For this reason, the historical context in which treatments are developed and used is extremely important, a point to which I shall return.

Sick roles, sex roles and depression

In terms of developing a coherent understanding of mental illness, the question of its meaning is one of the most analytically challenging, and practically important. Let's take depression as an example.

Definitions and classifications of depression vary considerably. The following quotations are from a standard textbook, *A Short Textbook of Psychiatry* by Linford Rees:

> Depression. . . affects the whole organism: feelings, energy, drive, think-
> ing, bodily functions, personality and interests. . . .
> The depressed patient is self-concerned. . . .
> He may blame himself for errors . . . and tends to be self-depreciatory and
> self-accusatory.
> The loss of interest may apply to work, home, family . . . and sometimes
> personal hygiene and *appearance*.
> Depression is twice as common in females as in males.
> Depressive illnesses are the resultant of genetic and constitutional factors on
> one hand with environment and other exogenous influences on the other.
> (Linford Rees, 1976, pp.181–6, my emphasis)

Another, more popular, work distinguished depressive *reactions* from depressive *illnesses*, where the former could be both normal and abnormal but the latter were always abnormal and pathological. The author, Ross Mitchell (1975), emphasised the physiological correlates of depressive illness, i.e., 'psychomotor retardation'. But in addition:

> He [the depressed person] will blame himself. . . He sees himself as full of
> guilt and self-reproach. . . . He will feel so helpless, ashamed and guilt-
> ridden that suicide may seem the only way out. (Mitchell, 1975, pp.54–6)

Similarly, Linford Rees states, 'Suicidal gestures tend to be associated with females' (p.192).[15]

As an evidently paradigmatic female illness, what insight does depression give us into femininity? To find out we need to view it from two perspectives which differ from the medical one: its subjective significance for the patient and the general features of depression as a social phenomenon. To take the second first, depression is not an expensive problem to treat, since it rarely involves institutional care, which is now one of the heaviest medical costs. It is also extremely profitable for the pharmaceutical companies with a large number of drugs currently on the market which are sold principally with the treatment of depression in mind. The therapy usually offered to depressed women, i.e. drugs, is typical of 'active, scientific management' of patients, who are keeping up a semblance of living a normal life. Within safe limits women are allowed to speak of their suffering and hopelessness. Depression is also a historically specific phenomenon, of relatively recent origin, and has a social specificity since it is found principally in working-class women.

It is also important to look at the subjective experience that 'being depressed' describes. If we see the depression of housebound mothers, one of the major groups affected, as communicating information about their social/psychological situation, and their reactions to it, then a detailed examination is called for which concerns itself not just with which women in the population get depressed, but how and why. Why is it that women on the borderline of coping express themselves through the passivity and hopelessness of depression? Is it anger made self-destructive? Is it a bizarre distortion of the image of themselves which women see portrayed around them? Is the inactivity of depression a metaphor for their feelings of powerlessness?

I am purposely not posing questions about individual lives. Studies of individuals have been done which show what we would expect, that women with depression have experienced life crises, unsupportive relationships, poor housing and so on.[16] But the fact remains that their families (partners and children) have also experienced those conditions, by definition, yet we are not speaking of a wave of depression among working-class men with young children.

It may be that men have other forms of expression open to them, while women have the 'sick role'. It has in fact been argued that their child-like dependency suggests a congruence between the sick role and the female sex role.[17] Women consult doctors more often than men, and more of them are admitted to psychiatric hospitals. There are problems with this over-simplified view. There are sick roles which men primarily fill, such as those associated with diseases such as heart attacks, ulcers, hypertension, strokes and bronchitis and asthma. I am not referring to morbidity and mortality rates so far as they are known, which for some complaints do show marked sex differences, but to the popular images of diseases seen, for example, in advertisements, soap operas and magazines.

Drug advertisements are a particularly good example.[18] Among the diseases for which drugs are advertised with a clear sexual association are, for women, depression, anxiety, constipation, sleeplessness, migraine, varicose veins and acne; for men, asthma, strokes, bronchitis, hay fever and hypertension. Advertisements portraying women convey the serious state of existential suffering of the patient, and their difficulty in coping with day-to-day life. The pictures show ill-defined anguish for which specific pharmaceutical remedies are promoted. The copy often tells the reader that such drugs simultaneously alleviate anxiety and depression *without* impeding normal functioning. By contrast, the 'male' diseases, which are presented as more dramatic and acute, are controlled by drugs which enable the patient to triumphantly transcend the disease. They are frequently advertised through sporting metaphors and images, suggesting the power to conquer illness and celebrating recovery. For example, an advert for a drug for asthma shows a man doing butterfly stroke, with the caption 'Intal keeps asthmatics in the swim' and another for a drug to combat hypertension depicts two men playing tennis.

It would be a mistake to identify these two images of disease with a sick role for women and a healthy role for men. In terms of the Parsonian sick role it seems the positions are reversed. Parsons (1951) identified 'four aspects of the institutionalied expectation system relative to the sick role'. Briefly these were; (1) that the patient gains exemption from normal social responsibilities, (2) and also from being responsible for the illness and its cure; being ill is an undesirable state which therefore (3) obliges the patient to seek technically competent help and (4) to co-operate with the treatment (pp.436−7).

If we continue to take depression as a paradigm of female illness in our society now, it is striking how little exemption the patient gains from day-to-day burdens. The whole point is that depression elicits a low-key medical response since it rarely involves the acute character-istics which commonly invite the deployment of high technology medicine. Rather, it is treated with a continual flow of medications which do not disrupt day-to-day life, and so do not entitle the depressed woman to the sick role.[19] It is hard to say to what extent depression represents an active response by women to their situation, a protest as far as is permitted against their conditions of life. Despite the possibility that depression may be a decisive withdrawal, the fact that being depressed and coping can go on simultaneously is sig-nificant. Thus, depression does not routinely provide sanctioned immunity from responsibilities and work, as a heart attack would for a man.

With respect to the second feature of the sick role, the patient's responsibility for sickness, mental illness is uncomfortably ambiguous. Although the release from responsibility has been claimed by Siegler and Osmond (1974) as a major breakthrough resulting from the appli-cation of the 'medical model' to mental problems, the actual situation is much more equivocal. The extent to which people are blamed for their mental troubles depends on the beliefs about the causation of mental illness of those around them, and the precise form the illness takes. It is important to stress the lack of consensus even among medical practitioners about the aetiology of mental illnesses, so it is hard to believe that the passivity of depression is nowhere regarded in our culture as grounds for blaming the sufferer. While at an explicit ideological level physicians may exempt a female non-acute mental patient from blame, their behaviour may none the less tacitly imply it.

Turning to the third element of the sick role, women do, to some degree, seek technically competent help for their problems. Brown and Harris, in their recent study of a large number of women (1978), noted that many had symptoms of an equivalent degree of seriousness to those diagnosed as 'clinically depressed'. Without any studies of the 'actual' incidence of mental illness in women, it is impossible to estimate the extent to which 'technically competent' help is sought. Once again the problem of coping comes to the fore. A man whose work is visibly impaired by his illness will be under tremendous pressure to seek medical aid. Can the same be said of housewives? Isn't such a person more likely to buy a patent remedy over the counter and hope for the best? Why is it that unmarried women, and women with employment outside the home, are less likely to be depressed than the 'captive wife' (Gavron, 1966)? There are two key differences between women with jobs outside their homes and those without. The second group have a greater sense of social isolation, and less value is placed on the work they do.

A housebound mother may find it harder to make contacts with others to form supportive, peer group relationships than do women who work with others. It is worth remembering that many women who do 'alienating' jobs say they continue to work when they don't need the money simply for the company. Women at home with children also face a whole host of practical problems which exacerbate their sense of isolation; lack of childcare facilities, little or no public transport, the chores of housework and shopping for a family.

Although many women may find the full-time company of children very satisfying, it may not be enough to meet a woman's needs to be thought a valuable and useful human being by other adults. This leads directly to the second point about the value placed on housewifery (Oakley, 1976a). In the hierarchy of worthwhile jobs in our society, being a housewife does not come high on the list for most people. No doubt this is partly because it is unpaid, but other factors are also important, since many of the tasks housewives perform are not highly respected even when they are paid for. Neither babysitting nor house-cleaning are occupations with economic power or social prestige. Because of the infinite number of household tasks, a housewife's freedom may be seriously curtailed. Furthermore, to the extent that networks are built up, it is usually with other wives and mothers, which may support her to the extent she plays those roles, but not necessarily if she wishes to break out of them. Her isolation from her partner may be acute too, especially if there is little sharing of tasks and he is absent in leisure time as well. Such women will probably only be able to have short interviews with their GPs who are too harassed to give them much attention, they might attend overcrowded out-patient clinics in mental hospitals, often accompanied by their children, and receive prescriptions routinely renewed at regular intervals.[20]

Perhaps it is harder to generalise about the experience of illness and medical treatment which men receive. In any case I know of no studies which have attempted to understand how each sex feels about mental illness and the different ways in which men and women are evaluated as regards their suffering and their social esteem. I would emphatically reject the idea that women suffer *more* than men, but it seems clear that they suffer, and express their pain, *differently*. Is it possible that allowing greater emotional suffering to women actually clouds the material reality of the relentless need to perform menial chores?

The historical perspective

I argued earlier that a historical perspective helped to relativise mental illness by teasing out how it is constructed by each social group, in different ages and cultures.[21] Probably Michel Foucault's *Madness and Civilization* (1965) is among the best known attempts to locate madness in its cultural context. He traced over several hundred years a number of different attitudes to 'deviants', and he was particularly concerned with how far such individuals were tolerated in society at large or extruded from it into institutions.

Following Foucault, and the more recent work of Andrew Scull (1977), we may delineate four historical phases in the treatment of the mad by Western society. The toleration and integration of the insane until the mid-seventeenth century was followed by a period of about 150 years during which all undesirables tended to be indiscriminately incarcerated. Subsequently, they argue, only those defined as mentally ill were institutionalised, and it was usually anticipated that they would be successfully cured, and, like prisoners, rehabilitated to lead a 'normal' life. This third period, in the nineteenth and early twentieth centuries, was associated with the development of medical specialties like psychiatry which enjoyed increasing status, as distinct from the equally specialised but more menial occupation of insane asylum keeper. The last phase, which Scull argues has come since the Second World War, is characterised by a policy of 'decarceration', i.e. letting people out of custodial institutions. The mentally ill are released into the community, with inadequate support services, often controlled by psychotropic drugs. This has achieved dramatic savings in the very costly sector of custodial care.

Scull ties these phases to successive stages of capitalism, and to the need for a labour market with different characteristics at different times, and to the recent fiscal crisis of the State, which means that, as far as possible, costs are displaced into the private sector to save public spending. In many ways this is a challenging and stimulating approach which shows the total inadequacy of traditional accounts which emphasise increasingly humane treatment associated with the development of modern medicine and psychiatry as forces of liberation from superstition and witchcraft. But it provides little help in our project of understanding the experiences of the constituent groups of a community. Neither Scull nor Foucault offers clues as to how women specifically were affected by these broad transitions in social and economic structure. Their approach also has the serious shortcoming of ignoring all those cases, possibly the majority, which never reached a custodial institution or a psychiatrist.[22]

To overcome these limitations, we need to focus on concrete struggles around definitions of mental health and illness. The American historians John Haller and Robin Haller (1974) have drawn attention to the way in which an event like the American Civil War redefined the categories of health and illness for women (and for men too). In this respect the First World War would be similar, in that women temporarily assumed male roles out of necessity, and largely proved their capacity to fill them without detriment to their health.[23] After the wars, struggles ensued in both America and Britain over the physical and mental health of women, and the associated behaviour deemed appropriate. The Hallers also drew attention to the possibility of mental and physical illness giving women quasi-legitimate means of regulating their sex lives. They suggest that, far from being a mark of weakness, such complaints were a clear form of protest and an attempt by women to gain freedom and exercise more control over their lives.

Historians are only beginning to explore seriously the extent to which mental illnesses (and illnesses in general) are historically and sexually specific.[24] It is well known that physicians have characterised certain diseases as more commonly male (neurasthenia, hypochondria) or female (chlorosis, hysteria). Yet the fact that these disease categories have been used for centuries tends to blind us to different interpretations and definitions of the complaints from one period to another. Hysteria is an excellent example of an illness which, until Freud, was taken to be found in women alone, yet what was meant by hysteria differed considerably, and neither was it always associated with the womb. We need to know much more about the history of the clinical aspects of hysteria before we can understand how it was used to define women. In particular we must be critical of the assumption that women have always been characterised as more emotional and uncontrolled than men. The point would not necessarily be to reject the idea, but to show how this sexual polarity was sustained in specific historical cases.

We also need to document changing diseases from the perspective of women's mental suffering. In the early twentieth century depression was rarely mentioned in medical texts at all, yet now research into it receives vast amounts of money, millions are spent developing and buying treatments for it, and it, perhaps more than any other contemporary illness, is associated with the social condition of women. A similar argument could be made about anorexia nervosa which, like depression, is commonly seen as a woman's, or rather, a young girl's, disease, and it is also widely acknowledged to be a twentieth-century phenomenon.

Concluding remarks

The sexual specificity of illness and its subjective experience is little investigated and still less understood. To move forward I think we need to work on two fronts, one historical and the other contemporary. For the first we need to get away from stereotypical accounts of the control of women by male 'experts' which suggest that women are branded as emotional and hysterical merely to serve the interests of male professionals.[25] This is a simplistic and distorted account which does not do justice to the real complexity of women's mental anguish in a concrete context. I do not believe that women's mental health and illnesses can be isolated from that of men and children, nor from family structure, modes of work and other social and cultural features.

The same reservations apply to contemporary studies, such as the recent one by Brown and Harris (1978), which fails to locate women properly in the familial context which is supposedly responsible for much of their depression. In part the shortcomings of such work are caused by the attempt to elaborate a 'scientific and objective' methodology to study something which cannot be quantified. The statistical fetish makes Brown and Harris see depression as a clinical entity, and the whole conceptual apparatus of the book attempts to render mathematical the suffering and unhappiness of many women.

The feminist challenge, it seems to me, is to alter the terms of the debate completely without getting drawn into the false consciousness of either traditional scientific medicine or academic sociology. We must further say that proclaiming that women with shitty lives feel depressed isn't an adequate analysis of women and their mental illnesses. Doing justice to their suffering entails finding alternatives to such scientistic tautologies.

Notes

1   I would like to thank Karl Figlio for his comments on earlier drafts of this paper, Cathy Crawford and Ornella Moscucci for allowing me to read their unpublished dissertations, and the members of the Cambridge Medical Sociology group with whom some of the ideas in the paper were discussed in May 1979.

2   Two studies which fail in this regard are Miller (1978) and Skultans (1975).

3   There have been many excellent articles in *Spare Rib* on mental health issues. See also Orbach (1978). For a factual account of mental health in women with feminist sympathies see Leeson and Gray (1978).

4   For a spirited, but in my view misguided, attempt to defend the medical model see Siegler and Osmond (1974).

5   For examples of the use of physical methods see Groddeck (1949, first published 1923) and Reich (1968, first published 1942).

6   Among important feminist contributions to debates about psychoanalysis are; J. Mitchell (1975); Millet (1971), and the journal *M/F* (1978 on), see also note 9.

7   I do not wish to imply that family therapy commonly embodies the assumptions I describe, merely that it can do so. Particularly striking is the work of Richter (1974); see chapter 13 − 'A Thirty-Year-Old Daughter Grows Up'. For a totally different approach to family therapy see Minuchin (1974); Malcolm (1978).

8   For an example of the application of psychoanalysis by a feminist literary critic see Kolodny (1975); on psychohistory see the journals *History of Childhood Quarterly* (1973 on), and *Psychohistory Review* (1976 on), and de Mause (1976) and Poster (1978).

9   Among the classic writings by women on women are Chesler (1972); Deutsch (1973, first published 1945) and Horney (1967).

10   Studies of institutions include; Deyon (1975), Grob (1973), Ignatieff (1978), Rothman (1971), Scull (1977).

11   A useful critique of social control is Stedman Jones (1977).

12   Laing and Esterson (1970), Cooper (1972). It is worth noting that many of the young schizophrenics they treated were female, but this was not analysed with a view to understanding what role sexuality played in the genesis of the problem. On the other hand, the account by a woman who underwent Laingian treatment makes it abundantly clear how closely her anguish was tied up with her rejection, and denial, of her femaleness: Barnes and Berke (1973).

13   Breen (1975), specifically concentrated on the experience for women of bearing their first child.

14   The early studies of Freud and Breuer (1974, first published 1895), on hysteria are particularly relevant to the themes of the paper.

15 On suicide see Stengel (1970), and Alvarez (1974), the latter analyses Sylvia
    Plath's suicide in some detail.

16 The largest study is that of Brown and Harris (1978), see also Fagin (no
    date).

17 See Nathanson (1975), Chetwynd and Hartnett (1978), and in the latter
    especially the papers by Lipshitz and Litman.

18 Prather and Fidell (1975) and Goffman (1979) deal with the relationship
    between advertisements and sex, but from different perspectives.

19 On women and drugs see Stimson (1975 a and b). Scull (1977) provides an
    excellent summary of the development of the psychotropic drugs industry
    since the Second World War.

20 On the relationships between women and GPs see Barrett and Roberts
    (1978).

21 Crawford (1977) has provided a valuable survey of the literature from a
    critical point of view.

22 For a more extended critique of Scull's book see Figlio and Jordanova
    (1979).

23 Although not very satisfactory, Marwick's account (1977) mentions some
    of these issues.

24 The published literature is as yet rather sparse. In addition to works
    already cited the following may be useful, Moscucci (1978), Delamont and
    Duffin, (1978), Veith (1965), Ehrenreich and English (1979), should be
    used only with great care, Gilman (1973, first published 1892) is a short
    story which provides a vivid subjective account of a woman's mental break-
    down in the late nineteenth century. On chlorosis, see Figlio (1978).

25 Ehrenreich and English (1979) are particularly guilty of this type of
    distortion.

Further reading

M. Barnes and J. Berke, *Two Accounts of a Journey Through Madness*.
Harmondsworth: Penguin, 1973.

R. D. Laing and A. Esterson, *Sanity, Madness and the Family: Families of
Schizophrenics*. Harmondsworth: Penguin, 1970.

J. Mitchell, *Psychoanalysis and Feminism*. London: Allen Lane, 1974.

H. Richter, *The Family as Patient: The Origin, Nature and Treatment of
Marital and Family Conflicts*. London: Souvenir Press, 1974.

A. Scull, *Decarceration. Community Treatment and the Deviant – a
Radical View*. Englewood Cliffs, N. J. : Prentice-Hall, 1977.

Chapter Seven

Domestic Violence: Battered Women in Britain in the 1970s

VAL BINNEY

Violence against women within the home offers a useful entry for an exploration of the domestic oppression of women. By examining in some detail the conditions under which battering has occurred in Britain over the past few decades, I hope to reveal the inadequacy of the current idea that women can achieve equality in public life without a radical reappraisal of their subordinate position within the family.

It was the opening of refuges for battered women in the 1970s that threw into relief the widespread existence of violence toward women in their own homes. The initial public response was 'if it was really that bad, they would have left long ago'. But in looking at why women have stayed with brutal men, we uncover a web of constraints, both material and ideological, which affect all women to a greater or lesser extent. The issue of domestic violence serves to illustrate the way in which, at a particular point in time, factors such as money, the law, the sexual division of labour and State policies interact to shape women's lives and the choices open to them. And more optimistically, to illustrate too how contradictions between the forces structuring women's lives can sometimes make it possible for women to carve out new space for themselves. Refuges and the publicity surrounding them have secured a new space for battered women − space for a redefinition of what battering means and for a struggle against its invisibility.

One response to the evidence that 'wife battering' existed was to treat it as a new social ill, product of an urban evironment and the breakdown of old values, on a par with 'juvenile delinquency'. However, both Martin (1977) and Dobash and Dobash (1980) have documented clearly the existence of violence toward women across the centuries as a common and institutionalised part of marriage in European culture. A man's right to beat his wife was firmly entrenched in British law until the late nineteenth century, the only controversial issue until then being what the acceptable limits were to such treatment. However, during the latter half of the nineteenth century the ill-treatment of wives became an increasing source of social concern, with John Stuart Mill and Francis Power Cobbe amongst the advocates of legal reform to improve the position of women: 'The vilest malefactor has some wretched woman tied to him, against whom he can commit any atrocity except killing her' (J. S. Mill, in Sutton, 1979). A series of reforms around divorce, separation and women's property rights was won, and although there is no doubt that wife beating continued, it disappeared from public interest for almost a hundred years.

Why did battered women resurface as an area of social concern and policy making in the 1970s? Angela Weir (1977) points out that historically the issue has always been raised during periods of active feminism. It was a feminist initiative that led to the setting up of the first refuge in 1972 and feminists have continued to be prominent in the wave of activity against battering that has followed. This has had important consequences for the way in which refuges are run and campaigns fought (see, p.124). The current women's movement was not only sensitive to such aspects of women's oppression as battering but was prepared to do battle outside the conventional channels. In addition, there seemed to be an increasing reluctance on the part of women to put up with battering as an inevitable part of married life. In effect, wife beating was an age-old phenomenon which forced itself on public consciousness in the 1970s in the face of considerable resistance.

The major source of evidence about battering comes from women living in refuges, one of the few places where battered women become socially visible (see Dobash and Dobash, 1980; Pahl, 1978; Binney, Harkell and Nixon, 1979). Many of these women report a long history of violence, lasting thirty years or more in some cases. Most report attempts to find help at some point. Yet nowhere did battered women catch the public eye, in spite of the steady stream who must have come to the attention of the various health and welfare agencies over the years. Nowhere did they gain the platform in discussions of social intervention, in stark contrast to the concern over baby battering. It seems that agencies maintained a peculiar 'social blindness' to the problem, well illustrated by research into social service records. Liz Kelly (1976) cites a study of case records for 1974 in one London borough where 42 per cent of referrals involving battered women had been classified under 'Miscellaneous' and as requiring no further visits. Maynard (1979) found in a survey of social service records for 1976 in York that about one-third of the casework involved battering, in spite of assurances to the contrary. The responses battered women have received from agencies reveal not only a lack of resources to deal with the problem, but more clearly a marked reluctance to interfere in the relations between 'man and wife'. This reluctance, not so evident for example in cases of child abuse or social security snooping, seems to mask an acknowledgement of and respect for male power within the family, rather than a respect for the privacy of the individual (see Jeffrey and Pahl, 1979). Violence against women is often described as too trivial to warrant interference, but the evidence from refuges in no way bears this out:

> Some women are appallingly injured; they suffer broken bones, knife wounds and severe bruising; some are hit over the head with furniture, some are thrown down stairs and one had a nail hammered into her foot. Some women suffer in other ways and may have no bruises to show for it. One woman who had stayed the longest in the refuge . . . had never said what drove her from home; all she said was that she had not been physically battered; but her need of the refuge is obviously great. (Pahl, 1978; p.8; see also Pizzey, 1974; Dobash and Dobash, 1980).

Most women coming to refuges have tried to leave home before. It had usually been a case of a few nights in a bed and breakfast, offered by a social worker until things quietened down or a sofa with relatives until she was found and harassed into returning to the man who had beaten her. Housing Departments often turned women away on the grounds that they had a 'perfectly good home to return to'. Privately rented accommodation has never been an option for single parents on social security. But it was the police who had been most commonly turned to by battered women and they who have been consistently described as unhelpful (Jeffrey and Pahl, 1979). The police have a policy of non-intervention in 'domestic disputes' which effectively leaves a woman unprotected by law within her own home. When they do come out for a call of this nature, the police tend to restrict their role to one of a 'calming presence' and seldom press charges against the batterer. Added to all these obstacles was most women's ignorance of the few rights they did have — would they lose their children? Could they claim social security benefits? — and more importantly, the attitude they encountered from whoever they consulted that it was a personal problem, that it was their own failing as a woman which had caused their predicament. It is not surprising that so many women have put up with battering for so long. What should be called into question is why the institution of marriage allows for such treatment to be meted out to women.

As the number of refuges grew and gained publicity, pressure was put on the State to respond to the problem. The political and ideological contexts within which changes have been made will be discussed below after examining what has been achieved in concrete terms. One of the first responses was the setting up of the Parliamentary Select Committee on Violence in Marriage, (1975). It recognised the severity of the problem, estimating that one woman in every hundred households might be battered, and recommended the provision of one refuge place for every ten thousand members of the population. To date this has not been achieved, with only 150 refuges in England and Wales, mainly in metropolitan areas. Other recommendations focused around police response and education of the public. A further attempt to improve the protection of battered women was evident in the Domestic Violence and Matrimonial Proceedings Act 1976 (DVA). Prior to this Act, court injunctions excluding a man from his home had been available only under very restricted conditions and there had been few repercussions when orders were broken. The Act extended the use of exclusion orders to a wider range of women — not only those already seeking divorce — and made possible the attachment of police powers of arrest in the event of a broken injunction. In practice, few judges have been prepared to use the powers of arrest clause and most of the other limitations of injunctions, whether exclusion or non-molestation orders, persist: judges have to be satisfied that the violence is of a 'sufficiently serious nature' to justify such drastic measures and most women complain that in the face of attack, waving a piece of paper does not constitute adequate protection. In addition, the Act has been used by some local authorities as an excuse not to rehouse women who have left their homes because of violence. They argue that it offers sufficient protection for a woman to return home alone, in spite of much evidence to the contrary. It could be said that an important effect of the Domestic Violence Act, despite all its practical limitations, is that it chips away at that closely cherished belief that 'an Englishman's home is his castle'. Resistence to this implication of the Act was evident in the case of Johnstone v Davis (1977) where a Court of Appeal ruled that a man's property rights took precedence over an injunction obtained under the DVA.[1] This decision was later overturned by the Law Lords in the woman's favour, but only for a three-month period.

A further increase in rights for battered women was secured by the inclusion of domestic violence as a valid cause of homelessness in the Housing (Homeless Persons) Act 1977. This Act imposed a statutory duty on local authorities to provide accommodation for priority groups amongst the homeless, including women with children. While it has probably had a more noticeable impact on women's attempts to separate from violent men than has the DVA, there have been considerable problems for Women's Aid groups trying to ensure its implementation. There are loopholes which allow authorities to define women as 'intentionally homeless' or to keep them quibbling over which authority is 'responsible' for a particular woman. However, the Housing (Homeless Persons) Act does recognise more clearly than the DVA the realities of trying to escape from a violent man, in that it states that women should not be forced to return to an area where there is a risk of further violence.

Since the early days of refuges then, there has been an increase in rights for battered women, at least on paper, and an increased awareness of the problem in at least some of the agencies with whom battered women come into contact. But how far reaching are these changes and how likely are they to prevent the occurrence of battering in the first place? To evaluate this requires an examination of how battering occurs. Indeed, the sudden focus of public attention on battered women led to a heated debate about the scale and interpretation of the problem. The idea that battering could exist on a large scale threatened to call into question the popular image of the contemporary family as a haven of love and personal fulfilment, particularly for women. It undermined the comfortable view of sociologists such as Wilmott and·Young (1972), who would have us believe that, whatever its past, a form of the family had evolved in which the old roles of dominance and submission have been replaced by a more 'symmetrical' relationship between husbands and wives. Within the debate three main views of battering can be discerned, which I will call the *traditionalist*, the *liberal/psychiatric* and the *feminist*.

The *traditionalist* view of battering was more vocally expressed during the earlier years of the debate, at least at a policy level. It is still in evidence in the treatment of battering in the media and in popular sentiment. Traditionalists tend to dismiss as exaggerated the reports of systematic, severe violence toward women and where they admit to violence occurring, women are seen to invite and deserve it because of their behaviour − unwashed dishes, a meal not ready on time or the refusal of 'marital rights' are seen as justifiable provocation to violence. No claims are made, in this view, as to the desirability of equality for women; women who are beaten should ideally accept it as their due, as they did 'in my day', that golden age when women knew their place. Contrary to the evidence that battering occurs across class, traditionalists conveniently see battering as a normal part of working-class life in which middle-class do-gooders should not interfere.

While the sheer weight of evidence and possibly the increased sensitivities fostered by the women's movement have made this viewpoint less acceptable in public debate, there is no doubt that many individual politicians and administrators adhere to it in practice. Housing Departments, for example, are notorious amongst women in refuges for their suspicions that battered women who come to them are lying, exaggerating or just plain fussy about their relationships. These suspicions are used to justify a narrow definition of battering as 'persistent and severe assault', calling for lengthy and often humiliating interrogation sessions to establish the validity of women's claims. It seems that a certain level of violence toward women is considered acceptable — only beyond that level does it become an eyesore to the rest of society.

The *liberal/psychiatric* view of battering is one which recognises it as a social problem requiring intervention, but its solutions are ultimately inadequate to that problem. In keeping with the dominant view of all social problems within the framework of the Welfare State (see Wilson, 1976b), be it depression in young mothers or 'juvenile delinquency', the solution is limited to the level of the individual. Stripped of their wider social context, these problems are confined to deviant minority groups whose defining characteristics are carefully documented in order to demarcate the bearers from the rest of society. The work of Gayford (1975) embodies such an approach to battering; he names drinking in men and early sex without contraception in women as predictors of a violent relationship. The obvious flaw with this sort of argument is that it does not account for those who share the predictors but do not end up in violent relationships, for both these characteristics were common in industrial society in the 1960s and 1970s. More insidious is the clumping together of items which define what is basically a stereotype of irresponsibility. Gayford divided the women he interviewed into various types who each in some way 'invite' or 'need' violence:

> *Go-go Gloria* — provided she can be protected from her own stimulus-seeking activities, she is a likeable woman. *Fanny the Flirt* — early in life she learned to manipulate people and found the glory of being the centre of attention; with puberty she found new toys to play with, but unfortunately she did not learn the consequences of this action. . . . As Fanny advances in

years she has a long list of relationships and children, some still with her, some abandoned en route. (Gayford, 1976)

What Gayford's cheap stereotypes have in common is that in each case the woman has transgressed by exceeding the bounds of the expected feminine role, in terms of flaunted sexuality, assertiveness or lack of maternal devotion. Although the women are seen by Gayford as disturbed individuals in need of professional help, the moral blame implicit in his descriptions is not that far removed from the attitude of the traditionalist.

What are important in this view of battering are the implications for who controls the process of escape from violence. Since the women are seen as colluding in the violence by (unconsciously) seeking out violent men, it is a case of doctor knows best. And although the battering men too are seen as 'sick' and in need of psychiatric care, the sick model in practice has unequal consequences for the sexes. It is the women who seek help when they are beaten and are thus more readily available as victims for psychiatric treatment. Men who batter see 'their woman' as the problem rather than themselves and are unlikely to seek help or to perceive themselves as sick. (See Jordanova, chapter 6, for a more detailed discussion of the medicalisation of social problems and its consequences for women.) Gayford reveals starkly his inability to perceive social and political events in any but psychiatric terms in his racist remarks on immigrants, made to the Select Committee on Violence in Marriage:

> Basically what one is saying is that if people have a disturbed background they tend to want to emigrate, and of course they bring all their family history with them, all their emotional problems, and they are more likely to be the ones that will enter into this type of relationship. (1975)

Despite flaws both in methodology and logic (Wilson, 1976a) Gayford's work has been highly influential in the way in which battering has been assimilated by professionals, as the pages of a magazine such as *Community Care* will bear out.

To those who adopt the psychiatric approach, the most important objects of treatment are the children of battered women, since a 'cycle of violence' model is put forward to account for the origins of this masochism in women and violence in men. A boy, beaten by his father or seeing his mother beaten, supposedly learns the masculine role for himself, while a girl observing these events learns the role of victim from her mother. This view is expressed repeatedly by Erin Pizzey: 'You've only to watch the boys in the refuge to see the next generation's potential batterers. Many of them are extremely violent by age three. By age eleven they are potential criminals' (Pizzey, 1974, p.74). And more recently from Bill Bowder (1979)[2] summarising Pizzey's views:

> As Betty smiled back with pleasure at her mother giving her pain she was cementing the association between pleasure and pain which may surface in her teens as a compulsion to pursue violent relationships with men.

While it is undoubtedly true that the family is an important training ground in social relations, it cannot be seen in isolation from the rest of society. In this case, battering is seen as socially produced, but the family is the limit of its social context. The implication is that as long as attention is focused on those families where battering is known to occur, the problem can be solved. These families are seen as essentially different from 'normal' families and so questions which might otherwise arise about the relations between the sexes in general and about women's role within the family, remain neatly cut off. To confirm this demarcation from the rest of society, it is asserted that these women tend to batter their children too, although no connections have been established in this regard. Given the high level of child abuse in the general population, it would be surprising to find that there were *no* instances of battered women beating their children.

A further case of attention being deflected from the fact that women are battered by the men they live with is to be found in a recent trend in the United States toward the use of terms such as 'spousal violence'. In an attempt to balance the picture, 'battered men' have become the new cause for concern. A study by Straus (See Steinmetz, 1978), for example, claimed to find rates of husband assault which were almost as high as those of wife assault. What Straus failed to take into account was the severity of the violence as well as its context; most obviously, whether women were retaliating to an attack when they were violent. This work has been ably criticised by Dobash and Dobash (1977) who comment that 'it would be ironic if, in the current climate, some magical twist of egalitarian terminology were to be used to deny centuries of oppression and further repress contemporary women by obscuring the undeniable fact that spousal violence is to all intents and purposes wife beating.' It is true that women can be violent, but they are so from a position of powerlessness and are likely to incur serious harm to themselves by using violence. The so-called 'shrewish wife' is tolerated precisely because she knows she cannot go too far, without punishment. I would suggest that women tend to be violent out of frustration with their powerless position, in comparison to the assertive, instrumental use of violence by men. For women, persuasion and subterfuge have always been a safer means to an end than violence.

So the liberal/psychiatric explanation of battering, while it may initially have helped to make battered women more visible, has done so at the price of containing and diluting the problem, and it poses a serious threat to women's struggles for self-determination. It has to some extent become the officially sanctioned view, endorsed by the Select Committee on Violence in Marriage and runs through the way in which a minority of refuges operate. These refuges smack of a middle-class guardianship of social morality, handing out relief only to the deserving. They see themselves as stepping in to ensure a process of 'responsible' separation where they deem the relationship to be in a state of irretrievable breakdown. Proof of serious violence may be required before admission to such a refuge, and reconciliation can be an integral part of their practice. While no doubt they serve a useful purpose in terms of providing emergency accommodation to women who qualify for entry, these groups have little in common with the aims of the National Women's Aid Federation.[3]

The third view of battering — the *feminist view* — has been put forward by the National Women's Aid Federation (1977; 1978), and in the work of Weir (1977), Hanmer (1977) and Dobash and Dobash (1977), amongst others. There is no single feminist theory of battering, or of male violence toward women in general, but what these writings have in common is that they look beyond the individuals involved and locate violence against women within the broader context of women's subordinate position relative to men. From this perspective, what is of interest is not so much that one human being *is capable of* violence toward another, as that, overwhelmingly, within the family this violence is being used by men against women. It enquires not only into why a man might hit his wife in the first place, but why he may repeat this behaviour regularly without social constraint, and why women find it so difficult to leave such a man. Feminists have pointed out the contradictory nature of the family, which is seen as affording women protection while in fact we find that a quarter of reported violent crime is wife assault (Dobash and Dobash, 1977), and that a large proportion of reported rapes occur between people who know each other, perpetrated often by husbands, boyfriends, fathers and uncles (Rape Crisis Centre, 1977).

It is not within the scope of this article to offer an explanation for women's subordinate status, which is apparent, albeit in different forms, in all known societies. That is a question to which this book as a whole addresses itself. Instead, I wish to examine the way in which physical violence towards women draws on and serves to maintain this subordination and, indeed, cannot be explained without reference to it. Dobash and Dobash (1977, p.438) explain the patriarchal under-pinnings of violence in a contemporary marriage thus:

> in Western society a man feels that marriage gives him the right to expect domestic service and sexual exclusivity from his wife. The fulfilment of these behaviours is not only personally pleasant to him, it also becomes an outward sign of his rightful possession of authority over her and ability to control her.

They have carried out the most detailed study on battering to date in Britain and they conclude 'it was the real or perceived challenges to the man's possession, authority and control which most often resulted in the use of violence − a late meal, an unironed shirt, a conversation with a man' (1976). Not all women are physically battered, but because of the nature of marriage, most men have the power to batter 'their' woman if they so wish. Feminists therefore regard battering as the extreme end of a continuum of oppression suffered by all women to a greater or lesser extent depending on their class, marital status and degree of economic dependence on a man. Ironically, it is the women who are in a position to offer the least challenge to masculine authority, those dependent because of young children, who seem to be the prime victims of violence. This is contrary to the popular prejudice that it is women's aspirations to equality with men which inspires violence.

The two main foci of feminist activity around battering, apart from the central role of refuges in enabling women to escape from violence, have been first to challenge the traditionalist and liberal ways in which battering has been interpreted (see p.119) and to attempt to demolish the material barriers that face women leaving violent men. Feminist refuges see themselves as offering more than simply accommodation. They also aim to provide the opportunity for battered women getting together to break out of their previous isolation and to thereby recognise that their experience has not been one of individual personal failure. Women are free to enter these refuges on their own definition of need, with mental cruelty being treated as an equally valid reason for leaving home as physical violence. An open-door policy is operated, on the understanding that somehow, somewhere within the federation of refuges, space will be found for whoever asks. Refuges are seen as offering a chance for women collectively to rebuild the confidence and strength necessary both for their individual survival and as the best political base from which to combat battering at a societal level. Women's Aid specifically rejects the idea of a centralised and hierarchical organisation operating on behalf of battered women.

Five years on, where does Women's Aid stand? Politically, it is in a more difficult position than it was in 1974 when battered women were not recognised and refuge provision was minimal. It was a comparatively easy task to force the plight of battered women upon public attention, so obvious was it that nothing was being done. But having forced an acknowledgement from the State that the problem did indeed exist, Women's Aid now has to cope with the State's notions of how to deal with the problem. With the passing of the Domestic Violence Act 1976 and the Housing (Homeless Persons) Act 1977, battered women are deemed to have been taken care of, regardless of how these Acts work in practice. In fact, refuge provision is still very limited and of poor standard, and in some cases has been eroded. Local authorities bypass feminist refuges to sponsor groups who will toe their line, while others declare refuges redundant now that battered women are in theory eligible for homeless hostel accommodation. Limited legislation copes with the steady stream of women who manage to leave home, usually by keeping them busy jumping through the endless hoops it provides, while the majority of women may still have no idea that refuges exist. The battle has hardly got off the ground over the quality of housing that battered women, like all homeless people, are forced to accept when they are lucky enough to be offered anything. Once they have left behind the boisterous communality of a refuge, battered women are faced with all the problems of loneliness and poverty that beset most one-parent families 'headed' by women. And yet, ironically, as with abortion rights, one hears talk of women's rights having gone too far, of battered women receiving 'priviledged treatment'.

In the end, the success of a feminist attack on battering lies not so much in the admittedly important reforms achieved in the law, but in keeping the issue alive as a problem not yet solved. Ideologically, the specific battle is to combat the containment of battering within a psychiatric interpretation and to insist upon the very real powerlessness of women within the family. In this, Women's Aid cannot survive alone; its fate is inextricably bound up with the successes and failures of the women's movement as a whole. To the extent that the women's movement makes a lasting impact, the attempt to contain battering at 'acceptable levels' will be weakened.

Notes

1 The couple were unmarried and held a joint tenancy to the flat. See *Roof* (1977) for a fuller discussion of the limitations of the DVA.

2 See Dobash and Dobash (1979) for a thorough demolition of Bowder's article.

3 The National Women's Aid Federation was formed in 1974 to co-ordinate existing refuges and to promote the interests of battered women.

Chapter Eight

'A daughter: a thing to be given away'

A PENELOPE BROWN, MARTHE MACINTYRE,
ROS MORPETH AND SHIRLEY PRENDERGAST

We should like to start this paper on violence against women with the story of the death of a young woman in 1973 in a Sikh village we shall call Pind in the State of Punjab in Northern India.[1] The woman's name was Balwinder Kaur (Bindo for short). She had returned to her parents' home for the birth of her fifth child. Shortly after the birth, which had been a very difficult one by all accounts, Bindo's husband Jaswinder Singh visited her in a drunken state. There was a violent quarrel overheard by near neighbours, followed by a suspected sexual assault. Within a day Bindo died in great pain and mental torment.

The events leading up to her death are as follows: she was the only and greatly loved daughter of one of the richest Jat landowners in the village. Her marriage was arranged when she was 17 (in about 1963) to a husband whose family had a similar economic and social status to her own. They lived in a village called Budapur a few miles away from Pind. The marriage did not turn out well — Jaswinder Singh proved to be a drunkard and a violent man and in addition his parents did not treat Bindo well; they kept her short of food and adequate clothing. This upset Bindo's parents and brothers, but the person who felt it most was her mother, who encouraged her daughter to make long visits home and would always send her back to her in-laws with gifts of food and clothing. At other times she would visit Bindo in her husband's village, bringing gifts of food for Bindo and her children.

All these matters were, of course, common knowledge in both the villages, as was the tension caused in both the husband's and Bindo's parents' households. Bindo's two elder brothers and their wives and children were living in a joint family with their parents, farming the land together and running a communal household. They resented the fact that a portion of their shared resources was going to support their sister and her family. Her husband, Jaswinder Singh, and his family clearly found Bindo's mother's visits and gifts an intrusion into their affairs. It was from this background of tension and hostility that Bindo returned to her natal village (village of her birth) for the birth of her fifth child, and died. Her death was entered in the records as death from puerperal fever and her body was cremated as quickly as possible. No one in the village thought it strange that the cause of death was recorded as fever, despite the fact that many people were aware of the violent circumstances surrounding her death. The baby boy who survived his mother's death was put in the care of one of Bindo's brothers' daughters, a girl of about 15 called Sukjit.

The incident did not end with the cremation of Bindo's body, because almost immediately Sukjit became 'possessed' with Bindo's spirit. Several people were prepared to testify that Sukjit started to talk with Bindo's voice and very angrily ask for her baby back (she said that she wanted to 'eat' her baby). She also made demands for food, especially meat, and for new clothing. Bindo's spirit did not only enter Sukjit, it also visited other women in the village who started to manifest the signs of possession, speaking in Bindo's voice and demanding food and clothing in an angry manner.

At this point the male elders of the village decided to call in the village exorcist (the 'chella'), an old man called Balbir Singh. Balbir's method was to try and talk to the spirit and appease its anger by giving it the food and clothing it wanted. Bindo's baby had a black mark put on his forehead to make him appear unattractive to the spirit. The food and clothing were of course consumed by the woman who was possessed by the spirit, because she was the medium of communication with the spirit. The village 'chella', however, wasn't powerful enough to exorcise the spirit and after he admitted defeat another, stronger, 'chella' was sent for from outside the village. Using the same methods as Balbir Singh, he succeeded in expelling the spirit from the village and the symptoms of possession in the women disappeared.

Sukjit looked after the baby for a short time until Bindo's mother had recovered enough to take care of her grandchild. As far as we know Bindo's spirit never returned, but the strain of these events precipitated Bindo's two brothers and father into dividing the land between the three of them and splitting up into three separate households.

What are we to make of this story and what features of Punjabi society does it reveal? What relevance, if any, does it have for our concerns as feminists in our analysis of our own society? By the end of the paper we hope to be able to answer these two questions in a limited way. The main theme of the story is the use of male violence to keep women 'in their place' and the particular ways women have of responding to this violence.

A few remarks about the social organisation of northern Indian rural society are a necessary background to understanding the incident. The kinship system is patrilineal, with patrilocal residence as the norm (i.e. inheritance goes through the male line, and wives go to live in the village of their husbands, separated from their natal families). Many families live in joint households — generally an old man and his wife, his sons and their wives and children. Sex roles are rigidly defined, women are confined to the domestic sphere where their personal behaviour is supposed to echo and constantly reaffirm the dominance of men. Women are expected to value husbands and sons above all female relations, and should be obedient to all their demands and respectful of all their needs, both physical and emotional. A conventional Punjabi religious blessing says 'May God bless you and keep you a married woman with seven sons.' When a woman marries she usually moves to another village and relinquishes all direct claims on her natal family wealth (in land and property), which goes to her brothers.[2] She has a dowry, which consists of gold ornaments, clothing and household equipment, but she cannot convert these into cash, and is entirely dependent on her husband for sustenance and shelter.

The first thing to be said is that the events recounted here are not all that extraordinary in the framework of Punjabi society. Even though the murder of women is not culturally sanctioned or commonly admitted, its occurrence fits into the total structure of belief and action that affirms at every step the subordination of women to men, and in which physical control is the ultimate and logical resort. The murder of Bindo is thus the logical extreme, in this case made brutally explicit, of a society that has the concrete and unquestioned use of physical violence available at any moment to turn against women who are in breach of its rules of social action.[3] The acceptance by everyone in the village of Bindo's murder and its official description as death from puerperal fever, alongside the lack of public disapproval and censure of the murderer, her husband, underline this fact even more dramatically.

In the Punjabi context the woman's place, as mother/sister/daughter or daughter-in-law/wife, is completely at the disposal of her male relatives, first, by virtue of birth and second by marriage. The woman's role (and its limits and constraints) is therefore rigidly defined and maintained by the male authority structure. It is through men that access to the life-support systems flows — goods, shelter, social status and cash. A woman may not leave her family without dire consequences, for in order to survive a woman must, by kinship and later by marriage, be attached to a man. In Bindo's case the strong mother-daughter bond, denying as it did the supremacy of both the husband-wife and the mother-son relationships, was already the source of a division of loyalties within the family.

Women in this society have little or no social space in which to ease or bypass their allotted roles. Yet, as we have seen, owing to the very nature and degree of repression and control involved, women (at least those in unhappy marital circumstances) do sometimes feel angry and rebellious. Men, in contrast to women, have socially acceptable ways of expressing aggression as part of their social role. They inhabit the wider world of work outside the home and community involvements, rather than being confined, as women are, to the restricted universe of the household. They express themselves in speech and physical movement more openly than women. All men partake of the status and excitement of factional politics and feuding.[4]

We would argue from this example and from all the evidence available for this society that the definitions of transgression, the judgement and punishment of women's aggression in sex-role deviant ways, are always in Punjabi society ultimately controlled by men.[5] Looking at this point in a cross-cultural context, it has been suggested that the fusion of women's roles with the meaning and structure of kinship and the family has resulted in the denial of women's aggressive impulses and the definition of any expression of aggression as therefore 'illegitimate'.[6] We would argue further that men, in taking on the tasks of restricting and delineating the boundaries of the women's world in the negative sense, are thus controlling women's lives in a more fundamental way. The mechanism of control is that which sanctions the possible or actual use of force as a prerogative of the dominant group in upholding the norms of the society.[7]

The separate world of women, maintained by a rigid sexual division of labour and the restriction of women to the domestic sphere, has led many anthropologists to state that, for some societies at least, the world of women is one 'separate, different but complementary to that of men'.[8] That is, the worlds of women and men are distinct in their own terms but inextricably bound up with each other; the implication is that they are, therefore, not comparable in terms of status and power, and indeed that these are not relevant ways of viewing relationships between the sexes. While this argument raises many complex issues which cannot be dealt with here, we would like to point to one aspect of the women's world in Punjabi society which at first sight appears to be paradoxical. Even though the women's world is undeniably separate from the men's, women appear to have so accepted and internalised their roles as women that they have amongst them their own 'police force', for within their separate world women often act against one another's interests and in the interests of men. The aggression and hostility that they express in relation to their subjugation as women tends to become entrapped and contained within their female domain with the sanctions of gossip, ridicule and criticism of other women's behaviour.[9] Kinship structures in Punjabi society, by dispersing mothers and daughters, breaking the bonds between sisters, and setting daughters-in-law against one another and against their husbands' sisters remaining in the household, militate against any kind of collective female solidarity.[10] The mother-in-law in a patrilocal household is frequently the agent of control amongst the wives of her sons. Ill-treatment by women of women is common in this kind of situation — this is the private arena of verbal humiliation, beating and the withholding and control of food (and therefore, in a rural economy, of the means of exchange) by the mother-in-law. In addition, there is a very high rate of suicide amongst young married women in India. It would appear that suicide (in analogy to the puerperal fever label in the case study) might often be more accurately described as murder, although it rarely appears as such in official statistics.[11]

One might argue from this example that women do seem to be able to express aggression openly in at least one aspect of their lives, namely against other women. Although this is true to some degree, the real significance lies not so much in its existence, but in the *form* that the aggression takes, because the legitimate (socially condoned) expression of aggression by women is always turned *inward*. We are not saying that felt anger cannot be expressed but that it can only be expressed in ways which are, in the final analysis, advantageous to men. This occurs in at least two ways: first, by being expressed only against their own sex and never against men, and second, by taking place in the non-public realm of the domestic household — the women's world. These two forms of 'inwardness' to which the explicit use of aggression within the feminine role is limited, are related to a third form of 'inwardness', that of spirit possession, which may be seen as the *implicit* expression of female aggression. In the story of Bindo we pointed to one of the ways, i.e. physical violence and possibly murder, in which men regulate and control sex-role definitions by the use of force. The external features of Punjabi social organisation are at the service of men, in that they inexorably draw women into marriage; socially and economically women have no alternative. The proper role for a woman is to get married and to display the associated role behaviour in and before marriage as wife, daughter, sister, mother-in-law, daughter-in-law and sister-in-law. It is men who have the right, by virtue of being grandfathers, fathers and uncles, to arrange marriages, and it is men who have the public rights to transfer both property and women (although individual women, through the strength of their characters, may be able to influence these events). Men, therefore, control and define the 'exits' and 'entrances' to the social and economic world, and they also patrol its boundaries. This includes both the way in which feminine roles contain and structure their own internal violence against women, and the public and private control of the women's world by male violence.

As a mother-in-law, a woman who has herself been subordinate in her husband's household becomes more powerful with age and the adulthood of her own sons.[12] Her own natal kin ties gradually become less and less important and her interests become irretrievably connected to those of her husband, and especially her sons. It is in her interest to repeat these patterns with her new daughter-in-law. New brides pose a threat of potential breaches of family solidarity — they have to go through the dangerous process of aligning their interests with those of strangers and breaking the ties with their natal families. A mother in her turn must let go of her daughters. There are many Punjabi proverbs and sayings about daughters which illustrate this point:

'She is a bird of passage.'
'Another's property.'
'A guest in her parents' home.'
'A thing that has to be given away.'
'Bringing up a daughter is like manuring and watering a plant in someone else's courtyard.'

In a society where a woman's first obligations are towards her male kin, and the kinship system, via the mechanisms of exogamy (marrying out of the village) and dowry, forces a woman from her family of birth, the relations of mother and daughter are fraught with a peculiar ambivalence. A mother knows what her daughter's life will be like as a married woman, and it is her duty to prepare her for it.[13] In our example Bindo's mother was blamed for Bindo's behaviour, because she was acting outside her socially defined role as a mother in loving Bindo too much in the first place, and in nurturing her after she was supposed to be entirely dependent on her husband's family. Bindo's mother was clearly not behaving as a proper mother should. In this sense the problem, coming to a head with Bindo's death, stretches backwards to her mother and forwards to her niece's aggressive behaviour when possessed.[14]

In all societies people manage to come to terms with the difference between ideal norms and actual behaviour, and Punjabi society is no exception. Bindo's disastrous marriage − and her mother's continuing to support her − could and would have been tolerated had it not been made public and taken out of the officially invisible realm of the household. By coming to her mother's house for the birth of her fifth child Bindo was exposing her marital problems to public scrutiny; she thereby, as a visibly disobedient wife, brought shame on her husband's family, and as a drain on natal family resources, angered her brothers and their wives. One important component of family honour is the good behaviour of the women, and this constitutes the weak link in the chain of male domination.[15] It is possibly for this reason that transgression is punished so violently, as an example to other women.

It is interesting that the gifts of food were the focus of much anger and resentment, for Bindo's family was not poor, the reverse in fact. The food was symbolic of sustenance, mothering and love which, in Punjabi society, were being put to inappropriate use in going to a married daughter. Furthermore, the food reduced Bindo's dependence on her husband and his family. Bindo also exposed her husband's family to social shame by taking food from her mother, thus suggesting both that they could not provide for the members of their household, and that they could not control Bindo, a subordinate member, both as a woman and as a daughter-in-law. The gifts of food thereby made their ill-treatment of her socially explicit, when it should have been hidden. The last point is important, for Bindo in leaving her in-laws at this time publicly exposed what in Punjabi society is generally contained within the family. As such she became a visible and dangerous example of a woman who did not channel her aggression and misery within the violent and private world of male control, usually exercised within the domain of her husband's family. By flaunting her disobedience in this publicly visible manner Bindo was seen somehow to have brought on, and even deserved, death at her husband's hands. Bindo's niece took up this theme and carried it through to a new stage in her subsequent possession by spirits.

Sukjit was of marriageable age — was 'hot', as the Punjabi saying goes — and therefore at her most vulnerable in terms of sexual alignments in the society. Prospects for her marriage were an important issue at the time of Bindo's murder. Yet Sukjit was faced with the reality of a future as a married woman. In her possession she was displaying antagonism towards her obligations as a woman — the threat to 'eat' the new baby was interpreted as Bindo's desire 'to take it with her' — but undoubtedly Sukjit had internalised the community's resentment towards Bindo. At the same time she was meant to behave obediently and accept her responsibility without question, when she had just seen the dire consequences of her aunt's marriage. Sukjit, however, acted differently from Bindo, possibly as a result of the latter's example. She expressed her resentment and anger at her future life as a woman by becoming possessed. She could not be punished, because in cultural terms she was only acting as the agent for Bindo's spirit. Possession (like 'insanity' in our own society) is seen as something that 'comes over' people; it is beyond their control, external to them, and requires different forms of treatment than does wilful misbehaviour. Anger and aggression expressed through spirit possession are accepted as part of an illness, in which the person is 'not herself'. Given this diagnosis, in Punjabi society (and, we suggest, in most, if not all, societies) it is finally men (whether they be doctors, psychiatrists or judges) who cure the 'ill' woman, and return her to her appropriate place in the social system.

The formal structures of social organisation — political and judicial systems — are generally male-dominated, and the dominant ideology of a society relates to these institutions as the ultimate expression of social order. A corollary of this near-universal fact is that in the last resort, when domestic or informal structures (which are often female-dominated) fail, male representatives are called upon to restore or reaffirm the social and sexual order. Many recent studies which focus on the separateness and non-comparability of female and male spheres have neglected to situate these domains within the total patriarchal system. Our point here is that the crisis precipitated by Bindo's death could not be 'contained' within the domestic sphere, precisely because the crucial woman, the mother, identified with her daughter more than she did with the formal sexual hierarchy, i.e. husbands and sons. The fact that Bindo's spirit did not restrict itself to her niece but spread briefly to many other women in the village, crossing caste and age boundaries, suggests that Bindo's fate brought near to the surface a recognition by the village women of their common fate. But female solidarity of an informal and unconscious kind was no match for the combined pressures of social conformity and the need to exorcise the 'rebellious spirit'.

The failure of the village 'chella', the exorcist, to deal with the spirit possession in this case is itself of deeper significance. The 'chella' was the force which neutralised the evil generated by the illegitimate actions of the women. It seems that because Bindo's behaviour became so socially visible, when it should have been hidden at home in the family, recognition of the injustice inherent in her position (as the totally dependent wife of a drunkard) could not be totally repressed as knowledge in the village. It is for this reason, we believe, that the village 'chella' was not strong enough to cope with the case (i.e. at some level there was community recognition by women that Bindo had a right to be so angry). The village men were forced to appeal to a higher order of authority outside the village in order to uphold and enforce their control over the world of women in general, and of Bindo, her mother and her niece in particular.

To sum up so far, there are three points to be made about this case. The first is that women's aggression, if expressed openly and visibly, is highly dangerous to the social order. Concepts of honour, shame and 'face' are very important in Punjabi society.[16] One important component is the appropriate conduct of the women in the household as daughters or wives. Breaches of sexual morality or public disobedience to male members of the family are the most serious transgressions. A woman does have the power to destroy family honour to balance against her otherwise total powerlessness, although if she chooses to exercise this power it leads to her self-destruction as well, because she has to go on living in the household she has dishonoured. The expression of aggression is, therefore, more often turned inward against either herself or other women, because if it does appear overtly it is deemed illegitimate by men, who have violent means to control transgressing women. The expression of anger which is directed against other women suits the male structure of dominance because women act as a police force, controlling each other to the benefit of men.

A second point is that women are caught in a situation where all expressions of aggressive impulses are channelled *by definition* into the role of deviance. Women's aggression which does not fit neatly into the invisible world of the household is defined as 'madness' (or spirit possession, or some other similar form of 'acceptable unauthorised behaviour'). It can still come into the category of socially appropriate behaviour, because the afflicted woman is seen as 'sick' and is cured by male doctors or exorcists who return her to her social place as a 'normal' woman, while the structure itself remains unthreatened and unchanged.

Finally, it might be possible to 'short-circuit' or 'cut across' male control where there is solidarity between women, e.g. between mothers and daughters or sisters, sisters-in-law, etc. That this is the case in some societies is amply testified (see Richards, 1950; Maher, 1974; Paulme, 1971). But Punjabi society is so structured as to make this kind of solidarity as difficult as possible. Bonds between female kin are fragmented and dispersed via the mechanisms of kinship, residence, marriage and the inheritance of property; things are arranged so that a woman's strongest possible allies are her sons, and a son-less woman is powerless indeed.[17] Moreover, the Punjabi moral code is based on the assumption of women's vulnerability as women — there is no countervailing norm of kindness or protectiveness to the 'weaker sex'. The only safety as a woman is to be a wife/mother/sister/daughter/daughter-in-law; a woman unprotected by her men is free game for rape or attack by any male. Widows are vulnerable unless protected by their sons or husbands' male kin, and even within her family a wife is potentially sexually vulnerable to other male members of the household — a husband's sexual jealousy does not always extend to his own brothers, especially if he has a vested interest in keeping them in the same extended household. So wives may be shared amongst the adult males of a household.[18] The point is that whatever she does, a woman in this society is subject to male control; there is no space into which she can fit herself as a woman on her own. The positions available to her as a wife/daughter-in-law preclude the possibility of allying with other women to evade male control.

We hope we have demonstrated how the story of Bindo's death enables us to analyse the power relationship between men and women in Punjabi society. We do not offer our interpretation as the complete one, nor as the only possible one, but as one way of making sense of this incident within its cultural context. We are aware that the 'sense' we have made out of it is an interpretation using the categories and distinctions specific to Western society. It is unlikely that any of the Punjabi women in the village at that time would share our interpretation or make the same links between events as we have done.[19]

We turn now to consider our second question, of the implications this Indian case study might have for our understanding of sex-based social relations in our own society. What relevance could the life and death of Bindo have for us as feminists in a Western industrialised society? We would like to draw out two parallels. In Western societies there is also an 'invisible world' where legitimate male violence exists, and which is only now having a critical public eye turned on it, due to the efforts of feminists in the 1970s (see Binney's chapter 7). And second, the notion of mental illness in our society has certain parallels with the Punjabi notion of spirit possession; both are definitions which support men's control of women.

Before embarking on such cross-cultural generalisation, however, a *caveat* is in order about the general role which anthropological material — and cross-cultural facts in general — can play in arguments about the position of women in society. There is considerable confusion on this point in the feminist literature, where there appear many glib generalisations about alleged cross-cultural facts and where much is made of their bearing on the status of women cross-culturally and on explanations for this status.[20] There are real problems of comparability in discussing the status of women in different societies: comparability both of concepts (are 'marriage', 'mother', 'woman', 'authority', 'nature', 'culture', etc. concepts with enough elements in common in two societies to be the basis for comparison?) and of *values*. How does a particular culture evaluate the sexual divisions? Do women *feel* oppressed? subordinate? powerless? What do they make of whatever sexual divisions they operate within, as opposed to what *we* make of them? Dispute over such questions is the source of a major division among anthropologists, between those who believe cross-cultural generalisations can be made and therefore that 'universals' can be identified in the human condition or in the condition of women, and those who insist that each society has to be evaluated in its own terms.

Our view is that we can legitimately make structural comparisons between societies. For instance, the scope of the options available to women, the effects of patrilocality and the availability of alliances for women, the structural discouragement of female solidarity, are all features which influence the position of women. These questions are raised in more detail in Brown's chapter 14; here we simply want to stress that cross-cultural comparison is by no means as unproblematic as some feminist writing has suggested.

It is for these reasons that we have chosen to delimit the basis for comparison very precisely when making cross-cultural comparisons, and we have concentrated on examining violence against women within one society, so that this violence could be located within its cultural meaning. Here is a case, then, of an extreme male-dominated society where women have virtually no alternative role and where they clearly do (at least at times) feel oppressed.[21] How does this relate to our own situation, where women have many options (though they are all defined within a patriarchal system, and therefore none is ideal for women) and where many women still feel oppressed? There are a few points we want to focus on as the source of generalisations about the use of physical violence (or the threat of violence) to keep women 'in their place', and the particular nature of women's response to such violence.

The first is the role of male violence in containing women within the roles and behaviours that are allotted to them. Men beat (and in extreme cases murder) their wives. Such beating is socially sanctioned (to some extent) — men joke about it, condone it in each other, etc. It is seen as an acceptable form of control of errant women within the family. The social visibility of such violence is a sensitive issue: images of the family (in both Western and in Punjabi societies) don't fit neatly with beating, for it conflicts with the ideal image of the family as the haven of love, loyalty and personal fulfilment. So there is pressure to keep it 'invisible', and, indeed, a determined social blindness to violence against women — who are seen as getting their just deserts for wilful badness. Women are regarded as responsible for this violence against themselves by provoking a situation, walking in the dark or answering back. They even internalise this responsibility in a sense of guilt or shame. The economic, social and emotional bonds created by marriage and the difficulty of leaving the marital home are enforced by the 'blind eye' approach of the legal institutions. Hence, the Punjabi villagers' willingness to accept the official cause of Bindo's death as 'fever', indicating the official public invisibility of privately carried out sanctions against female transgressions. Only in special circumstances can the discrepancy between ideal norms and real behaviour be publicly acknowledged.

A husband's prerogative to control his wife violently extends to other male kin in societies where family honour is based on the sexual purity of women. Here violence perpetrated by the woman's own 'protectors' (husband, father, brothers, sons) is sharply distinguished from violence by outsiders. Rape of a woman in such 'honour and shame' cultures is cause for feud — a public display of men reclaiming their family honour; and the need to 'protect' women from such violence is a major rationale for circumscribing their movements and activities.

In both cases the violence is explicitly devoted to controlling women's sexuality and reproductive powers. The violence meted out to women who in some way reject the constraints upon their sexuality and fertility is often extreme, and there are many societies where women are killed for breaches of male control. In some Muslim societies adulterous women are stoned to death, while in some Amazonian tribes and among certain New Guinea peoples pack rape of a reluctant bride is the customary form of punishment.[22]

Such physical violence is explicitly referred to in many ritual and symbolic representations of sexual relations. There are symbolic statements of women's physical vulnerability to men which are especially tied to control of women's fertility and sexual access — for example, in rites of passage, which make statements about the newly attained status (especially puberty or marriage), and in judicial or informal acts of punishment for breaches of the female role, such as adultery or the production of illegitimate children. Marriage ceremonies where rituals of capture occur have often been interpreted as symbolic acts referring to natal ties which must be broken by force. In all these ritual statements, such as 'kidnapping' the bride, or tying her to the groom's wrist, the woman is the subject of male violence or subjection and her comparative physical weakness is exaggerated. In the Punjab, a bride is often so veiled and swaddled in bridal garments that she looks more like an animated parcel than a person!

A second general point to be drawn from these considerations of violence and aggression has to do with the nature of women's response to male control. Women's expression of aggression is usually turned inward. This is so both for the spirit possession in our case study (women responding to fear and tensions about their female roles by becoming invaded by the spirit of an angry woman), and for depression (of housewives, mothers of young children) in our own society. Both of these forms of response to role pressure are characteristic of women.[23] In both cases the 'illness' does not threaten the social order, or seriously incapacitate the woman and prevent her from performing day-to-day duties, and in both cases the cure is performed by a man — or a representative of the male order — in the guise of doctor, curer, psychiatrist, exorcist, etc.

When such aggression is turned inward in these ways, it is 'legitimate', it is defined within a system of roles which can be contained and coped with — the roles of 'sick' or 'possessed'. As such it contrasts with other less legitimate forms of aggression also frequently claimed (by anthropologists and by members of the societies in question) to be typical of women — for example suicide, destruction of family honour by sexual misconduct, witchcraft.[24] But these forms, it should be noted, are even more self-destructive, resulting in the woman's own death as the ultimate form of aggression. The more limited (and legitimate) forms — e.g. possession, depression — are allowable within the society precisely because they don't shake the social order. Women

are given room to suffer such ailments so long as they don't thereby
threaten the male system. Women thereby reap whatever rewards may
be associated with the 'sick' role — e.g. good clothes, food, catharsis
in the case of spirit possession, attention and social concern in depression. But both strictly limit the scope allowed to the 'sick' person; there
is social impatience with women 'malingering'.

An important fact here allows us to link these two points about
violence and madness with respect to women. One feature of madness
is that it is an attribute of individuals, defined as such by everyone in
the society — by other women as well as by men. Explanations of
madness will always be about the person, or at most the immediate
family and social environment of the woman: she went mad (became
possessed) because her baby died or whatever. It is then seen as *not* a
social problem, but a problem particular to the woman and her immediately concerned family. The same can be said about wife battering:
it can be defined (as it has been by some sociologists) as an individual
problem, due to the particular characteristics of the individuals
involved (she asked for it, she was insubordinate, he's a violent man,
etc., etc.). In both these cases, however, the possibility of bringing the
invisible (family-contained) manifestations of such events into the
open depends on looking beyond the individuals involved and locating
the violence against women and their response to it within the broader
context of women's subordinate and vulnerable position relative to
men. Feminists in our society regard battering as the extreme end of
the continuum of oppression suffered by all women; we would add to
that mental illness and the inward-turned self-destructive forms of
rebellion. Both only become socially visible and act as a focus for
efforts towards change in periods of feminist activity. This is happening now in our own society, and also in India. In both societies,
there is a long way to go.

Notes

1   The case study we present is taken from the unpublished fieldnotes of Ros
    Morpeth. It is a true story, based on reports from the local people involved.
    We are grateful to Lol Sullivan for his detailed comments on the early
    drafts.

2   This description is the ideal for most groups; it can, however, only be fully
    achieved by land-owning or other rich groups; in the case of Pind, these
    were for the most part Sikh Jat farmers. There have been recent changes in
    the laws of inheritance (see the Hindu Succession Act 1956) so that now
    sons and daughters can claim equal inheritance, but in practice the

sanctions against a girl claiming her inheritance are so strong — loss of the support of her father and brothers, the possibility of her own murder or that of her husband if he tries to farm the land in her father's village — that the right is rarely activated. Kusum Nair (1961, p.108) was told by an informant that the enforcement of the new law in the Punjab might revive the old custom of female infanticide.

3   The story of Bindo illustrates the sort of treatment a woman can expect if she acts in breach of the social rules. But in fact women are murdered or driven to suicide by factors over which they have no control; for example, the amount of their dowry. Recent cases of the murder of young brides have been given a great deal of publicity through political activity of women's groups in India. There were several articles in the British press in June/July 1979 describing the extent of the problem of the murder of young Indian women in the early years of marriage. It is recognised that the estimate of the number of cases — 'At least once a day a young bride in New Delhi is burned to death by her in-laws or forced to swallow poison because her dowry is judged insufficient' — represents only the tip of the iceberg, because 'complaints are almost never made in dowry cases, officials say, because the custom is so firmly entrenched in Indian culture' (both quotes are from the *Guardian*, 11 July 1979). Moreover, of the 200 cases which were reported to the police in 1975, murder was only proved in nine cases, an indication of the lack of official sympathy. In the case of a 24-year-old Delhi arts graduate, married for 18 months with a four-month-old baby, who was burnt to death, her father accused the police of trying to suppress earlier complaints that his daughter was regularly and severely beaten by her in-laws because her trousseau had not included a motor scooter (Sunanda Datta-Ray, in the *Observer*, 15 July 1979).

4   Pettigrew (1975) describes very vividly how for Sikh Jat men death in feuding represents excitement and drama and proof of their daring and bravery. Women are, in a sense, pawns in factional politics, because men insult each other by casting aspersions on the virtue of their rivals' women. Therefore this acts as a rationale for restricting the movements of women.

5   There are very few enthnographies known to us on Sikh Jat Punjabi societies. The main one is Pettigrew (1975), but Sharma (1978) makes similar points about a Hindu north Indian village, as does Mandelbaum more generally about India as a whole, in Mandelbaum (1972, vol.1).

6   See E.N. Goody's essay on witchcraft in Gonja (Goody, 1970).

7   Young and Harris (1976) extend this to make a stronger claim, that in the 'simpler' societies, physical violence is *the* dominant means of subordination of women by men.

8   Recent studies which focus on separate but complementary female and male spheres in particular societies include MacCormack (1972; 1974; 1975), Weiner (1976).

9   In fact women's gossip can also operate outside the female terrain, for instance in alerting men to another man's wife beating or a wife's

misbehaviour. Margery Wolf makes this point for another patrilineal society, that of rural Taiwan (1974, p.40), observing that even though young women may have little or no influence over their husbands and would not dare to express an unsolicited opinion to their fathers-in-law, women can make men whom they consider to be behaving wrongly 'lose face' by gossiping about them to each other, or to their husbands and sons. No man wants to lose face, and therefore men are not free to ignore the opinions of the women.

10 This point is developed by Young and Harris (1976), and is particularly relevant for Punjabi society. They say:

> In societies where women depend on their children — especially their sons — for their maintenance in the future (i.e. where they possess no rights to land, livestock or other means of production) women may be pitted against each other for command over sufficient resources for the maintenance of their children.

11 Even so, suicide statistics from the *Towards Equality* Report of the Committee on the Status of Women in India, December 1974, are revealing of the strain in women's lives. According to vital statistics on suicide prepared by the Registrar General's Census, twice as many women commit suicide as men. Suicide was reported to be highest for people in the 15—34 age group, and most suicides take place in rural areas where 80 per cent of the population lives:

> It may be assumed that in this age group suicides committed by females were mainly due to quarrels with parents-in-law and quarrels with married partners. The joint family system still prevails in India, therefore suicides by females may be taken to reflect the extent of oppression of the daughter-in-law in the joint family at the hands of the in-laws.

And this isn't the whole story, for many deaths are not even reported as suicide, and many of the suicides reported as such were murder (see note 3). For a discussion of the meaning of these statistics within the village of Pind, see Morpeth (in press).

12 Pettigrew (1975, p.52) supports this point, and goes on to demonstrate how a power struggle develops within the family, between the daughter-in-law and her sons posed against her husband and his mother.

13 The dislike of the mother-in-law and the sympathy but powerlessness of the mother are expressed in many folk songs of the Punjab:

> The mother-in-law told me to knead fine flour in ghee;*
> The flour I put in ghee was scant and she abused me.
> Abuse me not O mother-in-law,
> Who is there to console me?
> Beneath the mansion my mother stands,
> And there are tears in her eyes.

* 'ghee' is clarified butter

> Weep not, mother mine; daughters have always
> brought grief to their parents.
>
> from Singh Bedi, 1971

14 Paul Hershman (1977), writing about ritual and symbolism in a Hindu Punjabi village, mentions in a footnote that the 'curail' (the ghost of a woman who dies in childbirth) is distinctly anti-male in character.

15 Pettigrew (1975, p.51) describes how for men one of the components of family honour is being able to look after your family and especially its women. She goes on to explain the consequences of failure:

> Links with other families are established through women and if the honour of a family's women is lost, so also is the family's entire public position. Her children are also affected because no one would want to marry the children of a woman who was dishonourable because they would 'come from bad blood'.

16 The concepts of honour and shame are common in Mediterranean and Middle Eastern societies as well, and have similar consequences for women. See for example Campbell (1964), Makan (1954), Peristiany (1966), Pitt-Rivers (1968; 1977). Pitt-Rivers (1977, p.161) observes that 'by making men's honour vulnerable through the sexual behaviour of their women Mediterranean culture gives to sex a kind of political significance it lacks in primitive societies.' This observation would certainly hold true for the Punjab too.

17 Hershman points out (1977) that a woman as a wife has almost no status at all and if she fails to produce children, and most critically, sons, a *de facto* divorce may take place, with the woman returning to live in her father's household and never again being recalled to that of her husband.

18 Pettigrew (1975) notes that when a woman is married into a family she is regarded as a possession of the family. There is a proverb 'If one Jat boy in a family is married, all are.' In the area where she worked there were numerous instances of a woman being married to one brother (usually the eldest) but being sexually shared by those brothers younger than him, in some cases four or five. Sometimes a man would hand his wife over to a younger brother while he was on active service in the army. This sharing of wives among brothers is distinct from 'sexual hospitality' where the women of a household are offered to male visitors. This practice − said to have been traditional among the Eskimos (Spencer, 1968) and claimed by Pitt-Rivers (1977, p.159) to be found amongst 'many nomadic peoples, who use their women as a means of establishing relations with the sedentary population', would be abhorrent to Punjabi men.

19 Sharma (1978, p.266) makes the point that in the north Indian village where she worked, women, although dependent and subordinate (in terms of the framework Sharma used to analyse their position), did not experience themselves as powerless or feeble or lacking in self-confidence.

20 For example, see Davis (1973), Reed (1975), Firestone (1971), Mitchell (1974), Oakley (1972), and The Matriarchy Study Group (1977; n.d.).

21 This cross-cultural example is not being presented in order to titillate readers with the awfulness of Punjabi women's lives. We share the reservations expressed in a recent issue of *Spare Rib* (March 1979), in connection with their publication of a story dramatising the painful conficts of a Muslim Pakistani woman brought up in England — that stressing the oppression of women in non-Western societies can be seen as yet another instance of racism and imperialism by those who are 'different' from us. But our point is that they are not all that different, and that it's important to analyse the similarities and the differences in order to come to an understanding of women's oppression which will fuel revolutionary change for all women, everywhere.

22 See recent articles in the press on the Saudi Arabian princess (1978) and similar incidents in Iran. See also Chagnon (1977), van Baal (1966), Berndt (1962).

23 See Jordanova chapter 6, and the literature on spirit possession in anthropology — for example, Lewis (1966; 1970; 1971), Curley (1973), Lewis and Wilson (1967), Wilson (1967), Werbner and Lewis (1968).

24 For arguments about the use of illegitimate aggression by women — such as witchcraft or suicide — see Goody (1970), Harper (1969), and the references cited in note 23.

Further reading

For good ethnographic reports of women's lives in other non-Western societies, see:

E. Boserup, *Women's Role in Economic Development*. New York: St Martins, 1970.

J.C. Goodale, *Tiwi Wives: A Study of the Women of Melville Island, North Australia*. Seattle and London: University of Washington Press, 1971.

P.M. Kaberry, *Aboriginal Women: Sacred and Profane*. Philadelphia: Blakiston, 1939.

P.M. Kaberry, *Women of the Grassfields*. London: HMSO, 1952.

V. Maher, *Women and Property in Morocco*. Cambridge: Cambridge University Press, 1974.

D. Paulme (ed.), *Women of Tropical Africa*. Berkeley: University of California Press, 1971.

A.I. Richards, *Chisungu: A Girl's Initiation Ceremony among the Bemba of Northern Rhodesia*. London: Faber & Faber, 1956.

M. Strathern, *Women in Between: Female Roles in a Male World, Mount Hagen, New Guinea*. New York: Seminar Press, 1972.

A. Weiner, *Women of Value, Men of Renown*. Austin, Texas: University of Texas Press, 1976.

M. Wolf, *Women and the Family in Rural Taiwan*. Stanford: Stanford University Press, 1974.

There are also several useful collections of anthropological articles on women cross-culturally in:

S. Ardener (ed.) *Perceiving Women*. London: Dent, 1975.

S. Ardener (ed.), *Defining Females*. London: Croom Helm, 1978.

P. Caplan and J. Burja (eds), *Women United, Women Divided*. London: Tavistock, 1978.

S. Lipschitz (ed.), *Tearing the Veil: Essays in Femininity*. London: Routledge & Kegan Paul, 1978.

C.J. Matthiasson (ed.), *Many Sisters: Women in Cross-cultural Perspective*. New York: Free Press, 1974.

D. Raphael (ed.), *Being Female: Reproduction, Power, and Change*. The Hague: Mouton, 1975.

R.R. Reiter (ed.), *Toward an Anthropology of Women*. New York: Monthly Review Press, 1975.

R. Rohrlich-Leavitt (ed.), *Women Cross-culturally: Change and Challenge*. The Hague: Mouton, 1975.

M. Rosaldo and L. Lamphere (eds), *Woman, Culture and Society*. Stanford: Stanford University Press, 1974.

Section III

Politics, Sexuality, Choice

Chapter Nine

Sexuality and Homosexuality[1]

JANE CAPLAN

'A detestable and abominable sin, amongst Christians not to be named, committed by carnal knowledge against the ordinance of the creator, and order of nature, by mankind with mankind, or with brute beast or by womankind with brute beast.' This definition of sodomy from Chief Justice Coke's *Institutes of the Laws of England* (1629) has formed the basis of English law on homosexuality for over 300 years. It is notable not only for its obvious omission of any reference to carnal knowledge by womankind with womankind, but also for its refusal to give the sin a name. One effect of this silence was the cultivation of an official and popular ignorance as to the precise nature of various possible sexual acts: all were subsumed under a generic title of sodomy, with its comprehensive biblical evocation of nameless vice. The process of establishing identities and conferring names — opening the subject up to speech, but also perhaps to practice? — has been a long one, not only in this country. It is often presented as a simple movement from repression to toleration, from prejudice to rational acceptance (e.g. Hyde, 1972, p.304) but the theme of this chapter is to question whether it really is a straightforward matter of progression in this way. Can it be argued that homosexuality is a fixed quality, the passive object of the liberalising processes of a society growing in maturity and rationality? Or is there a more subtle inter-relation between the object and its observers: not, in other words, the crude scientific paradigm of a real world awaiting discovery, but a world empty of such fixed boundaries, a world at least partially created *in* the very act of classification? In order to explore this possibility, this chapter will not present a history of homosexuality, but will instead try to illustrate how homosexuality was produced as a concept, and then examine some of the consequences of that production.

To begin with, I want to indicate the main outward sign of this movement to name or produce the concept of homosexuality in Western society: the secularising and medicalising practices which, from the late eighteenth century, began to isolate sexual identities and behaviours for classification and study[2]. This activity cannot be dissociated from the manifold social changes that marked the transition in Western Europe from an ex-feudal to a bourgeois economy and society − a series of changes in productive and social relations, and in ideologies. Along with other sexual practices, homosexuality was inscribed in a series of definitions as part of this comprehensive transition, and in a fuller account it would need to be examined alongside the precipitation of definitions such as child, family, sanity, illness and many other terms that may superficially seem to have 'natural' origins rather than historical ones.[3] In fact, the production of sexual definitions, and thereby of permitted and forbidden behaviour, seems closely linked to and the production of the category of childhood, as a prolonged state of pre-maturity (Ariès, 1963). It has been suggested that in the nineteenth century, onanism (masturbation) replaced sodomy as the generic synonym for sexual, especially homosexual misbehaviour (Bullough and Voght, 1973). This must have allowed a transition from an adult-centred model of sexual transgression to a child-centred one, for masturbation is *par excellence* the sexual activity available to children of their own volition. The exercise of independent will would hardly be consistent with the concept of the child as essentially immature and dependent: wilful sexual indulgence could readily be seen both as a form of resistance to the discipline proper to the state of childhood, and, increasingly, as a dangerous (because pseudo-adult) disturbance of the delicate process by which the immature child develops into a mature adult.

Whether the crystallisation of a concept of childhood actually was the main factor behind the growing concentration on masturbation as the model of sexual impropriety can't be adequately discussed here,[4] but the emphasis in medical literature (and its popular vulgarisations) is clear enough masturbation was seen as 'the narrow gate through which nameless dangers could pour', as Jeffrey Weeks puts it in a rather masculine metaphor (Weeks, 1977b, p.25). The discussion of Krafft-Ebing below will present a clinical version of precisely this model of sexual precocity leading to adult abnormality. Masturbation, then, could be used as a synonym for homosexual practices, and could be regarded as the factor that, in a developmental sequence, precipitated a later homosexuality. Its identification also coincided with the construction of precise and elaborate classifications of sexual malpractice, conducted by medicine and by law. Once again, this relationship is a complex one. The modern codification and secularisation of law in Europe has followed different patterns in different countries, according to the variations in structural and chronological relationships between the establishment of a central State power, the diverse influence of Roman and common law, and the relative power and status of Catholic and protestant churches. In France, for example, the Napoleonic code of 1810 took a rationalist-utilitarian view of the social harmfulness of an act as the criterion for its status in law. Thus, adults were regarded as morally free beings, and were legally left to make their own individual choices whether or not these contravened some other (moral, ethical or religious) code, as long as this didn't involve assault on a non-consenting party. But children were 'protected' here: as minors, they could not be consenting partners, and thus any sexual act with a child was by definition an assault. In England, by contrast, the physically severe penalties of canon law were taken over into secular statute during the reformation, in 1533. Buggery (sodomy or bestiality) remained punishable by execution until 1861 (the death penalty was last imposed in the 1830s), when life imprisonment was substituted. This apparently more 'tolerant' attitude did not, however, represent any lesser condemnation of the crime itself, but only the changing concept of punishment.[5] In fact, the next step was to enlarge the range of offences covered by statute: as is well known, the 'Labouchere amendment' to a statute of 1885 brought into the scope of the law a new and undefined category of male homosexual offences called 'gross indecency' (though it also reduced the sentence for buggery). Masturbation, at any rate as an intersubjective act thus found its way into the penal code. The effect of the 1967 Sexual Offences Act was merely to exclude 'consenting adult males in private' from the operation of the law, not to abolish the offences as such.

The exact course of these and other legal histories would have to be specified in each case if their meanings are to be understood. But although the outlines for the main European countries can be found without much difficulty, there hasn't as far as I know been much work on tracing the reasons for these varying national patterns.[6] Most of the existing historical work on homosexuality has focused on the development of medical practice on the sexual 'perversions' or aberrations including homosexuality, and even here the absence of comprehensive national historical accounts no doubt disguises variations from country to country — not least where female homosexuality is concerned, for although penal provisions varied, the actual inexistence or ignoring of it seems to have been pretty universal.

The beginnings of a taxonomical analysis of sexual 'perversions' can be roughly dated from the publication in 1844 of Kaan's *Psychopathia Sexualis*; and subsequent work — like that of Casper in Germany and Tardieu in France — seems to have been mainly intended to pin the subject down in a judicial context (Ellenberger 1970 ch.5; Weeks 1977b, Part I). Whether this was a co-operative project between law and medicine, or a competition for categorical priority, a central theme of debate was whether homosexuality was an acquired vice, or an innate congenital condition. This dualism was evidently open to further exploration along biological and psychological lines, or along both together, and was subject to endless ramifications as these two sciences themselves developed. As a dualism it also bears a more complex connotation, which has tended to become more prominent in recent work: the distinction between 'practising a homosexual act', and 'being a homosexual', or in social terms between a behaviour and an identity. Clearly, these distinctions (and, equally, their recombinations) are only possible if the spheres of biology, psychology, medicine, social organisation and so forth are themselves independently specified — which was of course beginning to be the case in this mid-nineteenth century era of burgeoning 'scientific' study. These distinctions/combinations have persisted in changing guises into the present, with the sphere of *social* causation and expression becoming increasingly the significant or 'privileged' one. (And of course there is not much to choose between any of the spheres, if they are paradigmatically equivalent in aiming to produce causal aetiologies of irreversible conditions.)

In their original nineteenth-century appearance, though, the specific context was found in the contemporary debate on the relations between, biology, inheritance and evolution (Burrow, 1966), and the issue of sexual 'perversion' had a clear relevance to familia issues of moral and legal responsibility, now being re-cast in terms of possibilities of disclosure, prevention and cure. For if homosexuality was acquired as a vice, there was no reason not to hold its practitioners responsible for their acts at law, especially because if not restrained they might go on to transmit the vice to others. But if it was innate, then the question of guilt was a good deal more complex (though not thereby banished — perhaps it could be displaced onto simple or complex parental failures?). And in either case, there was a strong indication that attention might usefully be paid to prevention as well as to punishment; while in the second case, cure became a possible concept too.

Rather than trying to compress the history of sexual study into a catalogue of names, dates and concepts, as if the story has a logical progression up to the better truths of today, I'm going to concentrate on two of the principal pre-Freudian writers on sexual practices; the German R. von Krafft-Ebing (1840—1902), and the English writer Havelock Ellis (1859—1939). The former is regarded as the founder of modern sexual pathology, and the latter was the most influential English writer on sexual behaviour, whose books were still being reprinted in popular editions in the 1950s (Weeks, 1977a; Brome, 1979). In summarising some of their principal ideas, I want to try to show how they were produced in the field of concepts outlined above, and how in turn they pointed in the direction of particular other concepts or practices, producing these as possible 'truths' about homosexuality.

As I've already implied, the dualism noted above is not necessarily a mutually exclusive one, and in fact Krafft-Ebing was the first to systematise the concept of two types or manifestations of homosexuality in his comprehensive *Psychopathia Sexualis* published in 1885.[7] He adopted the term 'antipathetic sexuality' for the acquired form of homosexuality, and 'inversion' for the innate form, which he regarded as an abnormal congenital condition. Krafft-Ebing was relying on a strictly organic model of sexual development: he believed that the normal course of events was for the development of 'sexual feeling' to take place step by step with the development of physical sexual maturity. Normal development, physical and mental, is regarded as depending upon inborn capacities or potentials, which need the correct environment if they are to thrive, and which may be upset or diverted if they are exposed to the wrong conditions. If conditions are correct, the body will mature physically through puberty, and the sexual capacities and sexual feelings will also develop normally. But abnormal conditions must produce an abnormal result (or, as we might say more critically of the method: an abnormal result must point to there having been abnormal conditions en route to it). The most potent and disturbing of abnormal conditions was childhood masturbation, through which the physical sensations appropriate to maturity were aroused in the emotionally immature juvenile (an act made possible by the (unfortunate) fact that the immature child is already equipped with physical sexual organs). Krafft-Ebing's hypothesis here was that, in the absence of what he called a fully mature 'cortex' of sexual emotions, the pre-pubertal child's actions were 'stripped of sexual meaning', and thus failed to find their true developmental path: 'the glow of sensual sensibility wanes, and the inclination towards the opposite sex is weakened'. So, 'antipathetic sexuality' was acquired through the disturbance of a normally linked process of physical and emotional maturation, and Krafft-Ebing divided its manifestation into four increasingly marked forms or stages: first, the perversion of the sexual instinct; second, the adaptative transformation of personality; third, the transition towards paranoid sexual metamorphosis; finally, full metamorphosis or delusion of sex change.

Krafft-Ebing's model of the other form of homosexuality, congenital inversion, stressed the characteristics of physical inheritance. In a famous phrase he defined it as 'a functional sign of degeneration and a partial manifestation of a neuro/psycho-pathic state, in most cases hereditary'. Just as a physical intervention, masturbation, was the precipitant of the antipathetic sexuality, so here a physical process, degeneration, is the pivotal concept, keying into the social nightmare that was the underside of contemporary evolutionary theory: the fear of the relationship between unfavourable environments and physical (eventually racial) decline. Here the reference is to a vast and complex world of nineteenth-century social and mental fears, inhabited by Malthusian scenarios of the degraded 'masses' and numerical class imbalances, crude social darwinisms, biologised versions of class antagonisms and the like. They can't be more than alluded to here,[8] but they were connected to the specific sexual theme by threads which also wove together the current conceptions of relations between the social, biological and mental spheres. Krafft-Ebing seems to draw on the evolutionary model in his proposition that, because (in his view) mono-sexuality in animals had developed from an earlier and lower stage of bisexuality, the organic dysfunction which produced homosexuality must therefore be a kind of primitive reversion to a lower state. His case-studies of inverts — an important part of his book — attempt to demonstrate his argument that 'in all cases of sexual inversion a taint of a hereditary character may be established' — these taints belonging to the vague category of hysterias and neurasthenias that populated nineteenth-century textbooks on mental illness. As with antipathetic sexuality, so with inversion four degrees of corresponding intensity are proposed: first, psychical hermaphroditism (bisexuality); second, homosexuality; third, 'viraginity' in women, 'effeminatio' in men (terms expressing the exchange of masculine and feminine characteristics); finally, further along the same path, 'gynandry' in women and 'androgyny' in men. Describing what these identities looked like, Krafft-Ebing suggested for example that viraginous women lacked modesty towards men, wore masculine dress, smoked and drank, neglected their toilet, even that 'perfumes and sweetmeats are disclaimed' by them; in the gynandrous stage, 'the woman . . . possesses of the feminine qualities only the genital organs'. Though most of Krafft-Ebing's labels have now fallen into disuse, it was his model which remained the basis for clinical work on homosexuality until Freud provided a potential systematic alternative, and it still echoes in the post-Freudian literature.

Although Havelock Ellis criticised Krafft-Ebing for his proliferating apparatus of categories and labels, and the disorderly presentation of his material, he too proposed a dual model of congenital inversion, and homosexual love (Ellis, 1897). However, the standpoints from which the two men wrote were very different: Krafft-Ebing was a forensic pathologist, whose 'cases' came to him from the courts, whereas Ellis's interest in sexual behaviour and morals was more personal and ethical in origin. He worked in a social milieu of socialism and feminism, he was a friend of Edward Carpenter and J.A. Symonds (both active in contemporary campaigns for sexual emancipation), and through his wife Edith Lees he met other women engaged in these campaigns. The whole tone of his book is more enquiring, suggestive and humane than Krafft-Ebing's clinical accounts, and seems more acutely poised between the rigid and moralising scientism of earlier work, and the intellectual adventurousness of Freud. Intentionally or not, Ellis's book contains hints of the significance of cultural practices and mores, in relation to the 'incidence' as well as status of homosexuality: it begins to suggest that definitions of homosexual behaviour rest upon real cultural relativisms, and are not fixed danger-signals on some evolutionary track of racial and social movement, in which the corollary of the promise of progress is the threat of decline. At the same time, as the following summary will try to show, Ellis couldn't pursue his perceptions beyond certain limits imposed by his basically organo-evolutionary understanding of sexuality. I'm going to concentrate here on his remarks on women, about whom he managed to assemble more information than did Krafft-Ebing.

Ellis begins his 1897 study with some remarks on the frequency of homosexuality among women in all-female environments like schools and prisons, and suggests some psychological and social explanations for this fact. As far as young girls are concerned, for example, it's argued that they need affection and devotion to another, that social convention allows them few emotional outlets with boys, that physical intimacy is socially more tolerated among women than among men, and that girls are more ignorant than boys about sex and are thus less self-conscious about behaviour that might embarass or humiliate the more informed. But even though these various facts raise fundamental questions about the social status of female sexuality, Ellis doesn't ask *why* they should be true for girls but not for boys. In any case, he dismisses these childhood manifestations as incipient or incomplete, and devotes his main attention to the real problem, which is inversion in the adult. Here he identifies two groups of women: one 'not strongly marked' homosexually, or what he calls 'the pick of the women whom the average man would pass by' and who have thus just missed being taken in marriage. These women are said to be attractive to the other group, the true inverts, who have a distinctive trace of masculinity in them and an active dislike of men: in these women, congenital neurosis is highly developed.

Towards the end of his chapter on women, Ellis presents another speculation based on empirical observation which, like his remarks on homosexual behaviour among girls, might seem to weaken his organic model. He concedes that female homosexuality is on the increase in his day, and agrees that it is at least partly the result of the movement towards women's emancipation. Although he approves this development, he notes that it also carries a number of unfortunate side-effects, for instance the increase in insanity and criminality among women (a direct parallel with the veiled critique of women's liberation in our own day). In the field of sexual relations, emancipatory trends meet considerable obstructions, he argues, for male-female intimacy is still discouraged, and men still have greater freedom in marriage than women. The explanation Ellis offers of these facts remains, however, tied to his basically constitutional model, which he does not want to forfeit: 'I do not say that these unquestionable influences of modern movements can directly cause sexual inversion, though they may indirectly, in so far as they promote hereditary neurosis; but they develop germs of it, and they probably cause a spurious imitation.' In other words, there is a core of 'real' i.e. organic inverts, surrounded by a periphery composed both of the constitutionally susceptible, and of those vulnerable to suggestion and imitation. The real-peripheral dualism is another that has continued to flourish in the 'scientific' literature.

Ellis's conclusion is in fact the logical outcome of his commitment to an organically evolutionist theory of sexual development as the gradual unfolding of a constitutional given. Thus he writes that 'The rational way of regarding the normal sexual impulse is as an inborn organic impulse, developing about the time of puberty' — an echo of Krafft-Ebing. In relation to abnormal sexuality, Ellis pointed out that

'The same seed of suggestion is sown in various soils; in the many it dies out, in the few it flourishes. The cause can only be a difference in the soil.' In other words, although many people have homosexuality suggested to them, only a few 'become homosexuals': thus, the significant difference must be some constitutional variation. Ellis clinches his argument:

> If a man becomes attracted to his own sex simply because the fact or image of such attraction is brought before him, then we are bound to believe that a man becomes attracted to the opposite sex only because the fact or image of such attraction is brought before him. This theory is entirely unworkable (p.130).

Ellis, then, is drawn by his own speculations further away from organic evolutionism than was Krafft-Ebing, yet cannot quite detach his arguments from it and let them move towards the dynamic conception of sexuality they pointed to. The quotation above makes his sticking-point clear, while his remarks on the ''spurious imitation' of 'true' inversion emphasise again the fact that for Ellis the 'real' remains the organic.

Despite their differences in other respects, Krafft-Ebing and Ellis resemble each other in proposing sexual theories which try to lock the organic and the evolutionary together, with the aim of demonstrating how both are inextricably tied to an already given and correct sexual object — and adult of the opposite sex. A critical break with this paradigm was made by Freud, whose working life overlapped with Ellis's. In this short essay it will be impossible to give an adequate account of Freud, and so some very compressed remarks will have to do.[9] Freud undoubtedly occupies a unique place in the history of the conceptualisation of sexuality, but it is also true that his work has frequently been misunderstood and misused; there are debased 'neo-Freudian' schools of thought whose flattened readings of Freud and reductive use of psychoanalysis misrepresent not only the problematic aspects of his work, but also its positive importance. It is at least partly for this reason that Freud has been such a controversial figure for feminists: for some he is the incarnation of patriarchal power masquerading as science, yet for others the pioneer of a genuine opportunity for deciphering the construction and meaning of sexual difference. I can't hope to adjudicate between these views here, because there is great difficulty in doing justice to Freud, especially in a short account (assuming that 'justice' means equal consideration of both criticism and approbation). For one thing, although the theory of psychoanalysis itself was a radical innovation, Freud's work and writings were strongly influenced by the contemporary state of research and debate; a properly comprehensive account would need to go into this context with great precision, and this can't be done here. Then, second, his theories were constructed along complex, overlapping and sometimes contradictory lines; his later work often explicitly revised his earlier ideas, or, worse, stood in implicit but not acknowledged contradiction to them. An intelligible account of Freudian theories ought to avoid both an excessive systematisation, and a smoothing-out of its unsolved difficulties. These caveats must be borne in mind in reading the brief account that follows, otherwise all it will do is to add to the confusion.

What I want to emphasise here is that Freud did actually open up the impasse in which Ellis was caught, by declaring that 'from the point of view of psychoanalysis *the exclusive sexual interest felt by men for women is also a problem that needs elucidating and is not a self-evident fact*' (Freud, 1977, p.57; my emphasis). Here Freud manages to problematise precisely what Ellis had refused. How was he able to make this conceptual leap? The crucial phrase in his assertion is 'from the point of view of psychoanalysis', for it is on the claims of this to be a distinct form of knowledge, a science of the unconscious, that Freud's credibility and innovatory significance finally depend. Like his predecessors and contemporaries, Freud's approach to the study of sexuality was via its 'aberrant' rather than its 'normal' manifestations; but although the project looked similar in form, the difference was that Freud's *means* of study effectively reversed the relation between normality and abnormality. For him, the perverse is not the distortion of the normal, but rather normality is the residual category left after all other possibilities have been blocked or discarded. Freud's case-studies forced him to break with the contemporary reluctance to accept the existence of a childhood sexuality (as anything other than itself abnormal). He postulated the child as 'polymorphously perverse', possessing a libido which was boundless, objectless, and aimless, and which required the specific intervention of certain moments — crucially, the Oedipus — to circumscribe it with limits, to give it an object and an aim — in short, to produce the 'adult' and the 'normal.' His *Three Essays on the Theory of Sexuality* (first published in 1905, but revised and amended four times between 1910 and 1924) record his discovery of infantile sexuality and contain his main arguments about the extraordinarily complex processes by which it may become fixed to a heterosexual object and a genital aim. In a useful summary, Juliet Mitchell has outlined these arguments:

Instead of accepting the notion of sexuality as a complete, so-to-speak

ready-made thing in itself which could then diverge, [Freud] found that
'normal' sexuality itself assumed its form only as it travelled over a long and
tortuous path, maybe eventually, and even then only precariously,
establishing itself . . . In other words, Freud put the stress entirely the other
way round: instead of the pool which released itself in different ways
[Mitchell's metaphor for Ellis's concept of sexual development], Freud
asked from what sources the pool was formed. He realised that instead of a
pool from which tributaries ran, the tributaries were needed in the first
place to form the pool; these tributaries were diverse, could join each other,
never reach their goal, find another goal, dry up, overflow and so get
attached to something quite different . . . In childhood, all is diverse or
perverse; unification and 'normality' are the effort we must make on our
entry into human society. (Mitchell 1975, p.17).

Normality, then, is not to be seen as a constitutional given, as the
end-effect of a correct and uninhibited development of an organic,
biological implantation. At the level of the unconscious, of the psychological construction of sexual identity, there are no 'givens', but
only particular forms of difference.

The novelty of this conceptualisation seems to me to reside in the
fact that it opens up 'spaces' between the spheres of biology, society,
and the unconscious. In contrast with the rigid correspondences of
earlier models, these spaces may in principle be occupied by otherwise
impossible questions about how sexual objects and aims are
constructed in theory and in practice. It was from this perspective that
Freud approached his study of the formation of sexuality, refusing to
allow reproductive biology the explanatory priority. Yet although he
thus released the interrogation of the construction of sexual difference
from an immediate biological correlation, he was also raising deeply
problematic questions which are not 'solved' in his writings — not
least the fundamental question of the relations between these three
spheres. Although Freud insisted that they formed different objects of
study, and that none was reducible to either of the others, they remain
in an uneasy tension in his work (as indeed they do in individual
subjects). Four problems in particular arise, at least as far as the
relationship between female sexuality and homosexuality is concerned. First, there is Freud's admitted inability to understand
women's sexuality, despite (or because of?) the fact that the subjects
from whom he first built up his theories of the unconscious were almost
exclusively female; second, a persistent organicism which erupts into
his expositions and explanations at unexpected moments; third, an
undertow of developmentalism which carries in its wake the teleo-
logical risks (of reading cause from result) that Freud was in principle
anxious to avoid; and finally, the problematic proposition of a unified

'entry into culture'. It won't be possible to do more than comment very briefly on each of these.

Freud's perplexity about women was excused in his earlier writings by remarks which can be construed as highly derogatory (e.g. Freud, 1977, p.63), especially when added to the conclusions about feminine ethical sensibility that he drew from his theory of their less inexorable super-ego (Freud 1977, p.342). It is partly for this reason that he has been derided (by the feminists of his own day as well as later) as simply an anti-feminist patriarch, whose so-called science is not worth the socio-sexual prejudices from which it is written. Freud's own self-defence here is not entirely convincing (e.g. Freud, 1977, p.377). This is one of the interfaces between the psychoanalytic and social levels at which Freud does seem unable to achieve a satisfactory final account of either their distinctions or their interrelations. Equally problematic are the related issues of developmentalism and organicism or biologism (see Riley, 1978). The former, on a simple linear reading, leads of course to the equation of homosexuality (or any aberration) with immaturity: the sexually aberrant person is one who remains 'fixated' at a point on a developmental path. This problem seems particularly blatant in the case of women, because the fixation appears to have not only a time of origination and fixation, but also an organic manifestation: the homosexual woman is locked into the 'active' clitoral pre-pubertal stage of sexuality, instead of having made the transition to vaginal passivity (Freud, 1977, p.374; Freud, 1920). Freud's inability to conceptualise the clitoris is peculiar; indeed, in terms of reproductive sexuality it is a peculiar organ. But although Freud seemed to see this as a biological problem (Freud, 1977, p.374), the issue and its irresolubility in his theory seem to me more essentially psychosexual. He cannot fully problematise the 'active' clitoris within his theory, unlike the 'passive' vagina, and unlike the penis which can be allowed 'its extraordinarily high narcissistic cathexis' because of its 'organic significance for the propagation of the species' (Freud, 1977, p.341). Finally, I have raised the question of proposing the entry into society as a moment of renunciation and unification. Recent research into non-Western societies has tried to question whether there is a single model of this kind (Thom, 1979); and one can also ask whether 'entry' has to be seen as a single moment in a process, or whether it might be represented as potentially a continuum of renegotiations and repositionings. I offer this merely as a speculation; some of the further meanings that have been attached to the concept of entry are discussed in Elena Lieven's chapter 15.

Setting Freud among the other participants in this society's history of sexual categorisation, there is not just a case to be made 'for' or 'against' the scientific plausibility of his theories. Rather, or in addition, we need to set his confusions, contradictions and awkwardnesses against his contribution to the dissociation of sexuality from a *simple* reproductive biology. Although there is no sense in which Freud marks a final stage in the development of concepts of sexuality, I want to move on here from the question of how homosexuality was produced as a separate category alongside the production of others, and take up the current attempts being made by those who find themselves the inhabitants of the category to seize hold of their 'own' existence and history.

The question of how anyone gets into that category, as an individual biography, is not under discussion here,[10] but the construction of an available social role is. An important academic stimulus to this was the development in the 1960s of the so-called 'deviancy' school of sociological and criminological theory. Broadly speaking, deviancy theory postulates that social stability is partly maintained by a system of 'social control', one of whose tasks is to demarcate permitted from impermissible behaviour. Models of normal and of deviant behaviour or persons are constructed and socially generalised, with the deviant side functioning partly as a negative image and thereby encouraging the maintenance of the norm. The boundaries between the two are supposed to be hard to cross, and although this has the aim of fixing people within the approved roles, it also has the unwished-for effect of actually creating and cementing deviant roles. In an article published in 1968, Mary McIntosh applied a framework of this kind to male homosexuality (McIntosh, 1968). She argued in particular that homosexuality ought to be seen not as a condition, in the medico-psychological tradition, but as a role. She then demonstrated the historical emergence of a male homosexual role in Britain from about the eighteenth century, and argued that its defining characteristic was its exclusivity, i.e. the homosexual role was inhabited by those whose sexual behaviour was exclusively homosexual. This role, she asserted, is found in few other societies or cultures outside of (roughly) Western Europe; thus the questions for investigation are why and how it developed here, what exactly its content is (matters like characteristic dress, speech, social grouping etc.), and how this changes over time. All this was applied to men only: the question for women would be why a corresponding female homosexual role didn't develop at the same pace — or, whether 'corresponding' would be the correct word anyway.

With this, we get back to the point made at the beginning of this chapter, when it was noted that Coke's definition of the vice 'not to be named among Christians' was framed in such a way as to exclude women from the operations of the criminal law. Even in those other European states where female homosexuality was defined as a crime, the incidence of prosecution was apparently minimal. Thus, although the legislative gap in Britain may have been 'accidental', the general European picture would suggest that this particular form of sexual transgression was not appropriated to what the deviancy model would see as a structure of 'social control'. Thus, whereas (according to Lafitte, 1958) the charge of homosexuality against a man tended to be invoked as the ultimate gauge of disreputability, and frequently accompanied and intensified other criminal accusations, women were perhaps more likely to suffer accusations of, say, witch craft as part of such a comprehensive character-staining.

The fact of the comparative 'invisibility' of lesbianism is emphasised in most kinds of writing on the subject, from the clinical investigation to current feminist discussion. According to the writer's standpoint, different explanations may be invoked − its actual lesser incidence, the denial of sexual autonomy to women, the social determinations just referred to, etc. Most of these accounts come, of course, from writers who are broadly speaking concerned if not with the suppression of homosexuality then at least with its categorical definition, monitoring or control. It is only in recent years that voices have begun to be raised on behalf of lesbianism as a self-defined sexual or political practice; and the characteristic of these voices is that they demand not toleration or social acceptance, nor just defensive solidarity, but insist on an active, positive occupation of the concept of lesbianism by those who inhabit it. In its most intense version, this is seen as the indispensable condition for feminists fighting the battle against male domination:

> Lesbianism is not a matter of sexual preference, but rather one of political choice which every woman must make if she is to become woman-identified and thereby end male supremacy . . . Lesbians must get out of the straight women's movement and form their own movement in order to be taken seriously, to stop straight women from oppressing us, and to force straight women to deal with their own Lesbianism. Lesbians cannot develop a common politics with women who do not accept Lesbianism as a political issue. (Myron and Burch, 1975, p.18)

Other feminists would object to this formulation on the grounds that it is wholly voluntarist, in the sense of reducing all the complex inter-actions of sexual, social, political, cultural and economic relations to a supposedly simple choice between lesbianism and heterosexuality.

From arguing, with evident justification, that 'lesbianism is political' (p.9), it moves by a swift and illicit reversal of the premise to the conclusion that there can be no feminist politics which is not lesbian. From the outside, deviancy theorists might well label this stance as a particularly comprehensive attempt to construct a defiant 'lesbian role' which has expanded to take in the entire social field.

Probably the most widely-shared approach to the placing of lesbianism in a feminist politics is the one which insists on 'the right of women to determine their own sexuality'.[11] This may also open up a perceived possibility for further stages of social and cultural transformation:

> It has been a long and painful evolution to develop the present homosexual identity. From the nineteenth-century struggle to articulate a self-consciousness in a hostile environment to the present large-scale movement has been a significant change. Homosexuals can begin to see the further possibilities of transforming the social environment itself. This could be the most significant change of all (Weeks, 1977b, p.237).

This quotation comes from Jeffrey Weeks' history of homosexual politics, in which he explicitly refuses to chart the history of homosexuality as any kind of movement (around a static definition) from repression to toleration: his subject is not 'society's' attitude to or treatment of homosexuals, but is the process of the emergence and capture of a social definition. This process is seen as one whereby identities initially defined and ascribed by 'others' have now begun to be actively taken over by those who, previously, had to live them out as the passive recipients of externally-established social labels. This account suggests that the specific homosexual identity may eventually be transcended and become redundant, and that the homosexual can be a contributor as well as an heir to this promised process of social transformation. Weeks' study is mainly about the male homosexual rights movement, and it is of course questionable how far a single model of the evolution and transcendence of identities can be applied from this to women, even by analogy. Indeed, the fragmentation of the 1960s and early 1970s male gay movement into varieties of rather helpless life-styleism reminds feminists seeking the exploration of a 'lesbian identity' that liberation through self-affirmation is by no means automatic. Sexual self-consciousness and (apparent) self-articulation guarantee nothing unless we know more clearly what might be meant in theory and practice by 'sexual revolution'.[12] This seems to me to be especially true given the degree to which (in a banal Marcusian sense) social paradigms can in fact shift to accommodate and de-radicalise previously unacceptable roles and behaviours, and purge them of much of their subversive authority.

In this chapter I've tried to indicate some of the complexities of the process of paradigm-formation; I have suggested that the issue to be explained is not why society moves along a simple axis from repression to toleration, but how we are to understand the shifts in the construction of categories of human behaviour and of strategies for their enforcement. This immediately raises the further question of why particular sexual practices are regarded as impermissible, by whom they are so regarded, and how 'norms' are maintained — and the argument of this chapter is that there isn't any self-evident relation between content, agency and means. Given the virtual impossibility of making adequate definitions of concepts like 'sexuality' or 'sexual identity', the use of these terms as weapons in current political struggle may carry certain risks — especially those of precipitating an image of seamless and total oppression, and of invoking personal choice as the solution. However, this is not meant to discount the fact that the gay 'coming-out' movement, along with personal politics in general, has had an enormously important political effect over the past decade, nor that this public fact contains within it thousands of individual journeys from ignorance, fear and misery to an otherwise inconceivable achievement of confidence, communication and political solidarity. The significance of this achievement is not in question, but that does not mean that we are thereby absolved from the need to question the limits of its theoretical or practical strategies. A crucial question for gay and feminist movements is, therefore, whether more is now to be achieved by pushing the occupation of a particular identity to its furthest limits, with the object of 'taking it over' and reformulating its meanings; or, on the other hand, by trying to fray the edges of this and other social ascriptions by refusing to participate in any definition which fixes boundaries between heterosexual and homosexual — whether these boundaries are proposed by 'orthodox' medical and psychological science, or by radical lesbianism. Given the weight of ascription under which women suffer overall (as this book tries to describe), this seems to me to be an even more vital question for women than for men, for it raises the whole issue of whether a position of objective weakness (or inferiority or oppression) can be effectively overturned by the affirmation of a contradictory 'strength'.

Notes

1 Apart from fellow-members of the Collective who read and criticised my

drafts, I would like to thank Jeffrey Weeks for discussing the general framework and letting me see some of his unpublished work; and John Forrester for his help with the section on Freud: I could not have written this without his advice, but I must absolve him from any responsibility for the end-product — for the inadequacies of this I take entire blame.

2   Michel Foucault's *History of Sexuality*, (vol.i, 1979), is certainly the most ambitious and interesting recent attempt to analyse the relations between the production of concepts and the history of society in the field of sexuality. Its flaws seem to me to reside principally in its use of an undifferentiated concept of 'speech', and an imprecise notion of 'power'. See the reviews by Philip Derbyshire, 'The regime of sex', *Gay Left* no.8, Summer 1979, pp.29–30, and Denise Riley, *Spare Rib* no.83, June 1979.

3   See Ludmilla Jordanova's chapter 3. Karl Figlio's article, 'Chlorosis and chronic disease in nineteenth-century Britain: the social constitution of somatic illness in a capitalist society', *Social History*, iii, 2 (May 1978), is a helpful case-study in the historicity of disease which also discusses current interpretations of the question.

4   One may also speculate that the prohibitions on masturbation came to prominence at this time as one theme in a many-sided discourse on individual continence and self-restraint, corresponding to the development of a capitalist mode of production which was highly individualist, and which emphasised restraint on spending in favour of accumulation. Here 'spermatic economy' would be a counterpart to the capitalist's material 'abstinence' (see Karl Marx, *Capital*, vol.i, 1976, pp.298–9). The precise relations between mutual echoes of this kind in 'ideology' and 'practice' are extremely difficult to define. Any model which tried to explore this particular set of relations would obviously also have to take into account numerous other factors, especially the terms of the existing Judaeo-Christian morality, and the class relations involved.

5   For a detailed examination of this process, see Michel Foucault, *Discipline and Punish. The Birth of the Prison* (1975).

6   European legal history is covered in Vern Bullough, *Sexual Variance in Society and History*, (1976). A detailed description of European legislation to the end of the nineteenth century in Dr Numa Praetorious (pseud.), 'Die strafrechtlichen Bestimmungen gegen den gleichgeschechtlichen Verkehr historisch und kritisch dargestellt', (1899). D. J. West, *Homosexuality Re-examined*, (1977 ch.7) contains a further account which though brief is fully referenced. For Britain, see H.Montgomery Hyde, *The Other Love* (1972); F. Lafitte, 'Homosexuality and the Law. The Wolfenden Report in Historical Perspective', (1958); the current legal position is described in the handbook *The Law and Sexuality*, ed. Steve Cohen *et al.* (1978).

7   It went through many editions, in which piecemeal amendments and additions were unsystematically incorporated. I have used the 1939 English

edition, i.e. the authorised translation and adaptation of Krafft-Ebing's final (12th.) edition.

8 The most lucid discussion of these themes I have encountered is in an unpublished paper by Gay Weber, 'Women and theories of degeneration' (1978). See also Gareth Stedman Jones, *Outcast London* (1976); Elizabeth Fee, 'The Sexual Politics of Victorian Social Anthropology' (1974, pp.86–102); some discussion also in Figlio, *op.cit.*

9 This account is based primarily on the following works by Freud: the *Three Essays on the Theory of Sexuality*; *Some Psychological Consequences of the Anatomical Distinction between the Sexes*; *Female Sexuality* (all in Freud, 1977); and 'The Psychogenesis of a Case of Female Homosexuality' (1920, pp.125–49). For an introduction to Freud from a feminist point of view, see Juliet Mitchell, *Psychoanalysis and Feminism* (1975). For a critique of Freud, Shulamith Firestone, *The Dialectic of Sex* (1979). See also Simone de Beauvoir, *The Second Sex* (1972).

10 Individual self-portraits form the substance of Angela Stewart-Park and Jules Cassidy, *We're Here: Conversations with Lesbian Women*, (1977); clinical case-studies in Charlotte Wolff, *Love Between Women* (1973). West, *op.cit.*, ch. VII, surveys the main clinical theories of causation.

11 The Sixth Demand of the Women's Liberation Movement (added to the original four in 1974) asserted women's right to a 'self-defined sexuality', glossed as 'a demand for greater freedom for women to be *truly themselves*' (my emphasis) in *Women's Liberation. An Introduction*, Women's Research and Resources Centre/Women's Information, Referral and Enquiry Service/A Woman's Place, London 1977. In 1978, this demand was split: the Sixth Demand now reads 'An end to discrimination against lesbians', and a preamble was inserted to the Demands as a whole, reading 'Women's Liberation asserts the right of all women to a self-defined sexuality'.

12 One recent exploration of this, Guy Hocquenghem's *Homosexual Desire* (1978), illustrates with particular force the difficulty of arriving at a concept of sexual revolution valid for both women and men, in that his discussion of a subversive male homosexuality is centred on the anus, though he admits that 'It would be futile to keep trying to deal with the subject of female homosexuality in terms of male ideology' (p.35).

Further reading

S. de Beauvoir, *The Second Sex*. Harmondsworth: Penguin, 1972.

A. Comfort, *The Anxiety Makers*. London: Panther, 1968.

M. Foucault, *History of Sexuality*, vol. 1. London: Allen Lane, 1979.

Gay Left Collective (ed) *Homosexuality: Power and Politics*. London: Allison and Busby, 1980.

Gay Liberation Front, *GLF Manifesto*. London, 1971.

A. Hodges and D. Hutter, *With Downcast Gays*, London: Pink Triangle Press, 1974.

A. C. Kinsey *et al.*, *Sexual Behaviour in the Human Female*. Philadelphia: W. B. Saunders, 1953.

J. Lauritsen and D. Thorstad, *The Early Homosexual Rights Movement (1864–1935)*. New York: Times Change Press, 1974.

Lesbian Left, A collection of papers by women in Lesbian Left for the National Women's Liberation Conference London: 1977.

K. Plummer (ed), *The Making of the Modern Homosexual*. London: Hutchinson, 1980.

A. Walter (ed), *Come Together: the years of Gay Liberation*. London: Gay Men's Press, 1980.

J. Weeks, *Coming Out: Homosexual Politics in Britain, from the Nineteenth Century to the Present*. London: Quartet Books, 1977.

Chapter Ten

Contraception and Abortion[1]

KAREN GREENWOOD AND LUCY KING

Women can only take charge of their lives if they can control their own reproduction. This means either sexual abstinence or the separation of sexual activity from procreation. The women's movement believes that the ability to make free choices in the expression of sexuality is an essential part of the liberation we are striving for. Therefore, one of the central demands of the Women's Liberation Movement is for freely available contraception and for abortion on demand.

The authors of this chapter are both active campaigners for this demand. One of us is a member of the National Abortion Campaign, and the other belongs to a women's group that provides information on birth control. In this chapter we will first give a brief history of birth control from the nineteenth century onwards, and then discuss to what extent the situation in Britain falls short of this aim of reproductive self-determination.

There is a tendency to look back from our current 'pill era' and regard birth control as a nineteenth-century invention whose history is that of a battle wherein the progressive forces of technology conquered the dark forces of ignorance and prejudice. And also to assume that the factors which have limited the efficient use of birth control have been the existing technology and the dispersal of information. This is much too simplified a story. For a start, there is evidence from old medical texts and other writing, and from anthropological studies, that women have almost universally sought to control their own fertility (Himes, 1970; Green, 1971). Furthermore, most of our present methods (i.e. cap, sheath, intrauterine device, spermicides, abortion) have had precursors in societies far less technologically sophisticated than ours. Generally speaking, the extent and openness with which birth control is practised is as much dependent on a society's attitude to sex, and the status of women, as it is on technology. For the use of birth control requires a morality that permits the separation of sexual intercourse from procreation, and is related to the extent to which women are valued for roles other than just those of wife and mother.

In the Christian tradition from St Paul and, later, St Augustine, to Pope Paul's encyclical of 1968 ('Humanae Vitae'), sex without the purpose of conceiving a child has been judged a sin. Most protestant churches now approve of contraception, but this was not always so. At Lambeth conferences in both 1908 and 1920 the Anglican bishops condemmed birth control and only in 1930 did they give it very guarded and limited acceptance.

As well as this ecclesiastical disapproval, Hippocrates, whose oath drawn up in the fourth century BC forms the basis of medical ethics even today, specifically condemned abortion. Despite such condemnations, birth control, especially abortion, has been persistently attempted by women.

What was new in the nineteenth century was a birth control *movement* that campaigned for the use of contraception, and also, a series of laws against abortion, which had previously been condemned morally but not legally. The start of the birth control movement is commonly regarded as marked by the publication in 1823 of Francis Place's 'diabolical handbills'. These advocated both withdrawal (coitus interruptus) and the use of a vaginal sponge, moistened with water, or a spermicide such as vinegar. Francis Place was an early socialist and trade unionist, who knew from his own working-class childhood what misery unwanted pregnancies caused, and who considered it unrealistic and inhumane to preach celibacy and abstinence as adequate solutions.

Place and the other birth control campaigners were ostracised as immoral and atheistic. It was not until the 1860s that the first organisation to promote birth control was founded: the Malthusian League.[2] They saw population control as a cure for poverty, unemployment and disease. Their views conflicted sharply with those of socialists, who saw economic and political factors as fundamental, and rejected the Malthusian League's assumption that the responsibility for poverty rested on the individual rather than society (Meek, 1953).

In the 1860s, most feminists seem to have been in favour of 'voluntary motherhood', via abstinence, but not contraception (L. Gordon, 1977). For when women did not expect to find sex pleasurable, contraception was seen as liberating only men, by enabling them to get sexual gratification without the responsibility of parent-hood.

The Malthusian League with its emphasis on population control, represents one strand of the birth control movement, a strand that has persisted intertwined with other strands, such as eugenics, and concern for individual welfare, up to the present day. In the early part of this century, Margaret Sanger in America and Marie Stopes in Britain both hoped to improve the welfare of women through sexual education and birth control; but there were crudely eugenic overtones in their writings (e.g. 'more children from the fit, less from the unfit — that is the chief issue of birth control', Margaret Sanger, 1919). The early free birth control clinics tended to be in poor areas and were started at a time (1920s) when there were fears that the working class were reproducing faster than the middle classes, and that society would therefore degenerate. As recently as 1974, Sir Keith Joseph as Conservative Shadow Minister of Health, argued for an extension of family planning services on eugenic grounds.

Since 1930 the chief birth control propagandists in Britain have been the Family Planning Association (FPA). For nearly 50 years they have pledged themselves 'to help individuals to avoid unwanted pregnancies'. They have been accused by some population planners of being over-dominated by 'feminists' with their 'middle-class individ-ualistic biasses' (Stycos, 1962). It is clear, however, from reading accounts (Wright, 1972) of the somewhat anguished debates that went on within the FPA during the 1950s and 1960s about whether they should open their clinic doors to unmarried women, and later even to under-aged girls, that at least some of these 'feminist' FPA workers were very chary of extending the right to birth control beyonds the bounds of the 'responsible, respectable' family. Even now, when local authority clinics are open to all women, married or unmarried, they are still known as *family* planning clinics. Their prime aim is to help space children in families, and it is all too easy to pick up feelings of unease from clinic workers if women seem to be opting not to have *any* children (Tunnadine, 1970; and personal experience).

It has been a common view that middle-class and working-class methods of birth control are different. In the nineteenth century con-traception was seen as mainly a middle-class method of birth control, whilst the working class were supposedly relying more on abortion. However, middle-class women certainly did resort to abortion — there were many adverts in newspapers for abortifacients at prices probably beyond the reach of most working-class women (e.g. Madame Frain's female pills 'on no account to be taken by persons desirous of becoming mothers')[3].

There are many possible explanations as to why contraception may have been used less by the working class:

(1) The publicised methods of contraception were not suitable for everyone: too expensive, or complicated and often requiring space, privacy and a suitable water supply.

(2) Most methods were either under male control or required male co-operation, whereas abortion could be under the woman's control.

(3) For many working-class families economic conditions were not stable and the desired family size differed with varying economic conditions. This militated against using methods of birth control which required planning ahead i.e. contraception.

(4) It has been thought that information about birth control had to percolate downwards from the middle class; the implication was that with time and education the working class' use of contraception would increase.

Certainly there was a sharper and earlier decline in the size of middle-class families during the nineteenth century[4] but there is evidence that working-class women could and did practise birth control when this was economically advantageous, for example when industrial employment for women was available.[5]

Despite the claims for differences between middle-class and working-class birth control methods there was much less of a distinction made between abortion and contraception in the early nineteenth century than there is now. This can be explained with reference to the concept of quickening which was retained by working-class women longer than by the middle classes or the law (see pp.176–77).

One major factor in the separation of abortion from contraception has been the nineteenth-century laws *against* abortion. It is only in this century that there has existed a movement in *favour* of abortion. Stella Browne, a socialist feminist, was one of the earliest to campaign for women's right to reproductive self-determination, making links between progressive reform of the laws against abortion, the sexual liberation of women, and socialism (see Riley's chapter 11).

In this chapter abortion and contraception will be discussed separately from now on, to cover their different specific histories in this country, and their present practice.

Contraception

One of the most obvious changes in the birth control situation during the twentieth century has been the extent to which contraception, and to a lesser degree abortion, has become respectable, and especially, medically respectable. In the nineteenth and early twentieth centuries contraception was practised almost entirely without the benefit of doctors. The clinic movement (the FPA and its precursors) finally placed contraception firmly in a medical context. Since the 1974 Family Planning Act, the clinics have been taken over by the National Health Service (NHS), and contraception has become an official part of preventive medicine.

So we now have contraception available under the NHS, free, for both married and unmarried women. The situation, however, is still far from ideal.[6] The problems lie both in the nature of the contraceptives available and in social attitudes which affect contraceptive services, i.e. distribution, publicity and education. The last two will be dealt with very briefly, first. Dissemination of information is hampered in a number of ways. For example, the Post Office still treats 'contraception' as a naughty word and will not use it as a heading in the 'Yellow Pages'. Authorities such as those controlling commercial TV and public transport have been extremely reluctant to accept contraceptive advertisements. Schools also seem reluctant to give birth control information, possibly through fear of encouraging sexual activity. Most secondary schools now give some sort of sex education, but less than half as much as mention birth control (Farrell, 1978).

Another source of difficulty is that contraception requires 'public' acknowledgement of sexual activity. This means that contraceptive use and, more especially, asking for contraceptive help is particularly problematic for people who are afraid that their sexual activity will be disapproved of, or even found ridiculous. These include both unmarried and no-longer married people, and people such as the middle aged, and the physically handicapped who may feel that they fail to fit the cultural stereotype of sexual eligibility.

This brings us on to the limitations of the services. Under the NHS, contraceptives may be obtained from GPs and birth control clinics. Unfortunately, some local authorities have been reluctant either to set up clinics or to allocate sufficient money to them and recently there have been threats of closure, in the name of economy. Clinics are often inconvenient both in their situation and in their hours of opening; and they are extremely busy, which means long waits both for appointments and at the sessions themselves. GPs, on the other hand, are not always well-informed, helpful, or interested in this recently expanded part of their work; for which many have still not received any special training. At present, training in contraceptive techniques is available for GPs but it is voluntary even for those who opt to provide a contraceptive service for their patients, and who receive special payments for doing so.

There are bad as well as good consequences of the 'medical expropriation'[7] of contraception. Some of these disadvantages are specific to birth control, while others are to do with oppressive aspects of the relationship between doctors and their patients — particularly, perhaps, women patients. For example:

(1) The medical contraceptive methods are largely female ones (the exception being vasectomy). While it is important that women *can* be in control, the growing assumption that contraception is a woman's responsibility means that if a contraceptive fails (or is not used) the woman not only bears the burden of the pregnancy, but is held entirely to *blame* for its occurrence.

(2) Doctors are seen, and often act, as authority figures who can give or withhold permission for sex by giving or withholding contraceptives. Such a figure may be difficult for a woman to approach for advice, or to talk to about her feelings, wants and needs. Women, therefore, often feel that the choice of contraceptive is the doctor's and not truly theirs.

Let us look now at the contraceptive methods available. In theory there is considerable choice, but since all have significant disadvantages it is a *negative* choice and in many important respects it is not really a *free* one. For example:

(1) Those methods most free of medical side effects and risks are also those generally regarded as less reliable as contraceptives (although estimates of failure rates vary considerably[8]). A method with an appreciable failure rate may be perfectly adequate for people who want to space their children but it is far less suitable for those who really do not want a baby, unless abortion is *freely* available as a back-up, *and* acceptable to those involved. In fact as Luker (1975) points out, the 'costs'[9] of efficient contraception may lead women to what she feels are *rational* decisions to run the risk of pregnancy by using less efficient contraception or none at all. But this rationality is rarely recognised. Recourse to abortion is stigmatised as due either to lack of contraceptive skills or to intrapsychic conflicts, in which case the unwanted pregnancy is seen as the result of unrealistic, neurotic and deviant behaviour. Doctors treat women with unwanted pregnancies as problem-women, rather than as women with problem-pregnancies.

(2) Many people equate contraception with the pill and/or the sheath. Doctors sometimes over-emphasise the pill, even, in one personally known case, to the extent of taking a woman off the pill for medical reasons and sending her away with no more than the admonition 'Be careful!' Also, women who regard the pill as the only acceptable method are liable to respond to side effects or scares about the pill in the press or elsewhere by ceasing to use any method of birth control and suffering unwanted pregnancies as a result.

On the other hand the sheath, whilst being the only relatively reliable form of contraceptive available from non-medical sources, is least suitable for the inexperienced and diffident — just those people who are most likely to be embarrassed or afraid to seek advice from a doctor, and for whom the choice may be the sheath, withdrawal, or nothing.

The sheath can be an expensive choice. GPs cannot normally prescribe them and some clinics are reluctant to supply them for regular use. It is particularly difficult for men to obtain them from clinics. They are quite frequently told to ask their wives to come for the supplies.

(3) Those whom some doctors regard as 'problem women', such as unmarried mothers and those who have had abortions, may be 'persuaded' to have an intrauterine-contraceptive device (IUCD), three-monthly injections of contraceptive hormones (Depoprovera), or be sterilised. Fairly coercive techniques may also be used to encourage some women to take the pill, e.g. 'if you don't take it don't come back asking for an abortion.' There have been reports that non-participant (IUCD, injections) and sometimes irreversible (sterilisation) methods have also been used in a number of controversial situations, e.g.:

    (i) for seemingly racist/eugenic reasons,

    (ii) where the woman is considered incapable of making responsible decisions about sexuality and childbearing, e.g. the mentally-handicapped and the 'severely disturbed'.[10]

(4) The fitting of caps/diaphragms and IUCDs requires specialised skills. Skills that not all doctors have learnt and which are rarely taught to lay people, although there are no good reasons why this could not be done.

(5) Apart from the controversial, 'social' use of sterilisation mentioned above, sterilisation is generally only carried out on people who already have children and/or are over a certain age. This means

that it is rarely available on request, for the young/unmarried/childless.

(6) Much of the above adds up to the pill being often the only method available from a GP, and it seems relevant at this point, therefore, to concentrate on the pill and some of the problems associated with its dominance as a contraceptive.

Apart from being an extremely effective contraceptive, the combined oestrogen-progestagen, oral contraceptive has a number of advantages. It has the psychological advantage, for some, of separating contraception from lovemaking, both in time and anatomically. It also frequently eliminates or reduces menstrual pain, excessive menstrual bleeding, and, for some, premenstrual tension. It may offer some protection against breast cancer.

One trouble is that just because the pill is so effective and has these beneficial effects, and because a significant number of women, freed from anxieties about unwanted pregnancies, report great feelings of well-being whilst on the pill, there is a tendency to dismiss complaints from other women as either unimportant or psychosomatic. At least one attempt to produce a male pill came to a halt because of fears that it would interfere with male libido. Many women experience loss of libido on the pill and the blame is put not on the pill but on the women, who are accused of failing to come to terms with their sexuality, etc. This is not to suggest that psychological factors are never involved, but that, all too often, physical causes that are unknown, or not understood, are assumed not to exist. Furthermore, a psychosomatic diagnosis not only carries implied moral disapproval but is often treated as if the diagnosis is also the cure − i.e. the complaint is imaginary, therefore go away and forget it.

Some doctors do not warn women about possible side effects or risks in the mistaken belief (Carwright, 1970) that women will then be less likely to complain of side effects. This, however, deprives women of the ability to make a real and informed choice.

Yet another difficulty is that many doctors regard the side effects of the pill as trivial, and indeed if this was a drug being given to cure a sick person this might be a valid point of view. But a woman seeking contraception is not sick and may, reasonably enough, object to being made to feel unwell.

Doctors favour the pill and may confine their contraceptive service to prescribing it, since (a) it helps to avoid the ethical dilemmas of dealing with unwanted pregnancy and abortion, and (b) it requires a minimum of time and skill whilst keeping contraception firmly under their control. For whilst, prior to special payments, many doctors were reluctant to give advice on birth control (Peel and Potts, 1970), they seem equally reluctant to lose control.

Medically there is tremendous confusion. It is recognised that the pill is a powerful drug carrying with it certain risks and that therefore users should have medical supervision. Yet in practice many women get such minimal supervision that even known contraindications must often be missed. Moreover, not all the risks can be lessened by routine screening of users (*Lancet*, 1974; Smith and Kane, 1975).

This has resulted in what may be a bad compromise. The pill is only available through restricted sources, which may deter some women from obtaining either supplies or information; but this restriction guarantees only token supervision. Quite possibly, if medical factors were the only ones involved, there would be less fear of loosening the medical hold over the pill. But while the pill and certain other contraceptives *are* associated with *medical* risks, anxieties about them are often compounded with moral as well as psychological anxieties about sex — anxieties that exist in doctors, patients and society at large. For example, the fear is commonly expressed that if the pill is too easy to obtain it will encourage promiscuity and a decline in moral standards (or indeed, has already done so). Confusion of medical, psychological and moral aspects of contraception means that many of the arguments about the merits and demerits of various contraceptives can never be resolved because, although they are couched in medical terms, the medical anxieties mask more fundamental anxieties about sexuality. Thus, there is a tendency to try to resolve moral anxieties by seeking medical reassurance.

Abortion

This section strongly emphasises the law, because the law is the battlefield for those holding differing views on the permissibility of abortion. The main British laws relating to abortion are the Offences Against the Person Act 1861, the Infant Life Preservation Act 1929, and the Abortion Act 1967. The 1929 and 1967 Acts amend the 1861 Act and set out conditions under which abortion was and is legal (of which more later). The present law can be better understood when viewed in relation to the earlier statutes. The 1861 Act was the last of a series of nineteenth-century laws which introduced restrictions on women's access to abortion. Before 1803 in British common law abortion prior to quickening[11] was not a crime, whilst after quickening it was a misdemeanour. In 1803 abortion was made a statutory offence punishable by death for anyone giving a woman an abortion if quickening had occurred. This law was part of a legal 'tidying up' (with abortion included in a long list of offences). However, it was eight years till the first indictment under it and then the drafting of it was torn to bits by the defence. Acts in 1828 and 1837 tightened up the law and dropped the category of quickening altogether. Prosecutions under these laws were relatively few and acquittals on flimsy grounds occurred.

Of the Act passed in 1861 (it did not apply in Scotland) sections 58 and 59 dealt with abortion. For the first time the woman herself was considered guilty if she tried to procure her own abortion.[12] The supplier of drugs or instruments was also guilty of an offence under this law. The law states that the attempt to procure an abortion by a second person is an offence whether or not the woman is pregnant, but if the woman herself tries to induce her own abortion this is not an offence if she is not pregnant − for her the crime in this case apparently does not lie in intent. She can, however, be convicted of conspiracy if, whether actually pregnant or not, she tries with others to procure an abortion.[13]

The 1861 law does not seem to have arisen out of strongly felt views in the country as there was no apparent public comment on it, and no debate in the House of Commons. The tone of articles, periodicals and newspapers for a middle-class audience in the 1860s makes it clear that much of the opposition to abortion was on social class and moral grounds. It implied that women were rebelling against the traditional role of childbearing and were therefore a threat to the hierarchical family structure. There was little discussion of the very high maternal mortality rate in childbirth and although the mortality rate from abortion was discussed, often with relish (e.g. Parry, *Criminal Abortion*, 1932) the question of why women persisted in attempting to abort themselves was ignored. For example, in the *British Medical Journal* in February 1906 a doctor from Torquay wrote: 'It is a disgrace that so many women prefer the evils and dangers of plumbism[14] to fulfilment of their natural function as women. . . . Are the girls of today properly educated to be able to fulfill the duties of motherhood?' (Tidswell, 1906) Abortion was seen as selfishness − seeking pleasure without responsibility.

The 1861 Act did not specify any conditions under which abortion was permissible, even those cases where the woman's life was in danger. Many doctors in the early twentieth century were performing abortions to save the mother's life, but were becoming increasingly uneasy about the lack of legal cover. The Infant Life Preservation Act of 1929 did give somewhat better guidelines in that it allowed the termination of pregnancy when the act was done in good faith to pre-serve the life of the mother and if the foetus was legally viable (i.e. at least twenty-eight week old)! It would have been unlikely at this time for a twenty-eight week foetus to have survived. However, this law still left the question of early abortions unresolved.

There was increasing debate over abortions throughout the 1920s and 1930s; this controversy spread to the British Medical Association and to the courts. In this context a doctor deliberately brought a prosecution on himself in 1938. Dr Bourne agreed to induce an abortion in a fourteen-year-old girl who had been raped by guards-men.[15] The judge in question gave a liberal interpretation to the law that abortion could be allowed to save a woman's life, extending 'life' to cover the mental and physical health of the woman. This judgement was never seriously contested in court.

This was the state of the law until the Abortion Act 1967 was passed in Great Britain during an era of social reform and under the pressure of opinion following the thalidomide scandal.[16] The 1967 Act allows women to obtain an abortion only if there is something physically wrong with her or the foetus, or she cannot cope mentally or finan-cially.[17] The law was meant to help in cases of 'severe social hardship', i.e. to be available (apart from when the woman's life is in danger) only for the 'deprived', the 'sick' or the 'inadequate'. A woman's own wish not to bear children (now or ever) is conspicuously not on these lists.

In V. Greenwood and J. Young's (1976), *Abortion on Demand*, it is argued that the Act was drafted as a reform and that in the reformers' view most 'normal' women do not want or need abortion, only problem women do. Those who drafted the Bill would therefore have expected little demand for abortion from the vast majority of women. This expectation was based on the assumptions that the decision to have a child is made rationally by all people and that the advances in contraception mean that everyone can avoid unplanned pregnancy.

The demand for abortion was much greater than expected.[18] Far from taking this as indicating that the abortion legislation uncovered a widespread need, the anti-abortionists have used the large number of abortions done as propaganda *against* the 1967 Act. Since 1967 there have been a series of unsuccessful Private Members' Bills which have sought to restrict the availability of abortion (James White's in 1975, William Benyon's in 1977 and John Corrie's in 1979). All three of these Amendment Bills gained support by proclaiming their purpose to be merely to outlaw abuses of the 1967 Act, but all, in fact, con-tained clauses that would have made it much harder for even the 'deserving' (in the reformers' terms) to obtain safe, early abortions. Furthermore, at least some of the sponsors of the Bills have openly admitted that their eventual aim is to outlaw not just abuses of the 1967 Act, but abortion itself.

The three main positions on abortion since the 1967 Act reflect attitudes to sexuality and to women's role as childbearers within the family.

(1) The Society for the Protection of the Unborn Child (SPUC) — this group (and also the Catholic Church) is anti-abortion except in a very few medical cases. Many people in these groups are also against contraception, advocating the inseparability of sex and reproduction.

(2) Reformers — progressive and conservative. The former (which includes the Co-ordinating Group for the Defence of the 1967 Act) are in favour of the 1967 Act in the main, apart from a few minor adjustments, whilst the latter, a miscellaneous group, suggest radical amendment to the law to cut out 'excesses' and restrict abortion to the deserving few.

(3) The third set is the only one committed to the goal of women's reproductive self-determination, and the only one which states their position in terms of *women's* rights. It includes the National Abortion Campaign (NAC), a group formed to fight the first of the Amendment Bills. This group has its roots in the Women's Liberation Movement and supports the feminist call for abortion on demand. The Abortion Law Reform Association (ALRA) also comes into this group although it differs from NAC in tactics and membership. A more recent group is Doctors for a Woman's Choice. The call for abortion on demand is a recognition that economic circumstances may force women to choose abortion; for many women there is no real choice regarding family size (see Riley's chapter 11) and, as we have tried to point out, contraception cannot prevent all unwanted pregnancies.

Despite the anti-abortion and conservative reformers' claims that there is now abortion available on demand, this is far from true. Most of the abortions carried out are granted under the physical and mental health clause. This clause can permit a liberal interpretation as it allows abortion if the risk of continuing the pregnancy is greater than terminating it, and early abortion is safer than childbirth. However, women have no *rights* to abortion, it is up to two doctors to decide whether they will be permitted to have one. Medicine is not neutral either politically or ideologically, and the decision to grant an abortion does not rest on medical grounds alone. Abortions can act as reinforcements of existing social values and arrangements such as monogamy and the family. So that, depending on the individual doctor, they may be more readily available for unmarried women, or ones with inadequate finance or housing. Black, Asian or white working-class women may find no difficulty in obtaining abortions and may find themselves persuaded into the decision, sometimes with a strong recommendation for sterilisation as well. Many doctors take up a role of benign paternalism in the belief that women should not have to make this sometimes difficult decision, so denying many women the control of their own fertility. When requesting an abortion (to *demand* would antagonise!) success may depend on the woman's ability to appear pathetic — but not too pathetic, else she may be sent off to a NHS psychiatrist — an effective delaying tactic. Abortions need to be done as quickly as possible as late abortions may be refused on medical grounds, and are more unpleasant.

An abortion is treated as a tragedy in a woman's life. The experience of being unwillingly pregnant is difficult, but there are also needless difficulties associated with the procedure of obtaining an abortion. The extent of the delay between an abortion being requested and being done varies between areas. For an operation that is safer the earlier it is done, long delays can be dangerous as well as unpleasant. The use of methods such as menstrual extraction for very early abortions is still extremely limited. Women are rarely offered the choice of a local rather than a general anaesthetic. Day care clinics where women need spend only half a day in hospital may well lessen the trauma associated with abortions but there are very few of these clinics in the country.

At present, less than 50 per cent of the abortions carried out in this country are done under the NHS. There is enormous regional variation in the availability of facilities, so that in some places it is much harder to get an abortion without paying large fees for it.[19] The legal position for both private clinics and the NHS is the same, so there is no *legal* reason why it should be easier to get an abortion in the private sector. The regional variations show the need for a great increase in the provision of NHS facilities, so that obtaining under the NHS does not depend on where you happen to live. Unfortunately, the threatened cuts in the NHS are likely to exacerbate the situation because those health authorities that already give abortion facilities a low priority are least likely to protect those facilities from the axe.

The combination of threats made on birth control services in the name of economy, and the repeated attacks on the abortion legislation, have forced groups such as NAC and ALRA to expend a high proportion of their energies on defending the current situation rather than having it available to campaign really effectively for the many needed improvements to the facilities.

We have considered abortion and contraception separately as this is the way they are considered within the NHS. However, when the actual methods are surveyed this division becomes blurred. Birth control methods range from those which prevent fertilisation (e.g. the cap, sheath and some pills), to those which may act after implantation has occurred (menstrual extraction, late insertion of IUCD). Some pills, the IUCD and the morning after pill are intermediate, acting between fertilisation and implantation. Logical anti-abortion arguments should apply to all methods that act after fertilisation. The overlap between abortion and contraception cuts across the prevailing attitudes. Contraceptive use is seen as the responsible choice and there is great condemnation of women who are thought to use abortion instead of a contraceptive method.

The incidence of abortion does go hand in hand with contraceptive use so that contrary to popular belief increased usage of contraceptives is *positively* correlated with increased requests for abortion.[20] Furthermore, improved contraception is unlikely to remove the need for abortion. Where women are seeking to control their fertility, abortion is, and probably will always be, necessary in some circumstances.

Abortion at present requires medical intervention. There has been some research on the use of prostaglandin gels, inserted vaginally, which would induce an early abortion. This could be used as a self-help method which would further undermine the distinction between contraception and abortion − there would no longer be a need for a hospital bed, or for anyone other than the woman to do the abortion. The necessary technological advance has already been tested but it remains to be seen when, if ever, these gels will be readily available to women. This raises the issue we mentioned at the beginning − that it is not the limits of modern technology which necessarily restrict the range of available birth control methods. The interesting questions to ask about technology focus on which technologies are being developed and to whom they are made available.

The histories of abortion and contraception run somewhat parallel, with that of abortion lagging about thirty years behind that of contraception and meeting with similar opposition to easy access, particularly for young and for unmarried women. At around the turn of the century there was a shift in the overt arguments against contraception from moral to medical grounds, although the underlying opposition to abortion remained moral. The medical arguments were not about the side effects of contraception, or the dangers of specific methods, but focused on the harm resulting when conception is prevented (by whatever means). For example: 'effects which included galloping cancer, sterility and nymphomania in women, and mental decay, amnesia and cardiac palpitations in men; in both sexes the practice was likely to produce mania leading to suicide' (C.H.F. Routh, 1878). Similarly, the anti-abortion arguments put forward by SPUC associate the practice of abortion with psychological breakdown, depression and madness. Other current anti-abortion arguments are also moral ones, but are made in medical terms with the implication that abortion is wrong because it is medically unsafe. The article by Wynn and Wynn (1973) is an illustration of the confusions between medical and moral arguments outlined above. The availability of safe, easy abortion methods (e.g. gels) would help counter these medical arguments and clarify the moral ones.

At present access to abortion and contraception facilities is dependent on the area a woman lives in, her GP's conscience, her race, social class and knowledge of her rights. This is still a very long way from the Women's Liberation Movement's demand for free contraception and abortion on demand. Not only that but there is a danger in fighting for improvements in birth control provision as an isolated issue, as this can lead to narrow and misleading interpretations of situations. Reproductive self-determination is itself not all that intelligible unless it is seen in a context of other social policies (see chapter 11). The shortcomings of the present situation are indicative of how far we are from realising women's self-determination. Furthermore, although we have talked here as if women have made steady progress towards the goal of reproductive self-determination since the nineteenth century, the well orchestrated opposition to abortion suggests that this ground is never perhaps decisively won.

Notes

1   We would like to thank all those who read and commented on the manuscript during its preparation, especially Paul Whittle and Mary Bernard.
2   The Malthusian League took its inspiration from the clergyman Thomas Malthus who wrote of the dangers of overpopulation (1798). He, however, disapproved of birth control and advocated only 'moral restraint' in the form of sexual abstinence. See Glass (1953) which contains essays on Malthus and his theories, as well as a reprint of Malthus' 'Summary of the Principles of Population' (1830).

3 See P. Knight (1977a and b) for further details.

4 The trend towards smaller middle-class families was often mentioned in the press in the 1860s in the debate on the 'flight from maternity' and this decrease in middle-class family size led to eugenic arguments for birth control.

5 See A. McLaren (1977) on Lancashire textile workers. He argues that these women used abortion as their main means of fertility control.

6 For some of the most recent statistics on unintended and unwanted pregnancies see Cartwright (1978).

7 This phrase is Ivan Illich's (1977).

8 See, for example, *Our Bodies Ourselves* (Phillips and Rakusen, 1978, p.241) in contrast to Peel and Potts (1970, p.47).

9 'Costs' include medical risks, expense, inconvenience, implications for sexual partnership.

10 E.g. Sue O'Sullivan (1975), Lyn Harne (1978), *The Guardian*, (12 February 1979).

11 Quickening was supposed to occur some time after three months — corresponding approximately to the time when the mother can feel the foetus moving inside her. Prior to quickening the foetus was not considered to be human. Aristotle was the originator of the concept — quickening was taken to be the time when the soul enters the foetus.

12 This law still stands and was the basis for the prosecution in 1977 of a fourteen-year-old girl. She had taken six laxative tablets in a hot bath to bring about an abortion. Since laxatives are harmless to the foetus this was not an offence.

13 See Parry (1932) for specific prosecutions.

14 Plumbism is lead poisoning and was often the outcome for women who took lead pills as abortifacients.

15 Bourne's decision to give the young woman an abortion, however, was based on his judgement that she deserved one and not on the basis of her desire to terminate her pregnancy. Although the court case in 1938 was a turning point in the liberalisation of abortion laws, Bourne himself was later opposed to the aims of the 1967 Act and joined the Society for the Protection of the Unborn Child.

16 Foetal abnormality was not sufficient grounds for an abortion before the 1967 Act.

17 See the Abortion Act 1967, HMSO.

18 Abortions/100 live births: 4 in 1968 rising to 17.6 in 1975.

19 In 1978 about 10 per cent of abortions were under the NHS in Birmingham whilst over 90 per cent were under the NHS in Newcastle-upon-Tyne.

20 Potts, Diggory and Peel (1977, p.454) cite several studies to support this.

Further Reading

E. Draper, *Birth Control in the Modern World; The Role of the Individual in Population Control*. London: Pelican, 1972.

Gordon, *Woman's Body Woman's Right: a social history of birth control in America*. Harmondsworth: Penguin, 1977.

J. Leeson and J. Gray, *Women and Medicine*. London: Tavistock, 1978.

M. Llewelyn Davies (ed), *Maternity: letters from working women*. London: Virago, 1978.

A.P. Phillips and J. Rakusen, *Our Bodies Ourselves: A Health Book by and for Women*. Harmondsworth: Penguin, 1978.

V. Walsh, 'Contraception: the growth of a technology', in The Brighton Women and Science Group, *Alice Through the Microscope*. London: Virago, 1980.

Chapter Eleven

Feminist Thought and Reproductive Control: the State and the 'right to choose'[1]

DENISE RILEY

The need for socialism and feminism to retain a strong critical and imaginative perspective on both the 'private' and the 'public' aspects of reproductive control is clear enough. Theoretical and political work of a socialist and/or feminist persuasion has long been occupied either with aspects of the politics of State interventions in population growth, or with the constraints on individual choices to have or not have children. But these as alternatives don't exhaust the issue. There's a need for a more systematic body of thought about the interface between conceptualisations of individual rights and governmental policies. The relations between the State, population policies (whether pro or anti-natalist), feminism and the 'right to choose' stand directly at this interface.

For example, the matter of a woman's 'free choice' to have children. Some version of reproductive self-determination, however problematic that is, is basic to feminism in the refusal to resign oneself to encroaching authorities, be they husbands, doctors, the government or whatever. And feminism, as the theory of one of the groupings of the 'oppressed', speaks of the rights of individual women versus the State or controlling agency, however defined. But at the same time, feminism also speaks from and about socialism. At the very least, that is, in the politically less-specific sense of envisaging a radically re-ordered distribution of power. And socialism does not, in ideal terms, entail the necessary opposing of individual to State rights or admit this as an essential antagonism of interests. Thus feminism, in so far as it's also socialism, can't tacitly assume a timeless irreconcilability between 'women' and 'State' on the point of reproductive choice. The question then becomes: what are the social conditions under which the most genuinely 'free' choices can be made by women, and how are the various constraints to be understood?

This is to speak abstractly. What I want to do here is to outline some of these arguments as they arise in particular instances — and to indicate ways in which a feminist analysis of 'choice' must encounter and challenge other suppositions about the nature of the State and the family in these areas. A complex conceptualisation of the State, as well as of the family, is needed to cope with this. States have hugely different population policies, and different intersections between, for example, welfare agencies, medical services, and population programmes. The relativity of women's reproductive choices has to be assessed in specific settings, and feminist analyses must find a necessary breadth and flexibility. This chapter has only limited objectives. I'll start by trying to place the most recent British feminist work on reproduction as produced reactively under the threat of legal erosion of abortion provision. I'll then spend some time discussing what 'choice' in reproduction means anyway. In the last sections of this chapter, Bolshevik and Stalinist Russia are used as illustrations of the vicissitudes of State reproductive policies, and of the problems these set for feminist and socialist enquiry with regard to choice.

Any adequate consideration of the State, choice, and feminism would demand attention to many other apposite questions which stand beyond the limits of this paper. These include demographic information and its uses. And to Third World economic and reproductive patterns which all clearly need full and separate analyses, so aren't mentioned here; my remarks refer only to Western and Eastern Europe. The essential question of imperialism in relation to population control isn't elaborated. I haven't dwelt on the fact that while the objects of reproductive policies are women, governments are largely informed by a male sensibility — although this point underscores everything else said here. Nor have I written about the part of men in making decisions about having children. (In fact it's noticeable in recent 'family planning' literature that decision-making, once removed from the anonymous powers of an unchecked female biology, is taken to be the province of 'the couple'.) The increasingly significant part played by sterilisation, a virtually irreversible choice, in influencing the British birthrate (Bone, 1978) is a change which needs attention. I don't develop the question of the emotional originations of the individual undertaking to have children; in the absence, that is, of material constraints not to do so and the grosser ideological pressures to do so. The psychoanalytic work is small and limited here (compare Antonis' chapter 4).[2] And feminist theory, has for good reasons, been more occupied with undoing the assumed naturalness of women's childrearing role than with the question of why women do 'anyway' have children. All these points are pertinent for a fuller understanding of reproductive choice and social policies.

Returning to my circumscribed objectives, I'll start with Britain. Here contemporary feminism has been on the whole − although by no means universally − working with a roughly Marxist-functionalist conception of the State. Such a conception, particularly dominant in late 1960s Leftist political thought, does tacitly or directly assume a somewhat monolithic version of the State − which, in the instance of reproductive control, is taken to have a direct interest in intervening to suit the needs of the labour market. The State is, in the area of reproduction, understood as a concerted block of invasive interests. (A more specific sub-thesis assumes that the State's exploitation of women in particular, as distinct from the population in general, is demonstrated in its use of women's labour-power in reproduction to extract the commodities of children from their bodies − thus running into a series of serious puns on 'labour'.) But in all versions of this widespread understanding of the relation of the State to fertility, the State is assumed to need to intervene one way or another, and thus to be the self-evidently legitimate target of political struggle for the reproductive self-determination of women.

There are several drawbacks to this model. It runs together questions of reproduction and questions of population need or assumed need too closely in some respects, and divorces them in others. It takes capital as always the most powerful influence on the State, so that capital can get the State to act directly on its behalf − which overlooks, for example, the ambiguities of the relations between 'welfare' and State. Nor does this model sufficiently distinguish between one State and another, or provide a basis for understanding the specific forms of, say, imperialist intervention in 'population policies'. However, my object here isn't to attempt a critique of this generally held concept of the State.

For such critiques are in the course of being developed; more and more attention has been paid recently to the nature of the 'Welfare State', and to the question of an international perspective on reproductive control. Feminist interest in national policies on fertility has in the past been turned largely to the practices of foreign governments. It has taken the form, for example, of attacks on experimentation on those least able to defend themselves against technical-economic imperialism − experimentation like the American Depo-provera trials. However, papers by the Women Against Population Control group (1973; 1974) both criticise population policies internationally and draw some conclusions for feminist politics and theory here, while also outlining the neo-Malthusian assumptions behind population control as a concept, and detailing the shapes of its manifestations in Britain. Most recently (at the end of 1978) there has been a fresh emphasis on the international aspects of fertility-choice campaigning, while opposition to the use of Depo-provera is now home-based too.[3]

In Britain, analyses of the State as trying to determine the rate of reproduction have not really been pushed into being, given the relative absence of any decisive *overall* pro- or anti-natalist policy exerted by the British government, as distinct from pressure from 'population groups' outside the government. And as distinct, too, from differential sectional treatment of women's access to contraception and abortion along race and class lines. That is, while policies about the birth-rate have by no means been *absent* from British politics and governmental debate, these have not, in the last two decades, been phrased in the terms of 'national growth' and 'national need', familiar from countries possessing an overt population target. Instead, they have been couched in parliamentary, legal-moralistic terms about individual rights and choices; while the need, under the Abortion Act 1967, for the consent of doctors has generated discussion about the function of the National Health Service, and the roles and powers of the medical profession. This relative absence of a hegemonic population policy being vigorously and visibly pursued by the State has meant that the obvious focus of British feminist attention to reproductive politics has been the preservation and the adequate implementation of the Abortion Act, and its possible extensions. The question of individual choice in those contexts continues to be a critical area of political struggle. The National Abortion Campaign, for example, has been characterised by the necessary defence against real threats of renewed restrictions of our abortion legislation (see chapter 10 by Greenwood and King).

The idea of the State as threatening Other, however inaccurate it may be as a description of the actual operating of the government with respect to reproductive control, is nevertheless a reasonable response to parliamentary threats to abortion facilities. For it's necessary to find an agency with a more direct political existence and influence than, say, the Catholic Church possesses; and an agency which can be politically engaged with, too. But the State as enemy has to be made more specific and broken down into its aspects of government, of 'welfare', of social work, of labour needs, of racist and class concerns. And its susceptibility to various pressure groups needs to be analysed. The

absence of those political conditions — e.g. a lack of a grossly interventionist policy — likely to produce a very active analysis of the
relation between reproductive control and State is clearly never
guaranteed or fixed. The 1978 proposal made by a Labour prime
minister to establish a Minister for Marriage is, however cynically one
understands that, none the less of interest to contemporary feminism
as one among several instances of the periodic re-entry of 'the family'
into party-political rhetoric, at however 'ideological' and merely
gestural a level. The labile nature of national policies on reproduction
can be demonstrated by the extensive wave of English pro-natalism
and eugenics in the post-war period — to give one relatively recent
example. Anxieties over the 'quality of the race' are by no means restricted to nineteenth-century conservatism.

But more recent arguments about pro-natalism, class and motherhood in this country are less familiar, perhaps. The anxiety about a
falling birthrate during and after the Second World War in Great
Britain was established enough to generate population commissions
and inquiries and debates, couched in eugenicist terms of 'quality' and
'race'. These included highly detailed proposals for measures to relieve
the lot of mothers in order to facilitate the having of more children.
Such debates and proposals were not the property of the right wing
only. The Fabian Society evidence to the Royal Commission on Population in 1946, for example, bears vivid witness to that. A 'bringing
home' of recent British racism and eugenicism is of interest not only as
an 'exposé', from a comparative cross-national perspective, but also in
so far as it raises questions about the ways in which contemporary
bourgeois feminist theories of the family and of motherhood entered
into pro-natalist debates.

There is a considerable recent history of interventionist concern
with reproduction on the part of socialist, capitalist, and fascist
States — a useful history, allowing for the incompleteness of evidence. For it exposes the degree to which the individual reproductive
'choice' is embedded within highly specific social and political
policies. Mao's China, for example, attracted a considerable amount
of (largely favourable) feminist and socialist attention which has
emphasised its communitarianism and work-emancipatory measures
for women. However, the firm anti-natalist policy which China has
operated since the Cultural Revolution has 'collectivised' women's
decisions to have children in such a way that no unrestricted 'right to
choose' to conceive exists.[4] But in the Chinese case, the enormously
different political-cultural framework also means that a part-collec-
tivisation of decision-making can't be simply opposed to what obtains
in Western Europe.

Concepts of both 'the State' and of the nature of individual rights and legislation are obviously dependent on particular histories of governmental policies, population movements, philosophies of rights, concepts of feminism, of waged labour, of collectivity and so on. To abstract a single one of such factors — which in themselves are by no means unproblematic definitions — and then simply to 'read it off' in isolation as it occurs from country to country, State to State, will produce unintelligible results.

Consideration of the relations between the State, population control and feminist theory produces questions about what is to *count* as 'a population policy'. How strictly is coercion to be defined? Should the lack of employment opportunities for women and a persuasive familial rhetoric be counted as constituting coercion, as well as the more obvious pressures of restrictive legislation on access, say, to abortion and contraception? Is *any* form of governmental intervention in the sphere of reproduction — encouraging or discouraging — to be understood as antagonistic to the 'interests' of women and so to be opposed on principle? Or is it instead necessary to allow for 'population planning' under certain political conditions, but to argue that the task of implementing such planning should be carried out in a way somehow congruent with feminist politics, — whatever that might mean? There is also the practical question of how far, anyway, women's fertility *is* susceptible to State policies, and if so, in what ways and under what circumstances, exactly. And on this last point, it's possible to turn from general speculations about the nature of hypothetical future socialist-feminist morality, to an examination of what's actually happened, and so fill out this notion of women's 'susceptibility' to interventions and to propaganda.

The appearances and eclipses of the feminist demand for 'self-determination' in reproduction (and sexuality), or for 'control' of these areas, are obviously open to criticisms that these ideas imply an isolated subjectivity operating in an impossibly free terrain of 'choice'. And, consequently, that they indicate a politically misconceived affirmation of women as pre-social 'subjects' (Adams and Minson, 1978). But it is nevertheless the case that the uncertain speech of the philosophy of 'rights' is the chief inherited discourse — whatever its deficiencies — for the framing of *any* demands for social reform or revolution. And demands for rights and choices are the expression of a critical refusal to leave the powers of decision to external authorities, be they doctors or government. The political significance of this refusal must override objections to 'the right to choose' which are based *only* on critiques of that slogan's apparent implications of a free individual operating on an uncircumscribed terrain, in an idealism of isolated 'choice'. For while 'choice' is obviously a complex concept, and while the right in law and social policy to 'make a choice' is by no means the whole story, nonetheless that right, minimal enough, is of a critical importance.

'The right to choose' has been invoked in Britain largely in a spirit of defence against threatened parliamentary encroachments on recently won territory as mentioned above. Such a necessarily defensive position has given abortion campaigning the appearance of 'a single issue'. But there is an obvious lack of congruence between the slogan and the campaign for abortion on demand, and the multiplicity of needs pertaining to 'choice' in lived life. If 'the right to choose' *is* taken as an assertion that an area of choosing 'really' exists (over and above the recapturing of the limited choice *not* to continue a pregnancy), the implication then is that women do live out their lives in an ideological and economic vacuum. Unconstrained, that is, by their lack of access to adequate housing, jobs, childcare provisions, by the weight of their own upbringing and familial-emotional histories.

'The right to choose' must imply the right to choose to have (not merely *not* to have) children; and this right is a very metaphysical assertion in a situation where provisions for the myriad needs for bringing up those children in a humane way are thin on the ground. And, of course, conspicuously thinner for some than for others. To follow through the 'positive' aspect of the right to choose would entail a many-faceted campaign, a generalising of the issue which linked it to a wider context of agitation for the reforms necessary to give more plausibility to the notion of choice. Nevertheless, it seems to me to be wrong to criticise an essentially defensive slogan, so heavily marked by its necessary strategical location, on the grounds of its incompleteness. (The ways in which campaigns of defence might also advantageously draw on other, less localised, campaigns, such as those for better contraceptive information and provision are a continuing ground of debate.)

Assertions about the right to control one's own body, to choose, are by no means manifestations of the most recent post-1960s phases of feminist politics. Their earlier appearances, transmutations, and eclipses are of great interest as part-pointers to the careers of earlier feminist movements. For instance, in England in the 1920s and 1930s, Stella Browne's writing provides an example of a socialist and feminist analysis of the imperative of free access to abortion (Rowbotham, 1977). She was not unique in this demand; what remains to be clearly determined is how 'representative' or not her position was of contemporary socialist-feminist thought, and how her apparent isolation inside the Communist Party fitted into this. In her contribution to the 1930 Sexual Reform Congress (Haire, 1930 pp.178–81), she argues for 'the full right of free motherhood', under which she includes 'the case for the absolute freedom of choice on the woman's part in the early months of pregnancy'. Some of her arguments are identical to those of most-recent feminism, including that from the unreliability and awkwardness of contraceptive methods.

> The present position of our contraceptive knowledge and technique indicates very clearly that an absolutely 100% reliable and otherwise acceptable preventive is not only as yet undiscovered, but possibly in many cases undiscoverable. The new demand for free motherhood is going to be the next step in feminism . . . not abortion, but forced motherhood, is the crime.

It was essential that abortion should be extended to married women too: 'the woman's need and wish, not a ring or a scrap of paper, should be the test.' And, like many radicals and theorisers on sexuality of her time, she argues — in this address at least — from eugenic grounds too: 'On the racial damage caused by unwilling maternity and pregnancy, I hold a very strong view.' Later she was to direct her efforts to securing reform in British abortion legislation.

In her address to the Sexual Reform Congress, Stella Browne also refers to 'the great Russian experiment' of liberalised abortion access, and to 'the work of those Russian and German pioneers who have made this cause practical politics in their countries'. Such an admiration for Bolshevik and post-Bolshevik 'pro-feminism' was common among British socialist feminists at the time. This was, however, somewhat misconceived; as, indeed, became clear after the restrictive Soviet legislation of 1936 which repealed the earlier liberal abortion laws, and which was unmistakably part of a population policy far removed from any respect for ideals of reproductive 'self-determination' for women. But the Bolshevik liberalising of abortion had hardly been done in a spirit of feminist right-to-choose. It is clear, rather, that the immediately post-revolutionary legislation had only been introduced as constituting a 'lesser evil' than the perpetuation of what was seen as a situation of hidden, widespread and physically harmful abortion practices. Thus, the Decree on the Legalisation of Abortions, 1920, describes abortion as 'a serious evil' which will disappear ultimately under socialism. But 'as the moral survivals of the past and the difficult economic conditions of the present still compel many women to resort to this operation', the Bolshevik government, 'anxious to protect the health of women and considering that the method of repression in this field fails entirely to achieve this aim', was therefore introducing free abortion on request up to the third month of pregnancy. (But this had to be done in hospitals and by doctors only.) That is, not at any point was the liberalising of access on abortion put in terms of women's rights or 'free motherhood'.

Indeed, the Bolsheviks distanced themselves explicitly from those whom Alexandra Kollontai, in her 1923 'Critique of the Feminist Movement', denounced as 'bourgeois equal-righters' (Schlesinger, 1949). 'Bourgeois feminism' was criticised for its emphasis on 'individual rights' and for a neglect of class-based demands and the material needs of women who did have children.

> Motherhood and its defence, the safeguarding of woman's interests as mother, were in no way included in the aims and programme of the bourgeois equal-righters and the bourgeois women who late in the 19th and early in the 20th century found the problem of safeguarding motherhood attracting their attention, were not of those who had been drawn into the feminist camp.

This critique, however, is made by Alexandra Kollontai as part of her insistence on the role of the new socialist society in both safeguarding and broadening the position of women with children, including through the collectivisation of housework and childcare. And her own stress on the new socialist morality in fact frequently rendered her subject to inaccurate accusations of propagating essentially bourgeois notions of 'free love'. Nevertheless, her comparative radicalism on questions of sexual morality does not include any mention of free access to contraception and abortion as part-constitutive of women's emancipation under the new socialism. The stress is instead on the protection of mothers and on child health; abortion is seen as a transitional evil, a residue of a capitalist inability to provide for all children. Alexandra Kollontai wrote in 1923:

> Soviet power realises that the need for abortion will only disappear on the one hand when Russia has a broad and developed network of institutions protecting motherhood and providing social education, and on the other hand when women understand that *childbirth is a social obligation*: Soviet power has therefore allowed abortion to be performed openly and in clinical conditions (Holt, 1977, p.149).

This insistence on childbearing as a social duty speaks from a general Bolshevik pro-natalism, more intelligible in the light of the fact that the population of Russia had been seriously depleted by war and famine and their aftermath, and the country continued to occupy an extremely beleaguered position (a fact crucial to considering the whole history of Soviet social policies). But a situation of economic scarcity and population depletion need not dictate descriptions of the imaginative impoverishment which characterise Lenin's conversation with the German Communist and women's political organiser, Clara Zetkin in 1920 (Lenin, 1972). The prominence given in the German Communist Party to discussions with working women on questions of sexual morality and the nature of marriage is criticised by Lenin as diversionary, in a classic text of 'after-the-revolutionism' and an equally classic stress on the self-evidence of socialist morality. (Compare chapter 5 on Left Critiques of the Family.) On the matter of contraception specifically, Lenin argued in 1913 against the 'neo-Malthusian pessimism' which timidly supposed that the new socialist State would be incapable of supporting its population: at the same time, though, he held that criminalising abortion laws should be annulled.[5]

Discussion on the pro-natalist legislation of 1936, which included the virtual abolition of abortion, made much of the 'lightminded' and bourgeois adoption of the 'disorderly sex life', and repeated Lenin on the point of 'timorous, selfish parents' who did not want children. Several contemporary Russian sociological commentaries on Stalinist family policies reiterated that the 1920 liberal legislation on abortion had been constituted only as a transitional measure, as a 'lesser evil'; while under a fuller socialism, abortion was not necessary. Increased material well-being guaranteed a future to all children, while 'the tragic cleavage where woman has to choose between productive work and the family does not exist in the USSR' (Wolffson, 1949). With socialism, true monogamy was possible. For Stalinist critics lumped together the collectivising of the functions of the family and 'free love', characterised them as bourgeois deviations, and condemned them together.[6] Whereas, as Lenin had pointed out, the socialisation of family labour need not necessarily go along with any sexual radicalism (nor, of course, conversely).

Modern feminism, like British feminism in the 1920s and 1930s, may have tended to exaggerate the sexual radicalism of the Bolshevik innovations, and to misunderstand the legislation on abortion in particular as evidence for a climate of respect for the sexual self-determination of women. On the contrary, it's arguable that to understand Stalinist socialist policy as an absolute ideological reversal is to over-state matters, and that in fact the absence of 'self-determination' arguments right through is telling. Thus, Schlesinger (1949) considers that Soviet legislation from 1936 to 1944 was really just in line with the general European and American moves to consolidate the 'modern family' and give it greater material encouragement – an analysis which itself gives rise to some interesting questions.[7]

Trotsky's sharp critique in *The Revolution Betrayed* (1972) of Stalinist stratification and bureaucratisation describes the new prohibition of abortion on the grounds that 'a woman has no right to decline the joys of motherhood in an ideal socialist society' as 'the philosophy of a priest endowed with the powers of a gendarme'. Yet his attack on the new Soviet familialism still characterises abortion as a qualified right associated with material lack. He writes of 'the right to abortion, which in conditions of want and family distress . . . is one of [woman's] most important civil, political and cultural rights. However, this right of women, too, gloomy enough in itself, is under the existing social inequality being converted into a privilege.' That is, no 'absolute' right of women to control their own fertility is referred to; and the implication remains that, under a situation of socialist material plenitude, the right might become redundant. Abortion gets characterised as a 'transitional' need by omission, when no 'absolute' claims for its free availability are made.

An unconditional guarantee of free access to adequate contraception and abortion, with no intervening official inquisitions, is a principle to which contemporary feminism is committed. Yet this is unlikely to be enshrined as a permanent legislative right. For only 'overpopulated' States, or States confident that their projected demographic needs, however understood, are being met, will tolerate an absolutely unrestrictive abortion and contraception policy in the long term. Fears that a falling birthrate entails a falling standard of living, a shortage of workers and consumers, conflict with principles of 'women's rights'; the rights are likely to undergo some redefinitions and emerge as, for instance, the 'right to bear children free from anxiety'. Here the example of Eastern Europe is relevant, where the liberalised abortion laws of the mid-1950s resulted in low birthrates in the Soviet Union, Hungary, Czechoslovakia, and Rumania in particular.

The shape of governmental attempts in these countries to reverse what was taken to be a dangerously low or sub-replacement population level is of depressing interest to feminism. Practical effects have included the erratic and often radically changing provision of contraception and abortion facilities, generating a climate of unpredictability, far removed from any sympathy to the idea of sexual and procreative self-determination for women. One example of the workings of shifts in population policies is afforded by Rumania. The recent history of this country's reproductive interventions is, admittedly, extreme; but it carries some implications for the question of women's 'susceptibility' to pro-natalist measures. To give only a rough sketch of what happened there; before 1966 Rumania had an unrestrictive abortion law. But the birthrate had dropped to such an extent that at the end of 1966 extremely limiting legislation was introduced, suddenly. This followed a nine-year period in which women, in the virtual absence of contraception, had become more or less totally dependent on abortion as a method of birth control.[8]

The immediate result was a near-doubling of the birthrate in 1967, in what has been described as the largest single-year fertility leap ever experienced by any one large human population. But this initial enormous increase in the birthrate was accompanied by a rise in deaths associated with illegal abortion, in stillbirths and in the infant death rate. And the effects of the drastic anti-abortion legislation were short-lived. By 1972, the birthrate had dropped right back again although that legislation still stood. Presumably safer and more widespread illegal abortions, and a picking-up on whatever contraceptive means could be used, account for the decline in births. The huge rise, which must have included a high proportion of conceptions begun before the repeal of the abortion facilities, had been not only temporary but also acquired at the cost of high infant and maternal mortality.

It's not possible, as this example indicates, to account for fluctuations in fertility in terms of crude economic determinations only. Nor, over longer periods of time, does repressive legislation retain its initial grip. The Eastern European experiences suggest that where women want or can only adequately house small families, or none, pro-natalist incentives like tax cuts and nurseries make little impact. The 'susceptibility' of women to various forms of State intervention in fertility is a difficult attribution, in so far as it collapses together both psychological and material elements. It might be asked whether there are situations in which an ideological identification with State policies is lived by women, so as to give rise to a demonstrable response to pressures to increase or curtail the birthrate. But it's hard to sort out mechanical outcomes of restrictive legislation from a concurrence with social policy, or, indeed, to understand the density of factors behind an apparent concurrence. The rise in the birthrate in Nazi Germany is a case in point; it did increase sharply after 1933. How far, though, this was a reaction to new curbs on abortion and the lesser accessibility of contraception or was due to pro-family social policies and welfare reforms, is difficult to assess decisively.[9]

Speculations about the influence of legal interventions on women's reproductive behaviour need evidence from several sources, including demography and economic history, to strengthen them. But it's probably safe to conclude that, as a general principle, attempts to raise the birthrate in the long term by either anti-abortion legislation or by the provision of 'social incentives' to reproduce, or both together, are largely failures. On the other hand it seems that some lowering of fecundity stems from increased chances for women to work, be educated, and have childcare provisions. The making of reproductive choices does not happen in an area of pure 'expectation' divorced from what's been known and lived; fresh experiences — of going out to work, say — will influence the breadth of possible courses. There are, of course, enough ambiguities in what, at an individual level, it ever means to choose or refuse a pregnancy — as chapter 10, by Karen Greenwood and Lucy King illustrates. And at a social level, 'choice' is always caught up in a dense web of possibilities and provisions, supporting and trapping it.

Any discussion of what it means for a woman to 'choose' to have children or not must include an analysis of the existing opportunities for meeting the multiplicity of associated needs: housing, work, nurseries, to name the most evident. This is the point at which campaigns for unrestricted access to the technical means of reproductive control — contraception, abortion — meet the more generalised feminist aim of bringing about a climate in which a more truly free choice can be realised. The problem isn't only that of maintaining access, both in law and in practice, to the means of control — although this is and will stay deeply important. There's also the allied problem of increasing the material circumstances for the implementing of the choice brought about, at a first level, by the availability of physical means. This is where a feminist critique of 'individual' provision meets a feminist critique of 'social' provision.

Notes

1 This is a revised version of a paper originally given to a socialist feminist conference in Cambridge in 1975. I am grateful to Joan Herrmann for her help.

2 See, for example, Helene Deutsch's category of 'compulsive motherhood' in *The Psychology of Women* (1946, vol.2, *Motherhood*).

3 Recent developments here include the formation, in 1978, of the British Campaign against Depo-provera, and of ICAR, the International

Campaign for Abortion Rights, committed to an internationalist perspective on abortion and sterilisation. See also 'Population Control, Racism, and Imperialism' (1978) by Janet Hadley, a paper given to the Socialist Feminist National Conference (London, 1979).

4   According to Western press reports, current Chinese practice in some areas is to assign a 'quota' of births, determined by the national population 'Plan', to locally based groups of women workers, who will then decide among themselves which of them should conceive. That is, neither the model of a purely private, 'free' choice operates, nor that of the lone individual standing against encroaching authorities. See *The Guardian* April 23 1979, 'China's Answer doesn't Lie in the Coil' by John Gittings, and May 2 1979, 'Chinese Birth Control Penalises Larger Families' by Jay Mathews.

5   In the article 'The Working Class and Neo-Malthusianism', reprinted in *On the Emancipation of Women*. Lenin's letters to Inessa Armand, in the same collection, criticise the vagueness, in her draft propaganda pamphlet, of the demand for 'free love'. But the terms of the criticism return to the familiar orthodox-socialist grounds of class-based morality; 'free love,' Lenin writes, 'is a bourgeois and not a proletarian demand' which can't be taken to mean freedom from seriousness in love, freedom to commit adultery, or freedom from childbirth.

6   Earlier 'Leftist' theories about the abolition of the family had really been counter-Marxist, discriminating against the needs of women and children, according to the Soviet sociologists of the later 1930s. Thus Wolffson in *Socialism and the Family* (1949), 'The disgusting attempts to disguise a bourgeois attitude of exploitation in the relations of the sexes, by causing it to masquerade in quasi-revolutionary phraseology, should be firmly dealt with.'

7   The question, broadly, of why different economic conditions should be accompanied by apparently similar forms of familialism. Schlesinger suggests that the earlier toleration by the Bolsheviks of, for instance, unmarried motherhood, wasn't unconnected with the then numerical discrepancy between the sexes.

8   Under the new law, abortion was allowed only for those over 45, those who already had at least four children, of whom four were still at home; and for medical reasons or where conception resulted from rape or incest. Simultaneously, divorce was restricted and tax incentives for having larger families were introduced. Imports of contraceptives were stopped. The general absence of contraceptive education and distribution of supplies which accompanied the abortion laws in Eastern Europe meant that abortion constituted the most available form of provided contraception. This may in part be ascribed to an official association between a systematic contraceptive policy, and neo-Malthusianism. Marx and Engels' critiques of Malthus, although produced in the historical and political circumstances of later nineteenth-century capitalism, were read as if they permanently guaranteed the impossibility of 'real overpopulation'. It was

assumed by Soviet political economists that full employment and State welfare provision would of themselves entail a rapid rise of the population to the desired level.

9   See Tim Mason's discussion in his 'Women in Nazi Germany' (1976). He considers that, whereas attempts to suppress the practice of illegal abortion probably were significant in their impact, positive pro-natalist moves did not work. 'Aside from the marriage loan scheme, however, and this only to a certain extent, none of the régime's positive policies can be demonstrated in any methodologically conclusive manner to have played any part in bringing about this result.'

Further Reading

L. Gordon, *Woman's Body, Woman's Right*. Harmondsworth: Penguin, 1977.

R.Meek (ed.), *Marx and Engels on Malthus*. London: Lawrence & Wishart, 1953.

H. Scott, *Women and Socialism; Experiences from Eastern Europe*. London: Motive Books, Allison & Busby, 1976.

R. Schlesinger (ed.), *Changing Attitudes in Soviet Russia; The Family in the USSR*, London: Routledge & Kegan Paul, 1949.

Section IV

Nature/Culture: theories of sexual difference

Chapter Twelve

'If it's natural, we can't change it'[1]

ELENA LIEVEN

This chapter deals with the attempts to provide scientific support for the view that there is a biological basis to the different tasks that women and men perform, and that because this basis is biological it is foolhardy, impossible and 'unnatural' to attempt to change it. A 'compendium' statement which incorporates the various ways of putting this position would run as follows: 'In all primate species it is the female who is biologically adapted to bear the young and feed them after birth. This has certain consequences for social organisation such that males and females tend to perform different tasks in the social group. Behavioural characteristics appropriate to these tasks have been selected for genetically during evolution; and evidence for this can be found both in the universal sexual division of labour found in human (and other primate) societies and in sex differences in human behaviours such as visuo-spatial tasks, language and aggression. Since there is a genetic basis for these behaviours which generates physical entities in the body — hormones and brain structures, for example — the behaviours are difficult or impossible to modify, and the sexual division of labour in modern societies which occurs as a result of them is both natural and desirable. Attempts to change it are therefore doomed to failure.'[2]

In challenging the logic of such statements, I shall organise my arguments around three central points:

(1) The dualism inherent in the contrasts between nature and culture, biological and social, is untenable and unscientific. Every human action is biological — we experience through our senses and we act with our bodies (including our brain cells). But every human action is also social — it is mediated from within (the body) and

without by social meanings which are created culturally.

(2) The evidence upon which statements similar to the one above are based is at best unclear and at worst downright distorted. Most of the behavioural differences between the sexes cited in support of such statements have either not been replicated in subsequent experiments and/or are not nearly as clear-cut as many who comment on them would claim. In addition, the conclusions drawn from such unsatisfactory evidence by biological determinists are completely invalid in terms of their consequences both for the individual and for society, even where there is reasonable evidence that a difference between the performance of the two sexes on some psychological task can be demonstrated. In view of this, the efforts of such writers to uphold a biologically determinist position must be put down to ideology rather than science.[3]

(3) There is a continual failure by those who address the issue of the social implications of behavioural differences between the sexes to keep to the appropriate level of explanation for the phenomena under consideration. This work is full of illegitimate leaps — for instance, from physiological data to conclusions about some social phenomenon. For, as Sahlins (1977) puts it: 'A fixed correspondence being lacking between the character of society and the human character, there can be no biological determinism.' (p.11)

It is important for those of us who wish to bring about radical social change to be armed against scientistic (seemingly scientific) arguments which seek to prove the impossibility of change. To be so armed means that we must avoid falling into the same traps as the determinists: those of dualism and of confused levels of explanation. This chapter is intended as notes towards such an armament.

1 Biological/social, nature/culture

This section challenges the view that if there is a genetic (and, by implication, hormonal or anatomical) basis to differences between the sexes, then this has determinist implications for individual behaviour. Since the arguments against this view are various and sometimes complex, I have put them under headings for ease of assimilation.

Genotype and phenotype

The genetic material in the zygote immediately after the fusion of ovum and sperm exists in isolation from environmental influence at the moment of fusion only. As this genetic material starts to construct the enzymes determined by the protein code (DNA) that it contains, there begins a continuous interplay between the current state of the organism and its immediate environment. Certainly the genetic material has been buffered against certain kinds of environmental variation through the process of natural selection whereby, for this material to remain in the gene pool of a species, the individual must survive for long enough to reproduce. But there is no absolute, unilineal relation between the presence of a particular gene and the existence of a particular feature in the individual whether this feature is anatomical (e.g. brain structure), physiological (e.g. hormones) or behavioural (e.g. mental retardation). The environment can effect quite different phenotypic outcomes from exactly identical genotypes. For instance, if two plants with identical genetic material (genotypes) are grown in different environments, one at the bottom of a mountain and the other at the top, they will have entirely different heights (i.e. they will have different phenotypes). To give another example, this time related to a more complex phenomenon − the human disease called Phenylketonuria (PKU) which, if left untreated, usually results in severe mental retardation. PKU is caused by the failure to metabolise, for use by the body, a substance called phenylalanine. This substance appears to be necessary for normal brain function and it is usually quickly metabolised for this purpose. People with PKU, however, have unusually high concentrations of it in their blood and urine because they lack the enzyme which metabolises it. In the foetus phenylalanine is metabolised by the mother's body, but as soon as a child with PKU is born, phenylalanine starts to build up in the body and most of these children become mentally retarded unless they are rapidly placed on an alanine-free diet. Nowadays, in countries with reasonable standards of health care, newborn babies are tested for the presence of phenylalanine in their urine and, if it is found, they are immediately placed on an alanine-free diet which, other things being equal,[4] prevents the development of mental retardation. The important point about PKU, for our purposes, is that it is known to be caused by a single gene which results in the lack of a particular enzyme present in people who do not have PKU. Thus it has a clear, unigenetic basis. However the *effects* of this gene can differ − the way in which the gene is expressed will take different forms depending whether the child is born into a society which can afford to test newborns for PKU or into one that cannot. Society has thus changed the mode of expression of this gene through conscious choice based on scientific understanding of the biological processes involved. Although genes are always expressed, *how* they are expressed will depend on the environmental factors.

Complex behaviour and multiple genetic involvement

The factors that go into making one person 'better' at some complex skill such as language or spatial orientation than another will *never* involve just one, particular 'piece' of genetic material, let alone one carried on the sex-chromosome (which it has to be in order for the claim for a genetic basis to a particular difference between the sexes to go through). To be sure, the genetic material can set limits of possibility, *given a particular environment* (this is called the 'norm of reaction' of the gene): those born deaf as a result of genetic factors will not learn to speak unless adjustments are made to their environment, those born blind will not be able to orient themselves visually, those born with PKU and not treated will be at the lower end of the range of 'intelligence'. Yet even in this last example, there will be great differences in the performance on IQ tests of a group of children who have untreated PKU and this will be due to the differences in their original genotypes and their mode of expression in different environments. The most simple psychological test involves a great array of behaviours for its proper performance – motivational, attentional, intellectual and social. In one sense both obvious and uninteresting, there is genetic involvement in all of these. But to claim that *one*, sex-linked gene is responsible for differences in performance between the sexes on even the simplest psychological test is highly misleading. When the claim is extended to differences in complex learned behaviours it is positively mischievous.

Genes, groups and individuals

Even if it could be conclusively shown that there was a genetic involvement in sex differences in performance on a well-defined task, this would have no implications whatsoever for the question of whether any particular individual could be trained to improve her or his performance on that task. Even where there is evidence of a reliable difference in performance between the sexes on some task *and* there is reasonable evidence that this may in part be related to a sex-linked gene, this tells us nothing about the limitations that any one individual will have in learning this task (Archer, 1976). This is because such limitations will be a function of the 'norm of reaction' of each genotype in a particular environment, and this cannot be determined *a priori*. There is no reason to suppose that the norm of reaction (the range of phenotypic variation possible for a given genotype, see above) will be the same for different genotypes in the 'same' environment. There is no necessary relation between a particular characteristic being available for selection at the level of the gene pool (which is what 'a genetic basis to the differences between two groups' means) and the possibilities for influencing it environmentally. In fact, in the enormous range of skills of which humans are capable, there is only *one* for which there is the remotest evidence for the involvement of a sex-linked gene; that is visuo-spatial performance on the Embedded Figure Test and the Rod and Frame test[5] (Maccoby and Jacklin, 1975, pp.120−2). Even here there is considerable argument about the evidence for a sex-linked gene, but for our purposes the important point is that even if it could be shown conclusively that such a gene existed, this would have no necessary implication for whether an individual could be *taught* visuo-spatial skills nor for how such a gene would be expressed in different environments. Indeed, there is some evidence that sex differences in visuo-spatial skills disappear with training (Chance and Goldstein, 1971). In addition, there is cross-cultural evidence that in some societies sex differences in visuo-spatial skills are not found (the Eskimo; Berry, 1966) and in others the difference in means between the two sexes is much greater than in the original study (India; Parlee and Rajagopol, 1974). Presumably if there is a sex-linked gene for visuo-spatial skills, environmental differences in these societies may be changing its mode of expression.

Defining the variable

At least when we are considering visuo-spatial skills, we can identify a set of specific tests on which performance by an individual relative to a group is highly correlated, and some writers are careful to confine their discussions of visuo-spatial ability to just these tasks (we shall return to those who do not in the next two sections). However, this is certainly not the case for most of the skills and behaviours discussed by determinists in support of their position. Even something as potentially susceptible to definition and measurement as 'language' has been 'measured' by a wide range of different behaviours, for instance amount of speech, complexity of syntax or semantics, vocabulary size and content, and very many others. Of course, the rank ordering of an individual within a group may be the same when some of these measures are tested, but may differ in some others. Thus it would be necessary to test individuals on a wide range of language measures and to be certain of a reasonable degree of inter-correlation for any particular individual before drawing conclusions about differences in linguistic skills between groups or individuals. When we come to a hypothetical construct such as 'aggression', which the determinists claim underlies a vast range of behaviours in both animals and humans, the problem of definition becomes acute. It is frequently claimed that primate males and females (and this includes humans) differ as groups in the 'amount of aggression' that they have and this in turn is thought to be linked to the greater quantities of the 'male' hormone, testosterone which circulates in males at particular points in development. 'Aggression' is taken to underlie such disparate activities in primate males as fighting for access to a female, fighting off predators and play fighting; in humans it encompasses the 'rough and tumble' play of small children, answers to personality questionnaires designed to 'measure aggression' and some of the behaviours involved in sport and capitalism. But, as far as I am aware, there is little or no evidence of any correlation between these various measures for a specific individual — yet surely such evidence is an absolute necessity before we can arrive at the conclusion that there is one underlying entity that is generating all these behaviours rather than that a number of different and interacting aspects of the individual and her or his social environment are involved? Nor, again as far as I am aware, is there any evidence of a correlation between the levels of testosterone circulating in different individuals and their levels of 'aggression' (however measured). There is some evidence for an effect on 'activity levels' of the injection of testosterone in *chicks* and on the adult sexual behaviour of *rats* which are subjected to different kinds of surgical and hormonal interference pre-natally, post-natally and in adulthood (Rogers, 1976). But, in the latter case this has nothing to do with 'aggression', and in the former, detailed research to establish a high correlation between 'activity level' and some measure of 'aggression' would be necessary for it to be possible to claim a relation between level of testosterone and 'aggression' even in chicks. In the one study that I know of in humans which attempts to correlate 'activity level' (in neonates) with 'rough and tumble play' (in pre-schoolers), there was an inverse correlation for boys (that is on average the boys who appeared most 'active' at birth (as measured by latency to respond to a bottle being removed from their mouth) were the most 'passive' in the pre-school situation (in the sense of standing quietly watching the other children rather than getting involved in games) (Bell *et al.*, 1971, reported in Maccoby and Jacklin, 1975, p.171).[6]

I have been arguing that to even minimally support a relation between a particular hormone (or its relative level) and certain behavioural phenomena, these phenomena must be clearly and explicitly defined. And to assert an underlying unity to a number of different behavioural phenomena such a unity must be clearly demonstrated. I shall now argue that *even if* a relation between a 'bit' of biology (e.g. a hormone) and a 'bit' of behaviour could be shown and *even if* some underlying correlational unity to various forms of behaviour could be demonstrated, *this would certainly not allow us to conclude that biology determined behaviour.*

Individual differences and social meanings

Individual differences between children which originate in the first instance in their genetic make-up will indeed be involved in the way that each child develops and changes, but such differences will always be expressed through social meanings — there is no other way for them to appear. Hormones certainly circulate in the bodies of individuals, but how the associated physical sensations are related to the conscious experience of the individual and her/his behaviour is a matter of the cultural meanings available to the child as she/he grows up. Sahlins (1977) makes this point convincingly:

> Thus, while the human world depends on the senses, and the whole panoply of organic characteristics supplied by biological evolution, its freedom from biology consists in just the capacity to give these their own sense. . . . Culture is not ordered by the primitive emotions of the hypothalamus; it is the emotions which are organised by culture. We have not to deal, therefore, with a biological sequence of events proceeding from the genotype to the social type by way of a phenotype already programmed by natural selection. The structure of determinations is a hierarchical one set the other way round: a meaningful system of the world and human experience that was already in existence before any of the current human participants were born, and that from birth engages their natural dispositions as the instruments of a symbolic project (1977, pp.12–13).

So, for example, a study by Moss (1967) found differences in the average amount of crying between a group of girls and a group of boys at three weeks of age. The boys cried more and their mothers spent more time in various caretaking behaviours with them. However, at three months, although the boys were still, on average, crying more than the girls, there were no differences in these caretaking measures between the mothers of boys and the mothers of girls. Most of the measures on which mothers showed differences at three weeks were on the sorts of behaviours that one would associate with attempting to prevent a child crying (holding, attending). It seems possible, then, that by three months, the mothers of the boys were responding differently to them by virtue of the fact that they *were boys* rather than as a function of the amount of crying. If this is indeed what was happening, we have an example of a response to the child based on a complex interplay between the child's sex, its actual behaviour and the mother's perception of it as a boy. I have argued at length in chapter 15 that membership by anatomy of one or the other sex is not a neutral biological fact but a complex social fact, and this study might be taken to support such an argument. Indeed, we know that adults respond differently to the *same* behaviour in an unfamiliar baby depending on whether they *think* the child is a boy or a girl but independently of whether *it actually is* a boy or a girl (Frisch, 1977).

To take another example of the social mediation of behaviour, let us look at 'aggression'. There is good evidence for wide variation both in the overall amount of different kinds of aggressive behaviour in different societies and in overall differences between the sexes in any particular society. Mead (1935) observed that men and women of the Arapesh tribe in New Guinea were not expected to differ in temperament and, indeed, did not. In contrast, for the Yanomamo of Brazil, 'aggressiveness' is even more part of the social definition of being male than it is in our own (Chagnon, 1977). A study by Ward (1970) of a Hongkong fishing village provides an informative example of one of the ways in which 'aggressive behaviour' may be socially mediated. Ward observed a high incidence of temper tantrums in 5-10-year-olds (particularly boys) in this village. When she investigated this phenomenon, she found that these tantrums were usually brought on by deliberate teasing of the child by an adult, for instance the adult would offer food to the child and then, just as the child was reaching for it, would snatch the food away. Children were thus put into situations of social stress in which they had no option but either to learn resignation or to indulge in repeated and unpleasant frenzy. Ward hypothesised that this was an unconscious strategy on the part of this society which was related to the fact that the people lived in very overcrowded conditions under which manifest anger and fighting among adults was thoroughly disruptive. She also observed that it was rare in the extreme to see an adult lose her/his temper, and when it did happen (usually when the person was drunk) it was a source of acute embarrassment to be quickly hushed up. Whatever the emotional predispositions of the young child in this society were initially, and whatever the contribution of specific internal and external factors to them, they have been transformed and translated into cultural reality by the symbolic transactions of the child's development in that society. Of course there are biological differences between individuals and between the sexes, but how each individual – female or male — expresses her/himself will be a matter of the social meanings available which become incorporated into that individual's subjectivity.

Biology may set limits and constraints in an unchanging environment, but what these are cannot be decided in advance of testing for them under environmental changes; thus there can be no determinism of behaviour by biology. What is more, and again I quote Sahlins 'a limit is only a negative determination; it does not positively specify how the constraint is realised' (1977, p.64). Finally, whatever these negative determinations of biology are, they are definitively not the ones claimed by biological determinists, as I shall show in the next two sections of this chapter.

2 Evidence

I shall not summarise here the evidence on psychological and behavioural differences between the sexes, since there exists in the literature a number of careful reviews of sex differences in cognition (Fairweather, 1976), sex differences in language (Macauley, 1978), sex differences in infancy (Birns, 1976) and the biological basis of sex differences (see chapters in Lloyd and Archer, 1976). In addition I shall confine myself to a discussion of what we might call 'behavioural' differences (sensory thresholds, language skills, visuo-spatial skills) and 'temperamental' differences (aggression, passivity) in contrast to 'attitudinal' differences (self-reliance, dependence, perceptions of others). Determinists tend to concentrate on the former and, if they discuss the latter at all, it is usually only to 'explain' them in terms of what they regard as these more basic differences between the sexes. Sayers (in press) provides an excellent review of the bias and distortion apparent in work on what I have called 'attitudinal' differences. In this section I give just one example of the kind of distortion that regularly occurs and recurs in the literature on 'basic psychological traits', and then consider what legitimate conclusions can be drawn in the case that a difference between the sexes on some behavioural measure has been convincingly established.

It is often reported that there are sex differences in all aspects of language skills throughout development, girls being 'better' than boys (Hutt, 1972; Buffery and Gray, 1972; Garai and Sheinfeld, 1968). Indeed, this was an accepted 'fact' in developmental psychology for many years. It was an important part of the argument for determinists like Hutt and evolutionists like Buffery and Gray that this difference between boys and girls manifests itself very early in development (since it was argued that it was therefore more likely to be innate). But the studies upon which this conclusion was based were largely carried out in the 1930s and 1940s (see Maccoby and Jacklin, 1975, pp.75−85).[7] More recent studies have not tended to support this finding. One apparent exception is the work of Moore (1967), cited by Hutt (1972). In this study Moore followed a group of children longitudinally, testing the same children on 21 different measures of language development in all, at the ages of 18 months, 3, 5 and 8 years. He found only *one* significant difference between the group of girls and the group of boys *at any age* and this was in something he calls the 'speech quotient', but does not define. Whatever it is, it can hardly be of great significance since, as Macauley (1978) points out, this measure showed a difference between the groups at eighteen months, but there were *no* significant differences between the *same two groups of children* at *3, 5 or 8 years*. Moore did find that the rank ordering of the girls on early measures of language skills predicted their rank ordering at the later test points, while this was not the case for boys. This may well be an interesting finding, if it can be replicated, but it surely does not allow Moore to conclude his paper in the following terms:

> The little girl, showing in her domestic play the overriding absorption in personal relationships through which she will later fulfill her role as wife . . . learns language early in order to communicate. . . . Her intellectual performance is relatively predictable because it is rooted in this early communication, which enables her (environment permitting) to display her inherited potential at an early age. . . . [Boys'] preoccupation with the working of mechanical things is less interesting to most mothers,. . . . Probably too, effective communication about cause and effect presupposes a later stage of mental development than does communication about household routines. . . . His [the boy's] language, less fluent and personal and later to appear than the girl's, develops along more analytic lines and may, in favourable circumstances, provide the groundwork for later intellectual achievement which could not have been forseen in his first few years.
> The girl, meanwhile, is acquiring the intimate knowledge of human reactions which we call feminine intuition. Perhaps because human reactions are less regular than those of inanimate objects, however, she is less likely to develop the strictly logical habits of thought that intelligent boys acquire, and if gifted may well come to prefer the subtler disciplines of the humanities to the intellectual rigour of science. (pp.100−101)

All this on the basis of one significant difference between the group of boys and the group of girls at eighteen months and no others on any measure either at the same age or at 3, 5 or 8 years, together with some evidence of differences between the sexes on the predictability of their later language skills from earlier measures!

I do not wish to claim that there are no differences between the sexes in language skills — there may very well be and it is possible that some of them may be in the areas that Moore refers to. But there is little evidence of it at present, at least in young children. Indeed, it is extraordinarily difficult to find reliable and replicable evidence of almost *any* difference between the sexes on measures of 'basic' psychological traits. Where evidence of such differences is cited it usually falls into one of the following categories:

(a) it is the only one out of numerous studies to show a significant difference (Maccoby and Jacklin, 1975, p.6);

(b) citing the evidence for a difference, the original study is distorted (see Birns, 1976, for the way in which Moss's 1967 study has been distorted in the literature);

(c) so many analyses of the data were made that the finding of a significant difference might well have occurred by chance (see Fairweather, 1976);

(d) the study in which a sex difference was found was not originally designed to test for sex differences but the experimenter decides to 'throw in' an analysis for sex differences as 'an afterthought' (again Fairweather, 1976, comments on this practice) — the point about this being that the conclusions drawn are often entirely invalid in terms of the design of the study.

In view of all this, it is difficult not to conclude that authors who insist on quoting distortions of the available evidence on sex differences are processing such evidence through an ideological filter (certainly unconscious in many cases) which 'needs' to find differences in psychological traits in order to claim their origin in biology and their significance in explaining the differences in occupation between the sexes in modern societies. But, and we now come to the second, and crucial point of this section: even where it *is* possible to establish an, on average, difference between the sexes on some psychological trait, this does not have any consequences whatsoever for our knowledge about individuals nor does it allow the conclusion that women and men are fitted to different types of occupation in our society — still less that they should be excluded from some and forced into others.

Sex differences between groups of females and males on some behaviour always refer to a difference in the *means* in scored performance on the task or measure. This gives the statistical probability of performance on the test by an individual drawn from the same 'population'[8] on which the test was originally carried out − it tells us nothing at all about the likely performance of any actual individual on the test unless there is absolutely no overlap at all between the scores of the two groups. For instance, suppose there was some trait which a firm absolutely required all trainees to have − perhaps a twitch in the left eyebrow to trip some photosensitive switch. Only in the event that a test of eyebrow twitching in groups of men and women randomly drawn from all parts of the population who might apply for the traineeship, demonstrated that no woman ever performed an eyebrow twitch and some men did, could the firm be sure that, in excluding women from the applicants, they were not losing a brilliant eyebrow twitcher! The largest and most reliable sex difference yet established is for a difference in the means of performance by females and males in some 'Western cultures' on the Embedded Figures Test and the Rod and Frame test. The difference in means (for the American sample) was about half a standard deviation, with boys on average better than girls (Maccoby and Jacklin, 1975, p.352). This is not a very large difference at all − i.e. there will be many girls who score higher than many boys. Thus one could not predict the *actual* performance of *any individual* girl or boy from this finding. If one wanted to predict the *statistical likelihood* of finding a certain number of girls or boys who performed at a particular level on these tasks then the findings of these studies would be helpful, but this would only make any sense if one was considering a very large group indeed; it would make no sense at all if one was selecting a group of say, ten people, who were required to show a particular level of performance on tasks of visuo-spatial skill. Indeed, studies to test for a sex difference, even on visuo-spatial skills, have to be carried out on very large and well-controlled samples before such a difference can be demonstrated and, even then, it is not always found.

It has often been claimed that the difference in means of performance on visuo-spatial skills explains why there are so many more male architects and engineers (e.g. Coltheart, 1975). Among the points to be made here are: (1) As Sayers (in press) points out, this claim is made in the complete absence of any research on the psychological traits that contribute to success in the professions under consideration. (2) It is quite probable that someone, female or male, would be unlikely to end up in the professions of architect or engineer if they showed a complete inability to do visuo-spatial tasks − and there are plenty of people who do show this inability in the present environmental circumstances. But there are also plenty of women who show perfectly adequate performance on such tasks: just as adequate, I would surmise (though, of course, this either has not been investigated or is not reported in the literature), as that of many men who currently occupy positions as architects and engineers. (3) We shall only be able to *commence* the investigation of the contribution of various psychological traits to performance in complex tasks when it can be shown that all other barriers to performance on these tasks (e.g. discriminatory education, discriminatory recruitment, different self-evaluations on the part of women and men independent of their *actual* competence) have been abolished. Until such time, statements such as Coltheart's above can only be regarded as ideological rather than scientific. (This is perhaps an appropriate point to note that the hypothesised greater ability of women in linguistic skills does not lead authors to argue for their greater involvement in all forms of work that might be considered to require such skills − advertising, the theatre, political oratory, foreign language teaching, translation, etc. − but only to confirm women in their traditional role of bringing up children and ensuring their adequate language acquisition! Hutt 1972; Gray and Buffery, 1971).[9] I have concentrated on visuo-spatial skills in this discussion because it is in these that reasonably reliable evidence of differences between the sexes have been found, and I wished to examine the implications of sex differences where they are convincingly established. It should be clear that precisely the same arguments will hold for *any* sex difference found under present social conditions.

Let me reiterate that I am not saying that, in principle, there *can* be no differences in psychological traits between the sexes. I am arguing that:

(1) where research on sex differences has been carried out 'in good faith', surprisingly few have been found;

(2) the conclusions about the current division of labour in society drawn from 'evidence' on sex differences have no substance both because of the nature of this 'evidence' and because of the illogical conclusions drawn from it;

(3) we can only discover whether there really are differences in psychological traits between the sexes when all other extraneous contributions to differential performance have been removed;

(4) if differences between the sexes are found on some task, this has no consequences for any *individual's* performance on that task and its consequences for the adequate performance of any job in society would need to be clearly demonstrated empirically.

We know that there is a wider variation of individual difference on any psychological trait within each sex than between the sexes, yet this has rarely been the object of study. We also know that human beings have immense capacities for learning and that many of the psychological traits that determinists are interested in can be greatly affected by training and experience. If science establishes that there is an, on average, difference in performance between two groups on some psychological measure, then obvious questions to ask are: how much can this difference be affected by training and how much has the difference been contributed to by differential experience between the groups? If the answers to these questions are 'greatly', then the decision not to train the group that is inferior on the trait is a *social* decision, based, presumably, on an estimation of the effort required, the resources available and the possible benefits to the individuals involved and to the society. Why is it that determinists never face these issues? Because, as Sahlins puts it:

> Between 'aggression' and 'Vietnam' . . . biology offers us merely an enormous intellectual void. Its place can be filled only by a theory of the nature and dynamics of culture as a meaningful system. Within the void left by biology lies the whole of anthropology [sociology and politics]. (Sahlins, 1977).

Let us examine this void.

3 Levels of explanation

What is it that determinists are seeking to establish by drawing attention to evidence for sex differences in behaviour? Here is a quotation from Hutt:

> This greater sensitivity to touch and to pain is an intrinsic characteristic of the female and has been observed from the moment of birth. Females also hear better than males: their auditory discrimination and localisation is superior at all ages. Males, on the other hand, see better. These sex-typical advantages in sensory capacities are not learned or acquired through particular forms of experience: they are evident in infancy. Even at a few weeks of age boys show more interest in visual patterns, while infant girls attend more to tonal sequences. Differences in sensitivity mean that males and females are likely to respond differently to the same stimuli (Kagan, 1969). In his memorable report, Kinsey commented on the greater susceptibility of the adult male to visually erotic stimuli. *The sensitivity first evident in the cradle is amply exploited by the strip-teaser and pornographer.* (1972, p.83, my emphasis)

Leaving to one side the issue of whether data on early sensory capacity is as clear-cut as Hutt claims (it is not, see Birns, 1976), this extract is a beautiful example of a complete confusion between different levels of description and explanation for the following reasons:

(a) there is, to my knowledge, no evidence of a relationship *in adults* between visual sensitivity (in the psychophysical sense) and 'response to visually erotic stimuli';

(b) Kinsey's work was conducted in the 1950s by *interviewing* men and women. Whatever the internal response of these people to erotic material, one could not possibly conclude that men and women would be likely to respond similarly to the request to reveal it;

(c) there is still a 'double standard' in society in respect of attitudes to pornography, which makes it impossible to treat the reactions of men and women to it on the same 'scale of measurement';

(d) most, if not all, pornography is sexist and exploitative of women – one would therefore expect on these, if no other, grounds that men's and women's responses to it would differ.

For these reasons, even if there were the clearest possible evidence for an absolute and opposite predominance of one sensory modality over another in infant males as opposed to infant females, Hutt's conclusion as to the origin of the supposed differential effects of visual pornography would be absurd. As things stand it is worse than absurd. This example is an extreme case and I have included it because I assume that most people would reject its logic out of hand. If this is the case, then it is not a particularly dangerous example of the logic I am criticising (although, as I write, memories of articles on pornography in newspapers and the 'natural' tendency of men to enjoy pornography prevent me from being too certain of its manifest absurdity to many people). However, arguments using precisely the same logic abound (they are extremely prevalent in Hutt's book), and these are very dangerous indeed since, despite the incoherence of their logic, they arrive at conclusions which many people want to hear – they give 'scientific' support to the status quo and argue against the possibility of change. If change is 'scientifically' impossible then one does not have to worry about whether it would be politically or ethically desirable.

Some of the best examples of these types of arguments come from those who claim an evolutionary basis for the supposed differences in various skills between the sexes. The evidence for a basis in evolution is drawn from data on present-day primate species, present-day hunter-gatherer societies (the assumption is made that these people live in 'simpler' societies which are in some way more similar to those of our ancestors than to our own) and from theories of hominid evolution.

This work ranges from the merely unlikely through the badly mis-informed to the downright absurd. Let us start with the work of Gray and Buffery (1971). These authors argue that the advantage of females over males in linguistic skills has been selected for in evolution as a result of the fact that it is women who have always had the task of rearing children (and language acquisition in children is of prime evolutionary significance). In addition, they claim that the advantage of males over females in visuo-spatial skills has been selected for evolutionarily since males have traditionally been the hunters and have therefore had more need of finding their way around. These conclusions are merely extremely unlikely. If there are sex differences in linguistic skills at all, they do not seem to be present in early development and they are definitively not of the order or kind to make any difference to language acquisition in children who spend their time with women as opposed to men (Buffery and Gray in a more recent article (1972) admit that where sex differences in size of vocabu-lary are found it is the groups of boys who have larger vocabulary ranges than the groups of girls!). As for the argument about the evolu-tionary advantage of better visuo-spatial skills in males, this too seems extraordinarily weak. In societies where there is a sexual division of labour in which men do the hunting, women do the *gathering*, and they range far and wide, often having to track down a particular kind of foodstuff on the basis of minimal environmental cues. A very much closer examination and analysis of the relative skills involved in the visuo-spatial orientation for both tasks would be crucial before any conclusion of the Buffery and Gray type was admissible. However, while Buffery and Gray claim that a genetic basis for these sex differ-ences is 'specified in the gene pool', they are careful not to draw any conclusions about present-day social organisation. Other writers are not nearly so careful. For instance, E.O. Wilson, the well-known sociobiologist, says:

> The building block of nearly all human societies is the nuclear family (Reynolds 1968; Leibowitz 1968). The populace of an American industrial city, no less than a band of hunter-gatherers in the Australian desert, is organised around this unit. In both cases the family moves between regional communities, maintaining complex ties with primary kin by means of visits (or telephone calls or letters) and the exchange of gifts. *During the day the women and children remain in the residential area while the men forage for game or its symbolic equivalent in the form of barter or money.* The men cooperate in bands to hunt or deal with neighbouring groups. (1975, p.553, my emphasis)

By asserting a unity across cultures and across time, Wilson here distorts the facts about the sexual division of labour in both the modern American city and hunter-gatherer societies. As I have just pointed out, the women of hunter-gatherer societies range far and wide in search of food, and there is an overwhelming amount of evidence for the involvement of women in the exchange of goods not only in hunter-gatherer societies but in almost every other 'type' of society which anthropologists and sociologists have studied. Wilson pays no attention whatsoever to the extremely complex factors responsible for the widely varying forms of social organisation and of the sexual division of labour found in different societies, and furthermore goes on to consider, on the basis of the sort of analysis cited above, 'some implications for the planning of future societies' (p.548). To move finally to an example of the 'downright absurd' level of argument that one can find in this literature, I turn to the work of Tiger (1969) which is extensively drawn on by Wilson:

> The hypothesis attempts to explain why certain social functions are performed by males and not females. I have suggested that the fact that males are stronger than females, that they are more directly socialised to accept and use violence, that they form the major structures of defence and police in all communities, all generally reflect a 'genetically preprogrammed behavioural disposition'. The cross-cultural incidence of the pattern is the result of more than inter-cultural diffusion of practices and the maintenance of tradition.
>
> The willingness to display 'followership' to males in situations of violence and disorder may be directly related to the apparently widespread unwillingness to appoint or elect females to posts of high responsibility. By analogy the leadership structure of hamadryas baboon troops can be seen to be male-dominated. The management of crisis is normally the function of males. While I am not saying there is a necessary connection between baboon patterns and human patterns (though it has already been noted that terrestiality may be central to the development of male dominance among primates), I am proposing that 'human nature' is such that it is 'unnatural' for females to engage in defence, police, and, by implication, high politics.
> (Tiger, 1969, p.86, Tiger's use of quotation marks, parentheses and caveats is all his own)

and again:

> Even a but partly female-dominated polity may go beyond the parameters of 'healthy' possibility, given the basic conservatism of the species. (p.205)

The first quotation from Tiger is a classic example of the evolutionary determinism that I am criticising. Almost every word in it requires adequate definition (as Tiger himself seems to be aware judging by his use of quotation marks): to give a few examples: 'followership', 'management of crisis', 'terrestiality', 'human nature', 'unnatural', 'healthy'. The unity which (for all his caveats) he asserts between hamadryas baboon troops and human societies would be an entirely inadequate and misleading characterisation of the social structure of all primate groups, even excluding man. As a description which is intended to encompass the breadth and variety of all human cultures, it is nonsensical (see Brown's chapter 14). But it is an extremely good example of the attempt to read into 'nature' characteristics which the author thinks are desirable in the human race (and which he would like to show to be unchangeable) and then to assert that since they are 'natural' they *are* therefore unchangeable. I can do no better than to quote Sahlins again:

> Since Hobbes, at least, the competitive and acquisitive characteristics of Western man have been confounded with Nature, and the Nature thus fashioned in the human image has been in turn reapplied to the explanation of Western man. The effect of this dialectic has been to anchor the properties of human social action, as we conceive them, in Nature, and the laws of nature in our conceptions of human social action. Human society is natural, and natural societies are curiously human (1977, p.93).

But, as he also points out, using an elementary law of logic:

> Of course it is true that all Americans are humans, but it is not true that all humans are American — and still less that all animals are Americans. (p.87)

The kinds of arguments that we are considering here impose a unity across species — for instance, in the 'aggression' of males — and then proceed to explain the phenomena of the social world and to argue for their inevitability by an appeal to this 'fact of nature'. In the first section of this paper, I argued that there was no necessary relation in the individual between some biological event and some social event (for instance, between the circulation of testosterone and the expression of 'aggression'). Precisely the same argument applies here where the attempt is being made to argue from some hypothesised behavioural feature of individuals to a social phenomenon such as war, capitalism or competitiveness. Not all people (or even probably most people) who engage in war do so because of 'feelings of aggression' — most are probably terrified, and to argue that wars are the result of male aggression is to ignore all the economic, political and ideological factors which are involved in war. An argument which moves from some hypothesised individual propensity to some complex social phenomenon leaps the 'void' that I referred to earlier. This void is filled with the systems of symbolic meaning upon which cultures exist — they are studied by anthroplogists, economists, historians and sociologists to name but a few. There is, what Sahlins calls 'a critical indeterminacy' (1977) between these symbolic systems and the motivations of the individuals who engage with them and restructure them.

Conclusion

In examining the style of argument of which Tiger is such an excellent example, I am not primarily concerned with the distortions in the evidence — though these abound, whether the authors are discussing early hominids, primate species, hunter-gatherer societies or modern industrial societies. It is the structure of the argument that interests me here. It goes as follows: 'Impose a false unity on complex facts of social organisation in early hominids, primates, hunter-gatherer societies, then claim that, since such a unity exists, it must be specified genetically (draw on psychological evidence for sex differences where you can — where you cannot, imply that such evidence exists). Then claim, either by implication or explicitly, that such biological underpinnings for sexual divisions in societies mean that these differences are desirable, natural and, in any case, unmodifiable.'[10]

I hope that, in this chapter, I have provided some tools for countering such arguments which, though illogical and ideologically loaded, are also extremely convenient. In my opinion, it is vitally important that those seeking to change sexual divisions in our society challenge the kinds of work that I have been criticising here. It is not as if such work was confined to the more obscure academic journals — quite the reverse. It is one of the few areas of the behavioural sciences which receives widespread attention and popularisation, not only by journalists and commentators but by the 'scientists' themselves. However, the arguments are complex and can be superficially very convincing, and their (spuriously) scientific nature may also make them seem hard to refute. The problem will not be solved by countering with arguments cast in the same mould — for instance by denying sex differences where they have been shown to exist, or searching for one society in which females hunt as well as males in order to 'disprove' the claims about male 'aggression'. What we must counter in particular is the false logic which allows erroneous conclusions to be drawn from the evidence (doubtful as it also often is). Biological determinism derives from an untenable contrast between 'the biological' and 'the social', and from the view that if something can be shown to be 'biological' then it is unmodifiable, while if something can be shown to be 'social' then it is easy to change. We affect, manipulate and destroy things we call 'biological' in hundreds of different ways each day (e.g. through the effects of the contraceptive pill, or the effects of atomic radiation). There is also extremely good evidence that it is enormously difficult to change certain aspects of our existence which are usually called 'social' (e.g. class; poverty; crime; the dynamics of personality, which most would agree are in some measure related to our earliest social experiences). We are never going to understand anything about the construction of 'females' and 'males' if we allow such deterministic and obfuscating distinctions and arguments to hold sway.

Notes

1   My ideas on this topic have been developed and clarified by working over a period of years in a group with the following people: Mike Beveridge, John Churcher, Graham Clarke, Graham Corran, Allan Muir, Chris Sinha, Cathy Urwin and Valerie Walkerdine. Gratitude is not quite the appropriate term but my life as a psychologist would have been considerably harder and more ineffective without them. The paper itself was greatly improved by the help and support of Dan Slobin. Any remaining errors of fact and argument are, of course, all my own.

2   This 'compendium' is an attempt by me to put all the different deterministic arguments together.

3   I am here referring to 'traditional' definitions of 'ideology' and 'science' and do not wish to become involved in recent, primarily neo-Marxist, discussions of the distinction.

4   Other things are not equal — it is extremely hard to *find* a diet which is completely alanine-free and children on such a diet suffer a variety of adverse nutritional and social consequences.

5   For some details of these tests see Maccoby and Jacklin (1975) and Sayers (1980). Essentially they are a measure of the subject's ability to visually orient her/himself despite the presence of confusing cues.

6   However, as Maccoby and Jacklin point out, studies of behaviour in neonatal period should be treated with extreme caution since they show little replicability even for the same child.

7   It is interesting to consider whether the substantially greater failure to find sex differences in children's behaviour nowadays as compared to two decades ago, is the result of different methods of research or whether it possibly reflects some genuine change in methods of raising children.

8   'Population' is here used in the technical sense of the group from which the sample of subjects who were tested was drawn.

9   I am indebted to Ann Thorington for this point which she made years ago at one of the 'Women in Society' seminars in Cambridge upon which this book is based.

10   This too, is a 'quotation' written by me.

Further reading

A great deal of further reading is supplied in the text. I shall not repeat these in detail but will just give some main references for the various issues covered by this paper.

Biological determinism

J. Archer, 'Biological explanations of psychological sex differences.' In B. Lloyd and J. Archer (eds), *Exploring Sex Differences*. London: Academic Press, 1976.

R. Brown, *Social Psychology*. New York: Macmillan, 1965. (Has a good section on the determinism of temperment as a function of sex; pp. 161–72.)

D. S. Lehrman, 'Semantic and conceptual issues in the nature-nurture problem.' In L. R. Aronson, E. Tobach, D. S. Lehrman and J. S. Rosenblatt (eds), *The Development and Evolution of Behaviour*. San Francisco: Freeman, 1970.

V. Reynolds, *The Biology of Human Action*. San Francisco: Freeman, 1976.

M. Sahlins, *The Use and Abuse of Biology*. London: Tavistock, 1977.

Sex differences

B. Birns, 'The emergence and socialisation of sex differences in the earliest years.' *Merrill-Palmer Quarterly*, 22(3), 1976.

H. Fairweather, 'Sex differences in cognition.' *Cognition*, 4, 1976.

R. Macauley, 'The myth of female superiority in language.' *Journal of Child Language*, 5, 1978.

E. E. Maccoby and C. N. Jacklin, *The Psychology of Sex Differences*. London: Oxford University Press, 1975.

J. Sayers, 'Psychological sex differences.' In Brighton Women Science Collective (eds), *Alice Through the Microscope*, London: Virago, 1980.

Chapter Thirteen

Oppressive Dichotomies: The nature/culture debate

PENELOPE BROWN AND L. J. JORDANOVA

Introduction

The distinction between nature and culture is basic to recent Western thought. It has so many varied manifestations that it takes consider-able effort to make them explicit. Since the mid-nineteenth century, the opposition between nature and culture has become central to evolutionary theory and allied sciences, to debates on heredity and environment, nature *versus* nurture, the measurement of intelligence and educational methods. All these areas are informed by a distinc-tion between unmediated, intractable nature, and a realm of human mastery where conscious social and individual action is accorded an important measure of power. The belief in human capacity to control nature is, in our culture, linked to the development of science, medi-cine and technology, and to the rational, refined analysis on which they are based. Our science-based culture depends on abstract studies, mostly in the physical sciences, and on techniques relating to engineer-ing skills. Both science and engineering are identified with male accomplishments, with the capacity for mathematical and logical reasoning, with mechanical skills; they are literally and metaphori-cally masculine activities. Women by contrast, are stereotypically identified with so-called caring jobs, nursing, teaching and social work. They are deemed to be uniquely gifted in the realm of human relationships by virtue of their greater emotional sensitivity. The model for female accomplishments is motherhood. The correspond-ing popular imagery is of soft, tender sympathy overriding reason and intellect. In the common emphasis on the unity of mother and child, the identification of women with nature is suggested. The biological functions of bearing and suckling children imply the priviledged status of women with respect to nature. This is further reinforced by their care of defenceless, unformed children who are not yet fully social beings.

It would be possible to devote an entire paper to detailing the various ways in which the nature/culture polarity functions both explicitly and implicitly in contemporary society. Our purpose here is different. We simply wish to note the pervasiveness of the dichotomy in our culture, and the power it has, and go on to suggest that we can learn a valuable object lesson from examining the history and use of these ideas, particularly as they are found in anthropological theories. Current debates in anthropology, like those in the natural sciences, rely on a certain approach to the interpretation of sex differences which we feel demands critical scrutiny. And it helps to realise that the presuppositions scientists and anthropologists use have a long and complex history. In what follows we shall outline the principal anthropological arguments, indicate some of their main problems and then briefly place these debates in their historical context in Western thought.

An anthropological debate as object lesson

As we shall make clear later in the chapter, the association of women with nature and men with culture is by no means new. The recent debates within academic anthropology draw on assumptions and stereotypes which have been deeply embedded in our culture for several centuries. Currently, debate centres on the dichotomy between women being seen as closer to nature and men as closer to culture, and its use to 'explain' the apparently universal secondary status of women in all societies. The controversy is of interest to feminists for two reasons. First, it sheds light on the difficulties of generalising about alledged universals in the position of women — an issue which is taken up in more detail in the following chapter. Second, it illustrates the prevalence and the persuasiveness of what we shall call *essentialist* thinking about the sexes. By this we mean the common conviction that sex differences in the sense of gender ultimately refer to concrete, biological distinctions between men and women. We contrast this with a *relativist* position where, while granting biological sexual differences, emphasis is placed on the social construction of sexuality. From this latter perspective there is no such thing as woman or man in asocial terms; women and men, or rather femininity and masculinity, are constituted in specific cultural settings according to class, age, marital status and so on. We further contend that essentialist thinking about the sexes is part of a dominant ideology which is an impediment to our understanding of the ways societies construct the sexes.

The nature/culture debate has taken many different forms within twentieth-century social theory.[1] Among the most important contributions is the work of the French structuralist Claude Lévi-Strauss. For him the human mind works through series of binary oppositions such as nature/culture, wild/tame, raw/cooked. He alleges that the nature/culture distinction is a universal folk concept, based on the equally universal human propensity to bound society off from non-society. In analysing how we use such dichotomies to order the world, he distinguishes their *synchronic* use as sets of metaphorical contrasts which are mapped onto one another in myth and ritual, and their *diachronic* use whereby the first term of each pair is 'transformed' into the second. Lévi-Strauss explains this transformation by the incest taboo and rules of marriage exogamy (marrying out of the group). The incest taboo represents the rise of the human species out of nature and into culture. In his arguments, Lévi-Strauss makes two fundamental assumptions about human nature. The incest taboo, which forms the basis of culture, rests on the biologically based rule of exchanging siblings for spouses. He also assumes that the human mind is specifically constructed to perceive binary oppositions. When we examine the terms in which Lévi-Strauss speaks of human nature, his indebtedness to psychoanalysis and theories of language are clear.[2] For him these dichotomies are in the unconscious; they need to be decoded by the anthropologist, so that his model of what it is that social scientists do is of rational, logical deciphering.

A number of critiques have been made of Lévi-Strauss on the grounds that he bases culture in biology. They point out that nature and culture are not value-free terms which can safely be used to explain any phenomenon, for they carry the cultural biases of the meaning attached to them. Western ideas of nature and culture have, since the eighteenth century, focused on the origins and evolution of the human species. Thus, we take the 'natural' to be innate in our primitive heritage, while the 'cultural' is arbitrary and artificial. Furthermore, as will be made clear later, Western traditions lay particular emphasis on controlling nature by means of culture, especially through science, medicine and technology. But ideas of nature and culture can be entirely different in non-Western societies. So, in using our ideas of nature and culture to explain the beliefs and behaviour of other societies we run into the danger of confusing our theories with the cognitive structures of other societies.

The nature, culture and gender debates are best known to English speaking people through two articles published apparently independently in the early 1970s by Edwin Ardener and Sherry Ortner. They sparked off a heated argument which has resulted in a challenge, on both empirical and theoretical grounds, to the contention that women are universally seen as nearer to nature, men to culture. Critiques have come from two angles: theoretical ones which attack the logic of the arguments and the premises from which they start, and empirical ones using detailed ethnographic descriptions to show that in particular societies these concepts either do not exist in the forms claimed, or are not consistently associated with gender.[3]

In view of their importance, we shall briefly summarise Ardener's and Ortner's discussions, for, although they argue broadly similar theses, they employ quite different terms to do so. Ortner's argument (1974) begins with the premise that women are universally, in all known societies and at all known times throughout history, considered secondary, inferior to men. She does not seek to explain this by direct reference to biological factors but rather by 'universals of the human cultural situation'. There is, she argues, a universal symbolic identification of women with nature, while men are universally associated with culture and its products. Women are thus somewhat outside culture; they are part of the nature which is to be controlled by culture.[4] It is an easy next step, according to Ortner, for men to find it 'natural' to subordinate women.

Ortner suggests that woman's body and its functions, being more involved than man's in 'species life', places her closer to nature. Man's physiology, by contrast, leaves him relatively free to take up the projects of culture, thereby creating artificially, whereas women create naturally. Women's social roles, such as mother, feeder, nurturer, are considered a 'lower' order of culture than male roles, because the former are family-oriented and therefore particularistic, fragmenting and divisive, while the latter are supra-familial and therefore universalistic and integrative. Ortner further suggests that women are socialised into a distinct psychic structure, one which is closer to nature since it is concrete rather than abstract, and tends towards personalism and particularism.

Ardener (1972, 1975) starts from quite a different set of basic assumptions which concern the social relationship between 'dominant' (male) and 'muted' (female) groups. Men provide the dominant structures of a society which totally define reality for the members. Dominant structures therefore also define the bounds of society which distinguish 'us', 'human, social beings' from all other things, the non-social, non-cultural. Women present a bounding problem, for in some respects they are self-evidently part of society, and yet not part of it in others, since, from the point of view of men, they are 'other', 'not-self'. A parallel is therefore drawn between women and the wild or nature. Women are thus, according to Ardener, seen as 'the wild' by men, and, although they may not see themselves that way, the net result is that their muted structures do not get a voice.

The case of women, Ardener insists, is only a particularly prominent example of muting, others are the working class, ethnic minorities, and other subordinated groups. It is simply a matter, he suggests, of raising the distinction between self and not-self to a greater level of abstraction such as social/non-social. This means that the equation of non-social with nature is an empirical contingency rather than logical necessity, and is not uniquely bound up with sexuality.

Neither Ardener nor Ortner argue that women *are* closer to nature. Rather they try to explain how and why women are *seen* to be nearer to nature by members of very different societies. They agree in attributing the source of such a view of women to female biology as perceived by men, and to women's restriction to the domestic sphere. Both rely on the presumed readiness of human beings to attribute symbolic significance to female anatomy.

The underlying logic of both Ardener's and Ortner's arguments moves from the premise that the only unalterable sexual difference is reproductive structures and roles, to the conclusion that this must therefore be at the root of social differences based on the social identification of the sexes, i.e. gender. As we have already stressed, this is not a crude biological determinism where biology *causes* sex differences, as sociobiologists might argue. Both Ardener and Ortner dissociate themselves from this position. But in fact what they do is simply add an extra link to the chain of causation. *Biological differences* provide a universal basis for *social definitions* which place women closer to nature than men, and this provides the basis for the *universal subordination* of women. Indeed both writers simply assume that women are universally subordinate to men, and see their task as explaining this 'fact'.[5]

The claims of Ortner and Ardener have not gone unchallenged. All three of their basic premises have come under fire: (i) that biology provides a universal basis for social definitions of women, (ii) that such definitions invariably place women as closer to nature than men, and (iii) that women are universally subordinated to men. Here we shall mention two specific criticisms of arguments which associate women with nature. The first is the charge of taking male and female as reified categories and searching for male and female essences, a complaint which has been made by Mathieu (1978) against Ardener. The second criticism is that made by MacCormack (1980), who argues that Lévi-Strauss is not only inconsistent in his arguments about universal polarities, but that he explains women in different terms from those applied to men in his anthropological theory.

Mathieu wishes us to examine the sexes as a social product of social relations, but she observes that we are accustomed to thinking in ways which are an impediment to this project. Her central point is that rather than assuming we know what a woman or a man is in all societies, we have to discover what they are in each society and in each discourse. The problem of female inarticulateness may be better explained by the characteristics of the anthropologist and his/her parent society than by those of the people who are being studied and their society. In other words, because *we* believe in the essential basis of sex differences, we are bound to find it wherever we look. The anthropological distortion takes this form: (i) conferring attributes on each sex, (ii) speaking about the models and symbolism peculiar to each sex, (iii) reifying these attributes, making certain attributes universally associated with each sex, and (iv) attributing *naturalness* to these alleged differences.

Like MacCormack, Mathieu argues that the sexes should not be treated as separate entities, nor explained asymmetrically, one in biological, the other in sociological terms. Rather, for Mathieu, the sexes 'define themselves *by and in* their relationships' (1978, p.58). It is this asymmetry which leads Ardener to assert the universal dominance of male structures over muted female ones. Mathieu insists that we need to enquire in each case whether women share male models of society or not. If they do share them, why should we posit with Ardener that the models are male ones which women have taken over? They are simply the models of the society as a whole. It is only when women's and men's worldviews differ that sex differences need be invoked. Mathieu argues that, rather than saying with Ardener that women live in a world of male speech, representations and models, we should say that the discourse is masculine, the referent is men. And, the referent of the dominant discourse is sociologically, not biologically defined. The issue is power not anatomy, and the alternative to Ardener's essentialist approach is a dialectical one which examines power and social relations directly.

In her analysis of Lévi-Strauss, MacCormack suggests some ways in which symmetry should be restored to social theory. She wants both men and women to be viewed as *mediators* between nature and culture, as cooks, cultivators, domesticaters, tool-makers and so on. This accords better with the ethnographic record which shows that in many cultures both sexes are mediators, and that whether men or women are seen as nature or culture depends on the context. It is in fact quite possible to rephrase the structuralist argument so that *both* men *and* women undergo social transformations, such as culturising their natural sexuality through marriage. Both men and women are both nature and culture.

MacCormack, like Mathieu, takes the debate away from putatively natural sexual differences and towards differences of power which derive from social relations. In this she takes Lévi-Strauss's recent ideas (1977) a stage further. In considering the pairs coloniser/colonised and capitalist/proletarian, Lévi-Strauss claims that simplicity and passivity are not *intrinsic* properties of the colonised or the proletarian, but result from the historical process which marginalises them and deprives them of power. MacCormack adds male/female to the list. The implication is that we should study the message of property relations, not the code of naturalness.

As we mentioned earlier, ethnographic material has also been used to attack the identification of women with nature (MacCormack and Strathern, eds, 1980). Recent accounts show that nature and culture are *not* universal native categories, at least not in the form in which they are conceptualised in our society. The notion of culture as superior to and dominant over nature is not universal. Nor, in societies which do have such concepts, is there necessarily a simple or consistent relationship with male and female. In both empirical and theoretical critiques of the debate, there is an implicit denial of the value of a rationalist discourse. Nature and culture are relativised concepts, their meaning derives from their place within a particular metaphysics; neither has a unique meaning either within Western thought or cross-culturally.

Many people dislike the ways in which the pair nature/culture has been associated with woman/man in anthropological theory.[6] But it is not the belief that social groups tend to define themselves as 'us' and others as 'not us' which they object to. It is the assertion that 'not us' is equivalent to nature, and is therefore inferior, that they take issue with. The split between 'us' and 'not us' can be into two symmetrical halves rather hierarchically ordered.

Of course we now have to study the formation of 'not us' groups. It is plausible to suppose that at least some of the criteria differentiating 'us' and 'not us' will be sex based, but in gender, not in strictly biological terms. The placing of marginal persons such as childless women, widows, 'hermaphrodites', men who opt out of male activities, is highly culturally variable, and biological sex is not necessarily the determining factor.

Many of the comments we have made relate to the extraordinarily difficult question of the use of dichotomous pairs in social theory as both explanations and descriptions of social behaviour. In part this brings us to the heart of philosophical disagreements about the form social theories should take, and of psychological disagreements about the way the human mind works and how psychoanalysis and theories of language are used. We are concerned here, however, with some rather simple errors which we believe are commonly made in analysing women. Even if we granted that there was a universal association of the form women are to nature as men are to culture, that would not sanction slipping into assertions about universal judgements of *value* (good/bad, superior/inferior), nor from there into issues of *control* (superordinate/subordinate). And this danger is not confined to anthropology.

The slippage referred to above is possible because of the way we conceptualise women and men as each possessing common features which constrain their lives. The feminist argument against this view is that what cultures make of sex differences is almost infinitely variable, so that biology cannot be playing a determining role. Women and men are products of social relations, if we change the social relations, we change the categories 'woman' and 'man'. On both political and intellectual grounds we would argue that, to put it at its bluntest, social relations determine sex differences rather than biological sex producing social divisions between the sexes.

The idea that biological differences between men and women cause social ones is, of course, extremely pervasive, and it has gained prominence through the recent spate of writings on sociobiology. Earlier we called it a dominant ideology. Now we want to argue that it is grounded in Western thought, and especially in science, medicine and technology; hence its dominance.

Science and sexuality

For many centuries there have been attempts to separate out what seemed intractable in the environment (nature), from what could easily be altered by human agency (culture). This division was bound up with notions about the form of God's power over both the natural world and over human beings. Only relatively recently, it has been

argued, did the idea that human beings had mastery over their surroundings assume more importance than the belief that they were
impotent by comparison with the deity and were merely guarding the
natural world on his behalf (Glacken, 1967). The examples we use are
drawn from the mid-eighteenth century on, the period when a secular
and self-consciously scientific language began to be employed and
when interest in the study of the physical and social aspects of 'man',
nature and the environment began on a large scale (Jordanova, 1979).
During the nineteenth century, the nature/culture distinction seems
to have been applied more consistently to sexual divisions, with the
result that stereotypes of women became more rigid. The ways in
which this hardening of the divide between the sexes came about are of
great interest, and all the more so as the rigid stereotypes were closely
linked with a biological definition of sexuality.

As the anthropological material alluded to in the previous section
suggested, the relationship between the metaphors people use and the
aspects of lived experience they allegedly express are extremely
complex. The metaphors contain contradictions, tensions or even
what strike us as logical inconsistencies, but these in no way undermine
the historical power of the images. For example, the eighteenth-
century use of women to symbolise truth in the sense of natural reason,
virtue and clarity, coexisted with their simultaneous use to symbolise
feeling and sentiment, also analogised to nature, but associated with
irrationality and superstition. The nature/culture distinction has
operated in Western traditions at many different levels. In addition to
myths, pictures and symbols of all kinds, a coherent scientific self-consciousness played a crucial role in reinforcing and redefining the
identification of female with nature and male with culture.

The scientific endeavour was linked with masculinity, while passive
nature, unveiled and revealed by male science, was identified with
femininity. The personification of nature as woman and as mother is
prominent in much writing in English during the eighteenth and nineteenth centuries. Furthermore, the very process of constructing a
scientific culture was conceived of as a struggle between the elements
of male reason and female superstition. For civilisation to progress, in
other words, the forces of intellectual and social order had to triumph
over the ignorant mysticism which kept back the human race. Men, in
the name of science, would assert their culture over women and their
religious creeds. For many people the battle for power between traditional and modern forces could be seen in the attempts by the
intellectual élite of philosophers, savants and enlightened medical
men on the side of science and reason, to undermine the authority of

superstitious and irrational practices exemplified by the Catholic church, and its main clientele — women.

Mozart's opera, *The Magic Flute* (1971), first performed in 1791, provides an excellent example of the ways in which men and women were represented as having opposed interests, the first based on reason, the second on superstition. Here, one of the most powerful metaphors of the Enlightenment was used, that of light. Darkness, both literal (the Queen of the Night is one of the principal female protagonists) and symbolic, is identified with women and an excess of emotion, irrationality of all kinds, and mindless superstition. On the side of light, Sarastro and the Priest of the Sun are the enlightened males who will ensure the progress and redemption of humanity through their secular rule. Politically this is represented in the feud between the Queen of the Night, the matriarchal figure, and Sarastro, who wishes to ensure that a male line of succession to power is established. In admitting the young hero, Tamino, to the secrets of the male priesthood, a body based on Freemasonry and not on the church, Sarastro is assured that the rule of justice can continue unhampered.[7] *The Magic Flute* is full of inventive and rich imagery and it provides some useful clues as to how the sexes were stereotypically portrayed. Its audience would have found its political message about the bankruptcy of absolute morarchy and the need for a new secular order built on reason quite obvious. Presumably they also took the point that those in power should be men rather than women; that social progress was turning matriarchies into patriarchies.

There were indeed many areas of life where struggles between men and women were explicit and some of these will be discussed below, but few were more dramatic than the extraordinary killing in 1835 of his pregnant mother by the Norman peasant Pierre Rivière (Foucault, 1978). His hatred of his mother's ownership of her land, her consequent power and her humiliating behaviour towards his father were so fundamentally objectionable to him that he felt compelled to take her life, and that of two of his siblings, to vindicate the honour and dignity of his father.

The struggle between the sexes was, for Enlightenment thinkers, part of the history of the human race. The ideology of progress so deeply entrenched in Enlightenment thought suggested the importance of the growth of a rational, humane and civilised society with the development of knowledge and science as motors of change. Allowing the male value system to prevail was therefore an integral part of the process of developing a culture with which nature, raw and unmediated, would be controlled. Human *mastery* over nature should ever increase, this was history, this was science. Women, as nature, were to be controlled, or rather channelled into the correct role for nature in the history of the human race.

Although we are concerned with the manner in which men and women were conceptualised as opposite and complementary using the nature/culture dichotomy, it is important to stress that nature and culture were *not* seen as necessarily incommensurable categories in the eighteenth and nineteenth centuries. Obviously, for human beings to have culture, nature has to yield to their manipulations. Nature, including human beings, is modified as a result of culture. We must be careful therefore not to construe the concept of nature as implying simply a view of the world as composed of intractable, innate qualities. Although nature was distinguished from environment, culture, civilisation and society, a continual interaction between them was envisaged. It is certainly true that what we have called essentialist thinking about the sexes is linked with a scientific view of nature, but it would be a drastic over-simplification to equate this with a crude deterministic position. In the natural philosophical and medical literatures of the eighteenth century there were extensive discussions on the ways in which behaviour, what we might call lifestyle, became incorporated into the body through diet, exercise, habits, occupation and so on. As a result, culture is continually affecting natural objects, particularly the human body; culture was identified as a major determinant of health and disease at both physical and moral levels. Both men and women were seen in terms of this continual dialectic between nature and culture.

Far from being defined exclusively in terms of their sex organs, women were, physiologically speaking, distinguished by the occupations and tasks of womanhood. Although these tended to be closely linked with their reproductive role, the emphasis on lifestyle as a determinant of the characteristics of the human body, provides important clues to the nature/culture relationship in the eighteenth and early nineteenth centuries. The emphasis on occupation as a determinant of health led to a radical boundary being drawn between the sexes. The theoretical basis for this was a physiology which recognised few boundaries; it conflated moral and physical, mind and body, and created a language capable of containing biological, psychological and social considerations. Physicians in late eighteenth-century France used these physiological presuppositions to argue that women were physiologically and anatomically quite distinct from men (Knibiehler, 1976). The total physiology of woman could, they argued, only be understood in terms of their lifestyle and the roles they ought to fulfill if they weren't doing so already. The occupational model of health tightly linked jobs performed in the social arena (for women, the production, suckling and care of children, the creation of a natural morality within the family) with health and disease. Of course the occupational model was applied to both men and women, but for the latter permissible occupation was tightly defined according to 'natural' criteria. Women's health therefore depended on their fulfilling a restricted social role which appeared to be an inevitable consequence of their ability to bear children. Men were members of the broadest social and cultural groups, while women's sphere of action was limited to the family — the ultimate guarantor of human stability since it was the essential *biological* unit of *social* life. These arguments led to women being conceptualised as physically feeble, unable to survive without male protection, frivolous and irrational. Women's minds worked differently from men's in making emotive associations rather than logical connections, a belief that became elaborated into a complex psychological theory in the nineteenth century which asserted women's incapacity for rational scientific thought and their superior talent for affective sentiments (Ploss, 1935).

Earlier we alluded to the fact that women were associated with traditional superstitious practices, and men with social progress through the application of reason. A particularly interesting case of the tension between so-called traditional and modern beliefs is childcare. Here the theme of the irrationality and irresponsibility of women's ways was articulated in both France and Britain in a simultaneous attack on midwives, wet-nurses and mothers. For example, William Cadogan's *Essay on Nursing* (1748) recommended a transfer from female to male responsibility for childcare methods. Nor was he simply co-opting the field for male medical practitioners, for he also wished fathers to take a more active role in preventing women imposing traditional techniques like swaddling, on newborn children. It was never suggested that men should take over the care of children, but that women should perform the childcare tasks allotted to them by men-physicians and husbands. Female functions were not denied or abolished but a hierarchy was envisaged where women acted under the supervision of men. So, men like Cadogan did not argue for a changed division of *labour*, but for an altered division of *power*.

There is no doubt that the question of power is the crucial one, and it holds the key to the apparently contradictory ways in which women were associated with nature. As we stressed above, femininity was commonly equated with superstition, that is, with irrational, illegitimate, mystical power. But it was also associated with moral regeneration; women as natural creatures held within them the possibility for growth and improvement, for the transcendence over evil by the forces of virtue. To be sure this feminine harnessing of positive power also, by implication, involved mystical elements, notably the special bond between mother and child, but here it was safe, even desirable. The idealisation of women as mothers and as founts of natural goodness was eloquently expressed in Bernardin de Saint Pierre's novel, *Paul et Virginie* (1788; 1966). The hero and heroine, Paul and Virginia, grow up in an ideal world, a state of nature, tended only by their mothers. Cruel calamities in the old world had separated the parents, and the mothers had, independently, set out for the new world to bear and rear their children in tranquility. Through their children they show the possibility of human beings achieving a state of total harmony with the natural world which guarantees their morality. Women were capable of intuitive instinctual love for their children, and the beneficial social effects of their special relationship with children made them the sex more appropriate for childcare. Bernardin's story even suggests that men are dispensable in the rearing of children. But if all tranquility, love, virtue and happiness come from women, so do the sorrow and pain. The story is a tragedy, for Virginia returns to Europe to be brought up by an old aunt as a noble woman, and when she refuses to marry the man of her aunt's choice, she is sent home in the hurricane season and drowns in a storm shortly before reaching her home. It is seldom pointed out that the reason her mother agreed to send her to Europe was Virginia's awakening sexuality which changed her behaviour and made her mother fear her adult sexual needs and her capacity to bring children into the world. At root, Bernardin's vision was equivocal; for him women were the saviours of the human race, but their sexuality was also a ripple in what might otherwise be a calm pond. However, Bernardin's book was an important and influential model of what might be called an adulatory style of writing about women as natural.

Of course, many writers saw women as natural in both its good and bad senses. One such person was the historian Jules Michelet, who, picking up many of the basic themes of Enlightenment approaches to sexuality, published a number of influential books on women and womanhood in the mid-nineteenth century. This heritage helps makes sense of nineteenth-century debates on the position of women. Michelet, for example, both adored the natural rhythms of female physiology and feared the consequences of giving political rights to women (Jordanova, 1980). Jules Michelet believed that giving women the vote would result in a move towards more conservative church-based government, since women were vulnerable to the manipulations of priests who would use their female parishioners to further Catholic interests. Ironically, the very qualities which made women the mainstay of society through their better developed feelings and *domestic* capacities, also made them liable to exploitation by powerful groups which preyed upon their vulnerability and credulity. Private virtues became social vices when allowed into the political arena.

Nineteenth-century interpretations of the nature/culture opposition which extend the argument into an evolutionary framework were sometimes quite explicit about the struggle for power between men and women. The struggle was hinted at in *The Magic Flute* where leadership was transferred to the male line precisely because of the rationality of men who are not prone to the irrational superstitions of women. These concerns came to the surface in a number of mid-nineteenth century works which dealt with the development of human society and attempted to grapple with the problem of whether all societies go through matriarchal stages (Fee, 1974). Such works considered the economic foundations of sex roles and were closely related to prevalent beliefs about women's limited capacities for participation in the labour market.

Late nineteenth-century debates about the entry of women into the medical profession employ the same sexual polarities of nature and culture in an economic sense, for it was considered unseemly for women to compete publicly with men. The argument that women could not become doctors because of their inherent lack of scientific ability is now well known. It was also claimed that only married women had the necessary 'experience' for the job, but they were the very ones who were excluded by virue of their childbearing and other family-based duties. Unmarried women, on the the other hand, might have the life style compatible with a profession, but lacked, by definition, the 'experience' required (Donnison, 1977; Delamont and Duffin, 1978, pp.46–7).

The division between married and unmarried women is of great importance. At the end of the eighteenth century the medical literature emphasised the superior health of married women, and contained pleas to married women not to leave the home but to consider motherhood their occupation. At the same period, working women came increasingly from the ranks of young, unmarried girls. In terms of work the division was not just between women and men, but between men and single women on the one hand, and married women who were reproductively active, on the other. Women who worked presented a problem, for by selling their labour power they entered a male world of abstract commodities with objective values.

They violated the neat category distinction. The common nineteenth-century concern for the modesty of women workers should be seen in this context. A working woman carried with her, through her sexuality, the associations of a private, mystified arena connected with feelings in the family, not the public routines of work. She brought the potential for uncontrolled emotion into an area of life which was held to epitomise control and objectivity, or put more concretely, men and money.

The economic inactivity of women was justified by the idealisation of the home and family life as women's preserves. The dominance of women in the family was itself explained in terms of their reproductive and nurturing role which had arisen during the course of human evolution. There was thus a pleasing harmony between the biological, psychological and social division of labour. Female biological rhythms, especially the menstrual cycle, were taken as examples of natural laws at their most beautiful. Women had to submit to the fluctuations and changes of their bodies which were watched over by the benevolent eye of the husband and the physician.

In its application to sexual divisions, the nature/culture distinction mediated forms of power. But perceived distribution of power was not simply a question of male strength and female submission. In fact, two forms of power were envisaged and both had their positive and negative aspects. The first, identified with women, was potency in the realm of feeling which made women good wives and mothers and general upholders of morality. These praiseworthy features were matched by destructive ones; the tendency to be over-emotional, superstitious and credulous made women vulnerable to dogmatic religious and political practices. These two sides of female power express an ambivalence towards nature itself: it was the source of all knowledge, the ultimate ethical arbiter, and at the same time, capable of unpredictable destruction. Male domination, on the other hand, came into its own in the public rather than the private sphere. It was based on an understanding of natural laws and abstract relationships; it was ideally suited to surviving in the complex economy of nineteenth-century Europe. Male power expressed contemporary notions of culture, that it had penetrated nature's laws, understood them and was now in a position to manipulate them. Its negative aspect was a lack of sympathetic identification with others.

One of the most noteworthy features of this ideological construction was the association of each sex with universal biological categories, as if all women and all men were really the same regardless of class or other social differences. In fact class differences are explicitly denied in this view, which we characterised earlier as an *essentialist* approach to the sexes. Furthermore, the ways in which the behaviour of men and women were spoken about implied the life style of a bourgeoisie as the fundamental human standard not that of the working people. A basic question remains: what interests were, and are, served by elaborating a set of biologically based, opposed categories which deliberately ignored (or conveniently obscured) social divisions? We argued earlier that during the eighteenth century male dominance was expressed through an area of human activity, science, which stands, then as now, for the capacity to control and manipulate the natural world. In this sense men possessed power through their identification with scientific knowledge. Simultaneously, women were conceptualised as the passive recipients of scientific manipulation. The dichotomy had implications for many areas of social life: the organisation of work, the division of labour, the ways in which political and social stability were envisaged, and the respective roles of husband and wife in marriage and childbearing.

We are not suggesting that scientific thought was conveniently co-opted in the service of male domination, but that scientific theories and practices have provided our culture with one of the most fundamental ways in which sexual divisions were perceived and understood. We would also say that notions of sexuality were basic to the ways in which science as an activity was thought about. These divisions between male and female, science and nature, did not remain at the level of theorising but set the terms for a whole range of concrete struggles which are still being enacted today in the Western world. It remains a task for feminist study to discover the situation in other cultures, and to be alert to the misuse of such ideas as the nature/culture dichotomy in the area of sexuality.

Notes

1   For more information on the meaning of the concepts nature and culture, see Williams, 1976; Oxford English Dictionary, 1971; Leach, 1978 (in Italian); Crocker, 1963; and Kroeber and Kluckhorn, 1952. Also useful are the entries for these terms in the *Encyclopedia of the Social Sciences*.

2   On Lévi-Strauss see chapter 1 by MacCormack in MacCormack and Strathern, eds, 1980; Leach, 1970. The whole nature/culture argument relies on the structuralist notion of nature and culture as binary oppositions; the academic criticism of the woman as nature, man as culture position is precisely against the binaryness and boundedness of categories. Support for the criticism has come from recent work in linguistics and

psychology, see, for example, Rosch, 1978.

3   Those who uphold, defend, or use the 'woman as nature' concept include Ortner, 1974; E. Ardener, 1972, 1975; S. Ardener, 1975; Stross, 1978; Needham, 1967. Those who have attempted to debunk it include the authors of articles in MacCormack and Strathern, eds, 1980; Mathieu, 1978; Llewelyn-Davis, n.d.; J. Goody, 1977; Leach, 1978.

4   There is an obvious parallel here with Simone de Beauvoir's approach (1972). For her, woman 'is defined and differentiated with reference to man and not he with reference to her; she is the incidental, the inessential as opposed to the essential. He is the Subject, he is the Absolute — she is the Other.' (p.16) Later, de Beauvoir distinguishes 'transcendence' from 'immanence', notions which closely parallel culture and nature: '[men] propose to stabilise her as object and to doom her to immanence since her transcendence is to be overshadowed and forever transcended by another ego (*conscience*) which is essential and sovereign' (p.29).

5   If women are not universally subordinated to men, then the need for an explanation in terms of symbolic associations with nature disappears. In fact, there is considerable evidence from recent linguistic studies that women are more 'cultural' than men when it comes to speech, in that women consistently display greater sensitivity to the social nuances of speech, and speak using more high-status forms and in a more prestige style than men do in comparable circumstances. See Labov, 1972; Trudgill, 1975; Smith, 1979; Brown, in press. For arguments against the universality of women's subordination, see Quinn, 1977; Kuhn and Wolpe, 1978; Strathern, 1972, 1980; and Brown's paper on 'Universals and particulars in the position of women' in this volume.

6   Strathern, 1980, sees an 'ideological intention' in attempts to hold these concepts rigid and produce sets of dichotomies out of them. Her point links up with the more general problem of empirical assessments of Lévi-Straussian claims. There is a difficulty in assessing structuralist arguments, since structuralists may claim that the 'deep structure' universals they seek are obscured by the variety of empirical solutions to life, therefore their theories are not disprovable by apparent counter-examples in the real world. MacCormack (1980) has challenged the viability of structuralist models which neglect consciously held folk models and actual statistical descriptions of real societies. For her, social anthropology is not a branch of semiology, as those in the tradition of structuralist anthropology would claim, but the study of the actual behaviour of human beings. Similarly, Strathern mistrusts the semiotic approach because it fails to take account of the embeddedness of notions like nature and culture in particular worldviews and prefers to construe them as universals.

7   Coser, 1978, has offered a feminist analysis of Bergman's film version of *The Magic Flute*.

Further Reading

S. Ardener (ed.), *Perceiving Women*. London: Dent, 1975.

S. Ardener (ed.), *Defining Females*. London: Croom Helm, 1979.

P. Caplan and J. Bujra (eds), *Women United, Women Divided*. London: Tavistock, 1978.

N. Chodorow, 'Family structure and feminine personality.' In M. Rosaldo and L. Lamphere (eds), *Woman, Culture and Society*. Stanford: Stanford University Press, 1974.

C. MacCormack and M. Strathern (eds), *Nature, Culture and Gender*. Cambridge: Cambridge University Press, 1980.

M. Rosaldo and L. Lamphere (eds), *Woman, Culture and Society*. Stanford: Stanford University Press, 1974.

Chapter Fourteen

Universals and Particulars in the Position of Women

PENELOPE BROWN

Theories of patriarchy, as they have developed so far, start from the assumption that the subordination of women is a universal phenomenon (at least at this point in history), and they attempt to construct an account which would explain this universal feature of human societies. There is, however, considerable controversy over the issue of the universality of women's subordination, both in terms of what is meant by 'subordination', 'inferiority', 'oppression', etc. such that these labels can be said to be universally applicable to the position of women, and in terms of the interpretation of ethnographic data. These two problematic areas are linked to a third, to do with the nature of universalistic claims about features of human social life: how can we bring such claims 'to ground', and relate universal explanations, phrased in terms general enough to encompass all societies, to the minutiae of facts about social life as actually experienced by women in any particular society?

In this chapter I take up a strand of theory and debate in anthropological circles which aims to bypass these difficulties by narrowing the scope of the explanation and attempting to state regularities in relationships between certain social-structural conditions and aspects of the position of women in societies displaying those social-structural conditions. Universal claims in this domain take the form of 'conditional universals', statements to the effect that 'If a society has feature X (a social-structural feature), it will also have feature Y (a characteristic of the position of women).' Claims phrased in this conditional manner do not suffer from the ahistorical lack of connection with material facts in particular societies which is involved in universal claims, though as we shall see they have their own set of theoretical hurdles to overcome. This chapter is intended as an introduction to the anthropological literature on the status of women cross-culturally; I simply summarise the arguments which have been made and assess their implications for an analysis of patriarchy. For a more comprehensive examination of such claims the reader is referred to several detailed reviews of this literature (Lamphere, 1977; Quinn, 1977; Reiter, 1979; Rogers, 1978; Tiffany, 1978).

Before examining the suggestions which have been made about the connections between particular features of social structure and the status of women, a number of preliminary clarifications are in order. What exactly do we mean by the two terms in our conditional assertion: 'social structural feature X' and 'the position of women'? In what sense can either of these items constructed within a description of a particular society be compared with those in other societies?[1]

These questions raise the fundamental problem of the viability of making cross-cultural comparisons, a problem which has to be confronted by any theory of patriarchy. This has been a continuing bone of contention amongst anthropologists of differing persuasions. On the one hand, anthropology has always been a comparative discipline, with an interest both in the extraordinary diversity of cultures and in the search for generalisations about the human condition. Anthropologists look at social institutions in a cross-cultural perspective which leads them to generalisations about the kinds of kinship systems humans construct, the nature of marriage rules, types of social organisation (including the division of labour and the role of hierarchy in social systems), the forms which ritual takes and the functions it serves, and even more abstract generalisations about the universal nature of human cognitive processes and the ways in which humans categorise and symbolise their world. This search for universals (including conditional universals such as those we shall be examining here) provokes a corresponding search for explanations for the pan-human characteristics of social life, and as such anthropological arguments are looked to by many feminists as a source of insight for theories of patriarchy.

On the other hand, there is a strong current of cultural relativism in anthropology which is highly critical of the sorts of cross-cultural comparisons which enter into arguments about universal features of social life. In our case, with respect to the position of women in society, such complaints focus on the problems of *definition* and of *values*. What exactly is meant by notions such as 'women's status', 'women's subordination', 'women's oppression'? Can we formulate an index which would measure such notions objectively, across all cultures? The criteria that have been used to identify the oppression of women in different societies vary widely; including, for example:

(1) Women are oppressed if they work for others' benefit, if the products of their labour are not theirs to use and distribute.

(2) Women are oppressed if they don't have control over their lives, decision-making ability, freedom of choice.

(3) Women are oppressed if they are culturally believed to be inferior to men.

(4) Women are oppressed if they are vulnerable to physical attack by men.

(5) Women are oppressed if there are valued cultural activities from which they are excluded.

It seems, then, that there are a variety of ways in which the social relations of sex can be oppressive to women. It also seems that women's position relative to men may vary independently of each of these dimensions, and that what the people of a particular society actually make of these placements (whether they are rigidly upheld, whether women and men agree in their evaluations) may affect what we would want to say about the position of women in that society. This problem of comparability casts doubt on the 'separate but equal' line taken by a number of anthropologists with respect to the status of women in the particular societies they have studied: the argument that women occupy a social sphere separate from that of men, but complementary rather than subordinate to it (see, for example, MacCormack 1972, 1974, 1975, 1980; Weiner, 1976). For there are many different scales along which 'equality' in social value can be measured. The following are several types of scale often confused in discussions of women's status, along with my rough gloss:

(1) *Status* – in lay usage, status is prestige; in sociological usage, status is any locus in a social structure occupied (temporarily) by an individual. So there is an ambiguity in the term as to whether or not hierarchy (status inequality) is being implicated.

(2) *Power* – ability to do what you want over and against others' wishes if opposed. Here there is a notion of competition, conflict and the ability to force others to do one's will.

(3) *Freedom of action* – ability to independently make choices and decisions that affect oneself; autonomy. Linked, but not equivalent, to power, since the domains over which each operates may differ.

(4) *Rank* — order of access to limited resources (including prestige), determined by a set of criteria particular to a society. Hierarchically ordered, with high rank commanding behavioural acknowledgment (deference).

(5) *Authority* — culturally legitimated power; the right to make decisions within a particular domain, and to command obedience.

(6) *Value* — degree to which care and protection or ritual attention is extended to social items, including persons.

(7) *Ideological value* — social beliefs about the relative superiority or inferiority of categories of persons (incorporating, for example, sexism, racism, classism, ageism).

(8) *Subjective (internalised) value* — self-image (as higher or lower, in relation to others); conscious evaluation of self.

There are several points to stress about these scales. One is that an individual's position is always relative to another individual's position — for example, a woman relative to a man of, say, the same social stratum. And these dimensions could be multiplied indefinitely, which is precisely what makes the comparability of such scales so problematic. Furthermore, in defining the position of women in any society all these factors should be examined, since a 'good' position on one dimension does not entail a good one on the others. There may also be factors other than those identified by scales of social value, more difficult to evaluate, such as the quality of social relationships, sources of emotional support, avenues to prestige and self-worth, which should enter into an assessment of the position of women in any society.

Given all these (and more) different dimensions on which one could choose to evaluate social position, there is a real question as to whether two categories of people perceived as different in a society are ever evaluated as equal on all such dimensions. If they are said to be equal, are they really being measured on the same scale? Does 'equality' mean equality on *all* these dimensions (and any others relevant in a given instance)? On most? One definition has been posed by Lamphere as an ideal-type:

> A situation of sexual equality would be one in which all men and women (regardless of social group or strata) could and actually did make decisions over the same range of activities and people, that is, exercise the same kinds of control. Subordination of women or sexual inequality would be a situation where this was not the case, where there were some decisions which women could not and did not make, some activities from which they

were excluded, and some resources which they did not control. (1977, p.613)

But given the universality of the sexual division of labour, there is no society where this description of sexual equality obtains; men and women invariably exercise control over different domains to some degree. And the restriction of some activities or resources to men is not in itself evidence of male domination, for this may be counterbalanced by the restriction of others to women.

In talking about the 'position of women', then, we are juggling with a notion of extreme complexity and elusiveness. My point in emphasising this is not to eliminate the question altogether and retreat into cultural relativism, for there are, I think, regularities and patterns in the position of women (on almost any scale of measurement you choose) cross-culturally. But I do want to emphasise (1) the necessity of being very explicit about the criteria on which such comparisons are being made, and (2) the dubious value of global claims that women are universally subordinate to men.

A second set of doubts arrives when we consider the ethnographic basis for many of the claims about cross-cultural generalities in women's position. A number of these come from studies based on the Human Relations Area Files, a computerised data-bank of putative social facts culled from hundreds of ethnographies, and there are particular criticisms of the material in these files,[2] but the problem is even more general. There are limits to the value of comparing societies on the basis of characteristics which have been reported by different anthropologists with different axes to grind — and mostly from a male eye-view — with different views of the nature of ethnography, differential access to groups (e.g. women) in their particular societies, different views about the boundaries of the social groups on which they are reporting (see Leach, 1978). It's a little like trying to compare the historical development of popular support for the American and Russian Revolutions, using only two source-books: one written by a bourgeois American about the Russian situation and the other by a Marxist about the American scene. It's not simply a question of overt bias in reporting (though that certainly exists); it's also a question of the *in principle* comparability of social concepts (e.g. clan, lineage, chief, matrilineality, marriage) applied in different societies and reported by different observers.[3]

Given these difficulties it is important to take with a huge grain of salt the claims found in feminist literature about cross-cultural generalities in the position of women. These difficulties have led some writers to argue that the generalised notion of 'women's status' is meaningless (Strathern, 1972b, in press; Quinn, 1977), and to abandon attempts to compare women's status cross-culturally. Others simply point to the weakness of the current data base, and emphasise the importance of women interested in the 'feminist problematic' collecting information themselves from the various societies in which they are involved.

Backed by all these caveats, it should be clear that I take the generalisations summarised below as tentative and preliminary, based in most cases on a 'hunch', drawn from one or two concrete instances with or without additional evidence gleaned from possibly unreliable sources. But these generalisations are a beginning, in the attempt to understand what systematic constraints social structure imposes on the social construction of 'women'.

Claims about factors influencing the position of women

I shall begin with the claims of the universalists, as a foil for the more specific claims that follow. These all rely on biological or psychological universals (sometimes, but not always, admitted to be mediated by social institutions such as childcare arrangements or socialisation). One of these has already been discussed by Brown and Jordanova in chapter 13 — the view that women are universally subordinate to men due to the universal association of women with 'nature'. To add the other biologically founded claims, I shall just mention the following: that the subordination of women is based in men's greater size, physical strength, or aggressiveness (see Quinn, 1977, pp.186−90), in the asymmetry of the possibility of rape (Young and Harris, 1976), or in the (hypothesised) suggestion that females are more 'compliant' than males, and more readily take orders from authority figures (Maccoby and Jacklin, 1975, p.371). Another line of argument focuses on women's role in childbearing and childrearing, suggesting that the desirability of protecting women and children from strenuous work, from the necessity for travelling long distances, etc., produces the universal features of the sexual division of labour (Brown, 1970); this in turn has been argued to affect the status of women dramatically. Rosaldo (1974), for example, posits a universal association of women with the domestic, men with the public domain, which she believes underlies the universal subordination of women. The different socialisation of male and female children (Chodorow, 1974) is a third source suggested. whereby the fact that both sexes are nurtured by a mother (and/or other females) provides different bases for personality development. The suggestion here is that boys have to break with the mother, go outside the family and identify with more distant male figures, thereby developing an achievement orientation and a universalistic perspective which girls, who can stay tidily encompassed within the domestic sphere identifying and role-learning directly from their mother, do not acquire. This achievement orientation is presumed (in conjunction with the association of women with the domestic, men with the public, spheres of social life) to underlie male dominance of political domains.

These 'key' explanations, which seek a unicausal basis to what is perceived as a unitary phenomenon – the universal low status of women – run aground on the problems of biologism and essentialism raised in chapter 12, and on the definitional problems discussed above. As 'explanations' which do very little beyond restating the premise – that women are universally subordinate because women universally do the kinds of things (or are the kinds of people) that women do (or are), they are too gross and too inaccurate to be very illuminating.

Turning to the more limited proposals of the particularists, about factors producing the great cross-cultural variability in the status of women, we may now ask: what social arrangements influence the distribution of social value with respect to women? Here I list briefly some of the determinants which have been claimed to be crucial, plus some hypotheses (or rather, predictions about expected correlations) that pinpoint the ways in which they are crucial, and followed by an assessment of their potential value as claims about the status of women cross-culturally.

Economic variables

Mode Of Production

The Marxist objection to these universalistic arguments is that the position of women – or more accurately, the social relations of sex – are grounded in the mode of production. Because the economic base clearly differs across societies, the status of women must differ correspondingly (see, for example, Kuhn and Wolpe, 1978). This perspective places human societies on a (usually evolutionarily ordered) line of development from (roughly) hunting and gathering societies, with no specialisation of the division of labour and with all members involved in production, through horticultural societies, where gardening is performed – usually by women – with a relatively simple technology, to plough agriculture, where men take over the major role in subsistence and women are relegated to household labour, to the beginnings of State organisation and modern capitalism. From this perspective (that the mode of production is the crucial factor in the social relations of sex) we find several kinds of claims, focusing on women's economic and familial roles as they differ in different modes of production

Engels' position (1973a) was that the oppression of women came with the advent of private property, which in turn came with sedentarisation and agriculture. He believed that property ownership determines women's status, and that getting women back into productive labour would bring about the end of women's oppression. Modifications of this argument have proliferated, in the face of considerable evidence that despite having a central role in productive labour in many societies, women do not necessarily have equality with men. As Friedl (1975) points out, in hunting and gathering societies, women as gatherers produce the bulk of the diet; in horticultural societies women also have a primary subsistence role. Yet in such societies women do not necessarily have access to political office, or control over the distribution of the fruits of their labour. This has led Friedl to suggest that it is control over the distribution of goods outside the household which is a necessary prerequisite to high status for women, not simply a major role in production. Slaves, after all, may perform the bulk of productive tasks in a society.

Division Of Labour

Another suggestion (by E. Goody, following Bott, 1954) is that in societies where women and men have segregated role structures, with women's work sharply separated from that of men, women are better off because they have a sphere of their own within which to elaborate their own criteria of self-esteem and social value. Women in societies like our own, where achievement and prestige are (at least today) defined in similar terms for both sexes, do not have the advantages of the separate sphere within which they can operate with relative autonomy.

A number of proposals have centred on the argument presented by Rosaldo, that the subordination of women is due to the universal association of women with domestic activities, while men monopolise the public, extra-domestic domain. Those who resist the universalistic interpretation of this hypothesis have suggested modifications. Draper (1975) agrees with Rosaldo about the depressive effects on women of relegation to the domestic domain, but argues that this dichotomy between public and domestic domains is itself a consequence of permanent settlement, with the corresponding investment in habitation and the accumulation of property. Martin (in Martin and Voorhies, 1975) extends this argument to suggest that the sharp split came with developed agriculture; Reiter (1975) believes it is associated with the rise of States and with industrial capitalism. Sacks (1976) stresses the significance of the reduction in the political importance of kin groups, and the relegation of many formerly kin-based functions to the State (see details in Quinn, 1977). Another modification to this notion of domestic as opposed to inter-domestic units and relations is proposed by Goody; she argues that men co-operate and share food between domestic groups; women co-operate only within a domestic group, to feed their own family. Hence men have the power of inter-group alliances, and develop a concern with inter-group status relationships — presumably because they can rely on the women to perform the basic subsistence tasks for maintaining the family.[4]

Social structural variables

Kinship And Residence Patterns

Whether a society is matrilineal or patrilineal, and whether residence after marriage is matrilocal, patrilocal, or neolocal, has been claimed to be significant for the position of women in a society. Friedl (1975) suggests that women are better off in matrilocal societies (where married couples go to live in the village of the bride's family), because women have the support of their own kin in the village; husbands are outsiders. But it is less obvious that matrilineality (where descent and inheritance go through the female line) is advantageous for women, for, although women are important as links in the lineage system, it is often males — related to the women of the lineage, especially brothers and sons — who control the political system in such societies. There is no necessary correlation between matrilineal and matrilocal systems; in many matrilineal systems residence is 'avunculocal', with the husband's mother's brother.

Women's Function As Childrearers

Another hypothesis focuses on women's reproductive role. The fact that women bear children and are primarily responsible for rearing them in all known societies is seen as crucial to women's position: it takes women out of the power sphere (since they are preoccupied with children), and limits their freedom of action. Brown (1970) argues that it produces the universal features of the division of labour (that men universally are the warriors, the clearers of fields, the stonemasons, the big-game hunters, the deep-sea fishers). A counter-argument, however, is produced by Friedl (1975), who argues that the time women spend in childcare is determined by their role in subsistence, and not vice versa.

Women's Control Over Their Fertility

The ability to choose a husband, to not get married, to get divorced, to have lovers, to control childbirth via abortion or contraception or infanticide, are also important aspects of women's status. There is a general view that women's position is better where they can exercise some control over their fertility, their sex life, their state of marriage — where they have options. An alternative view is that this is an effect, not a cause, of women's control over their lives in other arenas, especially the economic.

Women As Objects Of Exchange

The French anthropologist Lévi-Strauss (1969) has developed a theory of women as the objects of exchange in marriage transactions between the men of different social groups. This theory has been taken up by certain feminists as an explanation for the alleged universal subordination of women (Mitchell, 1974; Rubin, 1975). Lévi-Strauss's theory of women as objects of exchange is an abstract and technically complicated argument about the formal nature of unilineal descent systems of kinship, which, in my view, has been misunderstood and misused by those interpreting it as an explanation for the universal subordination of women, for it is entirely inadequate as a cross-cultural description of the actual status of real women in marriage transactions.[5]

However, a non-universalistic application of the theory to the position of women would suggest that in societies where such exchange is overt and consciously acknowledged, where women, as pawns in the marriage game, have no control over the process, women are in a worse position than otherwise.

Avenues To Legitimate Power And Authority

Friedl (1975) makes the controversial suggestion that in non-egalitarian societies (where social status is given by birth) women are better off, because they have access to legitimate power (as queens, noblewomen, high-caste women); whereas in egalitarian societies where power and prestige are achieved through competition, women are generally subjugated to men. There are limitations to this claim, however, as a general point about the status of women, for power in non-egalitarian societies is available only to the privileged few; the majority of women remain subordinate to men. And if you compare the position of women with the men of their own class (especially their husbands), they are generally subordinate in at least symbolic ways (e.g. they have to give deference to their husbands). A related argument is that women have access to illegitimate power where they have none to legitimate power; hence they are often alleged to be witches, to be ritually dangerous when menstruating, etc., and they may connive to influence the decisions of men by behind-the-scenes pressure, especially by strong ties with sons. But as illegitimate power manipulators (as seen through the eyes of men), they will be mistrusted, feared and (probably) circumscribed with ritual constraints on their actions.[6]

Ideological variables

Sex Antagonism

In a number of widely separated culture areas (in New Guinea and Brazil, for example), there is a belief that the two sexes are antagonistic, hostile, and in particular, that women are dangerous to men. This view is closely linked to pollution beliefs, that women (as menstruaters and childbearers, especially) are polluting to men.[7] Women in these societies have to follow strict regimens of seclusion and purification surrounding their reproductive functions. Such beliefs seem to be linked to male fears of women in other domains, that women can, for example, harm men cosmologically, or that they can (and will, if allowed) withhold their necessary services to men.

Women As Immature And Requiring Protection

Ideologies of this nature occur in 'honour and shame' cultures, where there is a belief that women are weak, helpless, or uncontrollable in their sexuality, and these beliefs are used to prop up severe restrictions on their freedom of movement. These are often linked with legal definitions of women as perpetual jural minors (see LaFontaine, 1978).

Women's Universal Association With 'Nature'

The claim made by Ortner − that the universal association of women with 'nature', the 'wild', etc. underlies their subordination to the 'cultural' men − has been discussed in detail in chapter 13. Its validity as a description of beliefs about sexual difference in all societies has been repudiated in cross-cultural studies (see MacCormack and Strathern, 1980). But the questions to which this argument was addressing itself − the relationship between ideologies of sexual difference and other aspects of ideology, and of social life − remain unsolved; these are questions at the heart of 'the feminist problematic'.

Conclusion

This brief survey of ideas and problems around the issue of women's status cross-culturally suggests that neither 'the position of women' nor 'patriarchy' are simple and self-evident concepts. Indeed, the pitfalls gaping at the feet of those aiming to produce an analysis of sexual relations — and a programme of action based upon it — are daunting to contemplate. In my view, explanations for the status of women are in a primitive state, for we have not yet learned to pose the questions we are asking in a form precise enough to allow meaningful answers.

Considering the particular question we have been raising here — what explanation can we find for the observable cross-cultural patterns in the position of women? — I have said enough to indicate that there are no easy answers. Simple economic determinist explanations don't work, because, as we have seen, women do the major productive labour in some societies, and yet are still subordinate (by some criteria) to men. It is quite possible for women to control food production almost entirely and still be largely left out of the society's political and ritual activities, or be required (at least within their own social stratum) to give public deference to men. Even in modern socialist countries, there has apparently been great resistance to changing the allocation to women of the primary responsibility for housework and childcare.

Other key explanations don't seem to work any better than economic ones — they frequently conflict with the data, and they are in any case too general to be of much use in understanding the particular forms of sexual oppression. We are left with some puzzles about very general cross-cultural patterns: the monopoly of men over formal political office; the exclusion of women from prestige spheres; ideologies of sex difference favouring men. Of course, the 'universality' of these may disappear under the impact of new ethnography, or the universality of each may be independently explainable, with no key explanation being required.

The prognosis is less gloomy for the more specific question of what social structural conditions influence the status of women. We can state correlations between aspects of social structure or social customs and the evaluation of women's position in certain respects, although the cross-cultural generalisations proposed so far are tentative due to the weakness of the data base (though that is improving). Greater confidence in stating such relationships will rest on detailed reports of the three dimensions of women's lives that are crucial to a theory of patriarchy: the structures of production, reproduction and ideology (as it operates in the unconscious, and overtly).

Feminist anthropologists are beginning to respond to the difficulties raised by the 'key' theorising produced by the first-generation attempts, and are turning to research focusing on the description and definition of particular aspects of women's position in particular societies. This change in focus has been fuelled by the recent increase in ethnographic reports by women about women, which have encouraged, as Quinn points out, more

> refined examination of particular domains of women's lives and activities and appreciation of the complexity and multiplicity of women's roles across these domains. If this trend continues then the 'key' theories which have initiated the anthropological study of women's status . . . will simply lapse or be incorporated into explanations of more restricted scope. (Quinn, 1977, p.183).

The main point I would draw from this exercise is this. There is no 'objective', cross-culturally valid, criterion for evaluating the position of women. This follows from the premise fundamental to this book, and the course on which it is based: that women are socially constructed. If we take this position seriously, then it means that the notion of 'woman' has to be interpreted *within* the parameters and definitions meaningful to the society that does the constructing. There is no essence of woman distinct from the definition of 'woman' within a society, and if a theory of patriarchy is to be developed which doesn't fly in the face of ethnographic fact, it will have to confront the variety and complexity of such definitions of 'woman' with a great deal of subtlety and sensitivity.

Notes

1   The terms 'society' and 'culture' are loosely used (more or less interchangeably) to refer to entities with relatively clear-cut boundaries, an internally coherent political and social organisation, a shared communicative code, and shared beliefs and customs. 'Culture' itself is defined in a variety of ways, beginning with Tylor's classic definition (1871, p.1) of culture as 'that complex whole which includes knowledge, belief, art, law, morals, custom, and any other capabilities and habits acquired by man as a member of society'. From this notion of the sum of human attributes acquired in society it was a short jump to talking about the society whose members hold

these beliefs, habits, etc. as a 'culture'. Culture, visualised as the sum of human-made creations, both material and ideological, is contrasted with those phenomena which humans do not create, the 'givens' of nature and the natural world.

The terms 'culture' and 'society' are often used in ways implying that these are discrete, bounded attributes of separate tribes. However, since beliefs and customs do not map one-to-one onto language, political systems, religion, etc., the segmentation of the human population into 'cultures', 'societies' or 'tribes', is not at all straightforward. The boundaries of these units are often difficult to specify, and the units themselves interrelate and affect one another in complex ways. In addition, all cultures today have been affected to some degree by the period of Western expansion and contact with missionaries. So cultures and societies are not genuine isolates, but are actually subsystems within larger systems, intricately interlinked, and all constantly changing and developing.

For those who read Italian, a good discussion of the use of these terms — culture, society and nature — can be found in Leach (1978). For English treatments, see Kroeber and Kluckhohn (1952), and the entries for these terms in the *Encyclopedia of the Social Sciences*.

2   See, for example, Leach (1978), who points out the non-equivalence of the units ('tribes', 'societies', 'cultures') on which reports are included in the HRAF files.

3   There are in addition particular sources of bias in this set of data in the ways in which aspects of women's lives are reported. Most ethnographies (anthropological studies of particular cultures) have been written by men, nearly all by Western-culture-biased anthropologists, who just don't report on the things they take for granted. Just as one doesn't write 'The Gururumba breathe air' or 'They tend to die when they get old', so in many ethnographies it is assumed that women do food-preparation and child-care tasks, and that men are the controllers of power and the manipulators of status and prestige. As a result, what traditional ethnographies have to say about women should be read with some scepticism. A list of exceptions — of excellent ethnographies by women about women — is given in the Further Reading following Brown *et al.*'s, chapter 8.

4   E. Goody made this argument in a series of lectures given at the University of Cambridge in 1975 and 1976; to my knowledge these have not been published.

5   For a clear exposition of the theory in Lévi-Strauss's own terms, see Leach (1970); Badcock (1975); Scheffler (1966); or consult Lévi-Strauss himself (1969). For a discussion of its limitations, see MacCormack (1980).

6   See, for example, Goody (1970), and other articles in the same book.

7   Such beliefs about women polluting men are in fact extremely widespread, occurring in entirely unrelated parts of the world (see de Beauvoir, 1972). They play a particularly important role in cross-sex relations in India

(Carstairs, 1967; Srinavas, 1952), and in New Guinea (Meggitt, 1964; Brown and Buchbinder, 1976). See also Douglas (1966) for an analysis of concepts of pollution and taboo.

Further Reading

Articles analysing the position of women cross-culturally (in addition to those cited in the text) include:

J.K. Brown, 'Anthropology of women: the natural history stage.' *Reviews in Anthropology* 2, 1975.

F. Edholm, O. Harris and K. Young, 'Conceptualising women.' *Critique of Anthropology, Women's Issue*, 9 and 10, 1977.

J. Ennew, 'The Patriarchal Puzzle.' *Review of Critique of Anthropology, Women's Issue. m/f*, 2, 1978.

E. Friedl, 'The position of women: appearance and reality.' *Anthropological Quarterly*. 40, 1967.

L. Liebowitz, 'Changing views of women in society.' *Reviews in Anthropology*, 2, 1975.

R.R. Reiter, 'The search for origins: unravelling the threads of gender hierarchy.' *Critique of Anthropology, Women's Issue*, 9 and 10, 1977.

S.C. Rogers, 'Female forms of power and the myth of male dominance: a model of female/male interaction in peasant society.' *American Ethnologist*, 2, 1975.

P.R. Sanday, 'Toward a theory of the status of women.' *American Anthropologist*, 75, 1973.

P.R. Sanday, 'Female status in the public domain.' In M. Rosaldo and L. Lamphere (eds), *Women, Culture and Society*. Stanford: Stanford University Press, 1974.

A. Schlegel, *Male Dominance and Female Autonomy: Domestic Authority in Matrilineal Societies*. New Haven: Human Relations Area Files Press, 1972.

M. Strathern, 'An anthropological perspective.' In B. Lloyd and J. Archer (eds), *Exploring Sex Differences*. London: Academic Press, 1976.

Chapter 15

Subjectivity, Materialism and Patriarchy[1]

ELENA LIEVEN

This paper is about the development, by Marxist-feminists, of a theory of sexed subjectivity. 'Subjectivity' is the general term for those attributes (intentionality, desire, awareness, etc.) which make us human 'subjects' — i.e. 'individuals' whose existence is bound up with that of our human bodies, and who reflect on ourselves as living among others. Materialist theories of subjectivity are opposed to the notion of a 'transcendental' subject, an individuality which somehow pre-exists social relations, or exists independently of them; rather, subjectivity is socially constructed, it changes historically as societies change, and is always being reconstructed.

The form of subjectivity that is discussed in this paper is seen as being constructed within a society by the various relations of power that exist and interrelate in that society. Marxists have traditionally been concerned with the ownership of the means of production and the class relations that derive from this — feminists with the relations of sexual difference. These two statements, while accurate, disguise a wide variety of approaches which widens still further when we come to the issue of the generation and location of ideology — that represen-tation of 'reality', as opposed to reality itself which, according to one view, is inaccessible in a non-socialist society and according to another is never completely accessible because it is a condition of our existence as subjects that we are cut off from the real — that is what it is to be part of society.

In this chapter, I shall concentrate on the attempt by some feminists to develop a theory of sexed subjectivity which is engaged with accounting for the seeming universality of various forms of sexual oppression while remaining located in historical materialism. My aim is to make some of this literature more accessible to the interested reader since it is notoriously difficult to understand at a first reading. Hopefully, the reader will then be able to make up her/his mind as to the usefulness or otherwise of this direction in feminist theory − an issue of some contention in the women's movement.

The chapter divides into three parts:

(1) Situating the attempts of Marxist-feminists in general and British Marxist-feminists in particular to develop a theory of the psychic construction of women and men.

(2) Critically presenting and analysing the use of Lacanian psychoanalytic theory to develop a theory of sexed subjectivity.

(3) Raising the problem of the relevance of such theorising to general issues of the relationship between theory and practice in the politics of feminism and the Left.

Situating Marxist-feminism

It has been clear for many years that although a theory of class can provide an analysis of the particular form of social relations that results from the capitalist mode of production, it is inadequate when it comes to accounting for aspects of the sexual division of labour in society: for instance, domestic labour as opposed to paid labour; the average wage for women as opposed to that for men; the different kinds of paid labour undertaken by women and men. Cousins (1978) says: 'the basic elements of a theory of modes of production do not require any specific forms of sexual divisions or of the sexual division of labour' (p.63). But are we therefore to assume that the sexual divisions we can observe are only accidental and transitory? Marxist theory deriving from Engels sees the entry of women into the paid labour force as the sufficient pre-condition for their emancipation (this is discussed in greater detail in D. Riley's chapter in Section 1 above). However, it is quite clear that even where this involves large numbers of women − as in some socialist societies − many aspects of sexual division remain unchanged: discriminatory wages; 'women's work' and 'men's work'; etc. (see J. Wajcman's chapter 1).[2]

From the late 1960s, Western feminists began to directly challenge the Western Left to face the inadequacy of Marxist theory and they began to address not only the silences in the theory but also the errors. But their analyses of these facts have taken very different forms. Firestone (1971), in one of the first analyses of the problem, sees the domination of women by men as *the* fundamental social division upon which all others rest and whose material basis is the appropriation by men of women's biological capacities for reproduction. Her debt to Marxist theory is evident in the extremely close analogy in her argument between sexual oppression as deriving from women's labour in biological reproduction, and class oppression as deriving from the proletarian's labour for the capitalist. Despite the criticisms that can be made of her position, her analysis of men's power over women is correctly angry, trenchant and detailed, and her emphasis on the need to delineate the material base of patriarchy is crucial — as we shall see below (see also Hartmann, 1979). Other feminists have tried to extend Marxist theory to include an analysis of women's domestic labour as a necessary part of capitalist production and this has led them to make the political demand of 'wages for housework'. This argument has by now become the subject of considerable debate, which is discussed in chapter 1 by J. Wajcman above. Yet another strand in Marxist-feminist theorising has been the analysis of specific aspects of women's position under capitalism, for instance the effects on women of economic recession, problems in the unionisation of women workers, the relationship between de-skilling, low pay, and the predominance of women in particular types of work. One thing that emerges clearly is that none of these different analyses can rely solely on economic arguments: a complex relation has to be admitted between economic factors and ideological factors. These may work together to 'keep women in their place', as when there is a move to keep women in the home and out of the job market; or they may work in opposition, as when there is a conflict between an economic necessity to expand the number of workers in a particular area and an ideological demand for women to stay at home to rear children (see Mason, 1976, for a discussion of both these aspects in relation to Nazi policies on women, the family and women's paid labour).[3] The problematic relationship between ideology and material structures therefore began to attract attention as a question in its own right. At the same time, a relatively independent development in British Marxism exercised a strong influence on the precise direction of feminist attempts to examine these questions in a Marxist framework.[4] This was the absorption into British Marxist writing in the late 1960s of Althusser's theories of ideology and Lacan's theory of psychoanalysis — two French intellectual currents which were themselves interrelated.[5] Feminists who were seeking a specifically theoretical basis for their political struggle against 'sexist' ideology turned to this increasingly available literature, and used some of its methods and insights in their own work. From this there emerged an independent body of Marxist-feminist theory. Why was it, then, that these French theories were utilised in the attempt to construct a systematic analysis of sexual oppression?

A materialist theory of social relations stands firmly in opposition to any theory that depends on essentialism in the attempt to characterise 'human nature' — the idea that there is something about being human, beyond the material biological base, which pre-exists society, something essentially human which transcends the terms of any particular set of social relations and institutions of a society.[6] Feminists were attempting to develop a theory which did not assume that there was anything essential about sexual hierarchy and oppression. They were attempting to place the sexual division of labour within identifiable, social conditions rather than within any kind of notion of pre-existing features of the human brain which might differentiate the sexes, or any statement about inherent sexual difference. This is not the total relativisation of all aspects of existence — humans, like other animals, have to eat, for example; and like other mammals, if they reproduce biologically, this takes place in the body of the female. These are physiological facts and to argue with them is futile, *but* they are always, in human societies, mediated by social relations: the social institutions of the production and consumption of food; the ideological significance, in different societies, of food and eating; the social construction of 'man, the hunter' and 'woman, the gatherer' and of 'man, the breadwinner', 'woman, the childrearer' are *not* essential and not part of biological reality. They are forged within a particular social organisation and its accompanying ideological constructions. Equally, the fact that some women can, and do, biologically reproduce is not open to question, but the idea that they thereby spend all of their lives doing it and that they have a mental make-up suited to such activity, is. A historical materialist (i.e. Marxist) seeks to uncover such ideological formulations by asking whose interests they serve, how they are maintained by the institutions of a society, such as law, education and medicine, and how definitions of so-called reality (e.g. the 'nature of woman') are constituted within them. A major component of the battles fought by the Women's Liberation Movement is the struggle against sexist ideology (for instance, the analysis of sexism in children's books and the education system; demonstrations against 'Miss World' competitions) which pre-dated the development of theories of patriarchy. However, such theories are partly concerned with giving a more adequate account of what sexism *is*, where it comes from and what effects it has. One theoretical approach to ideology sees it as 'false consciousness', that is, a consciousness induced by, and necessary to, the capitalist relations of production which will vanish in the aftermath of a socialist revolution. If ideology under capitalism is seen in this way (that is as something that *directly* reflects and legitimates the social relations of production) there is the implication that it is open to inspection by Left-wing groups questioning their own ideological assumptions, or by the consciousness-raising groups of the Women's Liberation Movement, and that it can be sloughed off either during such self-examination or, at the very least, 'after the revolution'. With such a formulation of ideology, it's tempting to see ideological struggle (for instance, against sexism) as something that takes second place to the struggle in the workplace (for instance, to get more women into the paid labour force).

This relegation of ideological issues to second place did not accord with either the political practice of many feminists or with the views of feminist theorists about the relative centrality and primacy of the struggles they were engaged in. Thus, a theoretical formulation of ideology, such as that of Althusser, as something that has as much real force and material effects as have economic or political constraints, was extremely attractive to feminists who had been experiencing and analysing both in every aspect of their lives.[7] To give just one example: the idea that children need their mothers at home with them for the first five years of their lives may well be bolstered up by the particular needs of capital in relation to the position of women in the paid labour force, i.e. by economic forces, but it is also quite clearly in contradiction to these at times; and yet, it presents real obstacles to every woman who wants to work, or has to, when her children are young. These obstacles are partly practical, such as the lack of easily available alternative childcare arrangements; but they are also ideological obstacles in the form of, first, the woman's own self-evaluation as a mother, and second, the evaluation of her by others. A theory that accounts for the existence and force of ideological obstacles such as these seemed tailor-made for the politics of feminism. Moreover, Althusser explicitly connected his theory of ideology to the psychoanalytic theory of Lacan (Althusser, 1971), to whom Marxist-feminists were also turning for an account of the way in which the relations of sexual difference and power were psychically constituted in the unconscious. In my view, there are both theoretical and political reasons for the incorporation, by some Marxist-feminist theorists, of psychoanalytic theory into theories of patriarchy. A major problem in Marxist theory has been the further elaboration of one of its original central projects — how to conceptualise the intersections between the structures of social relations and individual subjects. Economistic strands in Marxism have neglected this issue — by asserting the simple primacy of relations of production, they tend to dismiss the problem of subjectivity as an irrelevance, or at least see it as a secondary problem which will be 'solved' by a revolution in the mode of production. But there have been other attempts to take up this issue and develop a Marxist theory of individual subjectivity. Since Freud's work, these have often taken the form of attempts to fuse Marxist and psychoanalytic theory.[8] Examples are Reich (1972) and Marcuse (1972).[9] However, feminists have tended to be strongly critical of both Freudian and post-Freudian psychoanalytic theory, the latter particularly as exemplified in the works of American psychoanalysts. They have, correctly, pointed to the overtly sexist and unreflective nature of the biological determinism that one encounters on every page of such post-Freudian accounts. Both Millett (1971) and Firestone (1971) develop these criticisms in convincing detail. However, both also point to the *potential* importance for feminist theory of the level of description to which psychoanalytic theory is addressed — that of the construction of the unconscious in terms of power relations and sexual divisions, i.e. sexed subjectivity. The significance of Lacan is thus his claim to have rescued Freudian theory from the biological determinism both of its author and of his successors, and it is precisely because of this claim that some feminist theorists see in Lacan's work the possibility of a non-sexist psychoanalytic theory (Coward and Ellis 1977; Brennan *et al.*, 1976).

Another reason for the acceptance, by some Marxist-feminists, of a psychoanalytic dimension to a theory of patriarchy, derives from the emphasis on personal politics which has always been central to the Women's Liberation Movement. Consciousness-raising is an important aspect of feminist political practice, but in my view it was because some feminists felt that there were limitations to what could be achieved in consciousness-raising groups that psychoanalytic theorising met the acceptance that it did in some quarters. In consciousness-raising, we have tried to understand our 'socialisation' into the female role and femininity, by, for instance, analysing relations of dominance and power between the sexes. We have begun to see how we ourselves can use the 'possession' of children or of intellect as tools for putting each other down. But some of us also began to feel that there were ways in which we had been constructed into our femininity which were not accessible to public reflection in consciousness-raising groups. Relations of dominance and submission, of orientation to the male order, seemed to be locked into our very construction as people;

however hard we confronted this, there seemed to come a point when they were hardly available to consciousness but were as strong and determining of our behaviour as ever. Mitchell's *Psychoanalysis and Feminism* (1974) was one of the first attempts to confront these issues in terms of a psychoanalytic account. Although there are difficulties with her account (Brennan, *et al.*, 1976), its importance lies in her claim that Freudian psychoanalytic theory, rid of its biologism by Lacan, and reworked from a feminist theoretical perspective, can potentially provide a theory of the construction of sexed subjectivity in the unconscious of the child through the social relations of patriarchy and capitalism into which the child was inserted from the moment of its birth and, indeed, beforehand.

Patriarchy and subjectivity

I intend to concentrate on two aspects only of Freud's theory of psychic functioning: first, the Oedipus complex and second, his emphasis on the part played by symbols in the unconscious.

The Oedipus complex is important in psychoanalytic theory because it is here that the psychic differences between male and female are forged. Freud claims that it results from a recognition by both boys and girls of difference in sexual anatomy. From this moment on, according to the theory, the child's psychic development is sexually differentiated. Boys, threatened with castration for masturbation and seeing what they take to be real evidence of this in the absence of a penis in girls, are terrorised into giving up their desire to 'possess' their mother totally and to the exclusion of their father, in exchange for the prospect of one day possessing a woman of their own. Girls, with the same knowledge, accept that castration has already overtaken them and face a future in which the only way in which they can 'possess a penis' is through a relationship with a man who will give them a baby. This baby, particularly if it is boy, is the nearest they will ever get to satisfying their desire for a penis and overcoming the shame of castration. Thus, the child's psyche is forged through his or her knowledge of *anatomical* difference; the interpretation placed upon this; the desire on the part of both girl and boy to continue in the relationship of total symbiotic love with their mother; and, finally, their perception of, and relationship with, their actual family – mother, father, siblings and others. For the 'normal' boy this means competition with other males, proud, though ambivalent, identification with the father as a co-possessor of a penis and thereby member of a superior order, and fear, ambivalent love and contempt for women who do not belong to that order but who are, on the other hand, mothers. Freud frequently complained that it was much more difficult to delineate the psychic characteristics of the 'normal' female, since her options were very much less clear. Castrated from birth, her routes through hatred and identification with the mother could never result in anything other than some hard-won, unstable acceptance of her state. For both sexes then, the Oedipal situation is the beginning of the flight from the place that is female, castrated, impotent; and it is not difficult to see that this would be likely to cause different problems for females than males, since, anatomically speaking, females have no other place to be than in the female place.

This is a vastly oversimplified account of the basic features of Freud's theory of the Oedipus complex. It should not, however, be confused with the simplistic post-Freudian perception of women as castrating, permanently unsatisfied and unsatisfiable, but should be read against Freud's life-long struggle and acknowledged failure to adequately account for the psychic construction of women.[10] Most popularisations of Freud, both pro- and anti-, concentrate on more or less simplistic renderings of Freud's theory of the Oedipus complex; this is particularly true of the tradition of Freudian psychoanalysis in the United States. On the other hand, Freud's theory of symbol formation has been developed in much more detail by European psychoanalysts, who have, in the main, concentrated on psychic development in infancy. The best-known theorists in this tradition are Winnicott and Klein. It is from this tradition that Lacan has developed a highly sophisticated theory of 'signification', which he uses both to reinterpret Freud's theory of the Oedipus complex and to castigate those psychoanalysts who have gone well beyond Freud in the extent of their biological reductionism when discussing the Oedipus complex.

The biological determinism of Freud resides in his assumption that there is something 'natural' about the differential value given to male external genitalia, specifically the penis, as opposed to the female genitalia which are presumed to have only the negative attribute of invisibility.

Freud himself is both confused and confusing about the relationship between the real experiences of the child and the symbols which it constructs and represses into the unconscious and which carry its fears, wishes and desires. Does the child actually have to see and understand the significance of anatomical difference between the sexes in order to enter the Oedipal situation? Or is this a metaphor for the child's attempts to make sense of the anxieties raised by its desire for a totally fulfilling relationship with the mother, when it 'realises' that this is impossible and then in some way relates this impossibility to aspects of the 'real' world (one of the most salient of these being the presence of its father in some sort of relationship with the mother)? Many theorists of psychoanalysis raised these questions long before the post-Lacanian feminists and different solutions were attempted. For instance, one solution was to posit the existence of sexually differentiated psyches from birth, thus locating the psychological differences between the sexes not in the Oedipal situation but even further back in biology (see Jones in Chasseguet-Smirgel, 1970).[11] Another was to posit a stage prior to that of penis envy which consists in 'breast envy' (Stärcke, 1921). Similarly, Horney (1933) made the suggestion that boys suffer from 'womb envy' in much the same way as girls are meant to suffer from 'penis envy'. It was also pointed out by a few writers (Adler, Thompson, 1973) that what Freud has provided is a brilliant account of the psychological development of boys and girls in the bourgeois, capitalist and puritanical Viennese society in which he lived, but that this did not necessarily hold for all possible societies and all possible methods of rearing children.[12] However, it was not until Lacan provided a 're-reading' of Freud which emphasised and provided a much more detailed analysis of the formation and structuring of the *symbolic* function in the unconscious, that feminists had a potential means by which to relate highly salient sexual divisions in society to the symbolic structuring of the unconscious in boys and girls.

Lacan concentrates on the processes by which the infant, initially an undifferentiated blob of feeling (Lacan's punning (H)ommelette), first starts to separate itself from the mother through a primitive image of self and other; he argues that, because the images that it creates to contain its desire for the mother do not satisfy this desire, the child forms a chain of signifiers of desire (symbols which the child constructs to represent, and to some extent repress, its desire for complete fulfilment). This construction of a chain of signifiers is, in Lacan's theory, the precondition for the development of language and of subjectivity. Lacan makes a potentially useful distinction between the realms of the real, imaginary and symbolic in the child's dealings with the world. The real is that which exists objectively, hunger in the child, the mother as a body in the world, etc. But we can never experience the real unmediated by the imaginary (in the infant) and the symbolic (in the language-speaking human). From the moment of birth, the infant is going to experience moments in which it does not have its needs immediately satisfied. The child's response to this is to create a signifier for its desire which will both allay the terror aroused by lack of satisfaction and will also 'carry' that terror (e.g. Klein's 'good breast'). It is arguable that a capacity to make one thing stand for another in this particular way is what differentiates the human brain from that of animals since it is the precursor of the symbolic function which in its turn makes human language possible. However, according to Lacan, this capacity is inherently problematic.

The infant starts with biological needs, such as the periodic need for nourishment. Inevitably, these needs are not always immediately satisfied, and over time and in the repeated absence of satisfaction a substitute is found, in the form of a representation of some external object, i.e. of something separate from the infant, and capable of obstructing needs as well as of satisfying them: in Lacan's theory this object is the mother, and its representation Lacan regards as a 'signifier' (a symbol) of the missing satisfaction, its 'signified' (the 'thing' that the symbol is made to represent).[13] (This substitution is just the same as that whereby in dreams, according to Freud, the hallucinated fulfilment of a wish substitutes for its real fulfilment.) Moreover, the need whose frustration gives rise to a representation, is then transformed by that representation into something different, which Lacan distinguishes as *desire*. Desire is different from need, because being desire for a substitute, it can *never* be 'satisfied', and so it in turn must be substituted for by yet another signifier, of which it is now the signified. The infant thus continues to create a chain of signifiers of its desire for total fulfilment, none of which can ever satisfy it. Prior to the acquisition of language, this chain of signifiers is completely in the realm of the imaginary, as the child exists for itself in a relationship of symbiotic narcissism with the mother. In this relationship with the mother, there is no individualised subjectivity. That is, the child does not initially make a distinction between self and other but exists in a relationship of 'deadly dualism' within the nexus of its own feelings and its experience of the mother. Even when, in Lacan's mirror-stage, the child makes a primitive separation between self and mother, its imaginary signification of self is an all-powerful 'mirror' of its signification of the mother. Subjectivity proper is ushered in by language, when the child gives up its fantasies of self for a human form of subjectivity: in language, 'I' refers to the speaker — any speaker — its value as a signifier is neutralised by contrast with the child's imaginery construction of 'self'. In using language, the child by accepting one set of significations, excludes others — thus 'full meaning' is not possible in language. Language, itself a chain of signifiers, acts to contain the child's free-floating narcissim by privileging certain signifiers (for instance the 'I/You' distinction) and making others inaccessible (such as the child's fantasy of 'omnipotence' which becomes repressed). The realm of the symbolic, language, is built upon the realm of the imaginary; but, in language, symbols are cultural and conventional and in accepting them and becoming human, the child gives up others — for instance the possibility of access to its signifier of desire as total possession of the mother. Thus subjectivity is not given at birth but is acquired through a process of signification. According to Lacan, the importance of the Oedipus complex resides in the fact that the entry into the symbolic order is retrospectively interpreted by the child as a separation from the mother (female) by the world of the father (male) (i.e. language and culture) by virtue of perceived power relations in the nuclear family. Thus anatomical sex becomes a privileged signifier of lack and loss.

It is not possible for me to lay out Lacan's theory in detail here nor do I think it necessary for this chapter.[14] It is an immensely complex theory rooted not only in psychoanalysis but also in the French tradition of semiotics (theories of meaning). Lacan's theory of signification flows from Freud's comment that 'the unconscious is structured like a language'. Hence, Lacan observes that the counterpart of metaphor in the unconscious is the process of displacement, whereby one object is made to stand for another; and that the counterpart of metonymy (where the part is made to stand for the whole) is condensation, where a number of significations are held by one signifier.

For the purposes of the discussion presented here, we need to consider three central aspects of Lacanian theory. First, by contrast with Freud's theory, Lacan discusses in detail the ways in which the pre-verbal infant attempts to represent the world to itself in images and symbols into which it projects its desires and fears. In this, his work has similarities with that of Winnicott and Klein, both of whom developed Freudian theory in extended analyses of infant psycho-symbolic development. Second, Lacan maintains that the infant, in transforming its needs into symbolic projections, creates a situation in which it now desires those projections, but since they *are* projections and not actual needs, these desires can never be fulfilled. It is the impossibility of fulfilling its desires which leads the infant to set up a chain of signifiers, each one more distant from the original need; and it is this capacity which is the prerequisite for the acquisition of the chain of culturally determined signifiers which is language. Third, the condition of subjectivity is that the infant, in learning language, submits to culture and to its separation from the mother which it sees as having been effected by the power of the father. The point about this is that, in Lacan's theory, it is not the father and mother *per se* who are important in the structuring of the child's unconscious, but the projections which they come to hold: the mother in acting as the signifier of the child's wish for complete unmediated fulfilment; the father in acting as the signifier of the impossibility of fulfilling desire — as the signifier of that which separates the child from its signification of the mother as that which it desires.

It is precisely because Lacan replaces the real mother and father of Freudian theory with the significations which the child constructs for itself around them in order to contain its desires, that his theory raises the possibility that there might be different significations under different kinds of social relations. Thus the possibility is raised that a child whose primary relationship is not with one, female person will not come to represent its desires to itself in a fantasised image of one person, later and retrospectively seen as female. We might then ask what form the recognition of loss and unfulfillable desire, and the entry into language, would take in infants born into a society in which such social hierarchies as existed were in no way based on sex. Is there any reason to suppose that such a development of subjectivity would be crucially related to the child's sex? These questions are certainly not asked by Lacan himself who, while providing for their possibility with his theory of signification, assumes that it is the penis that comes to act as the privileged signifier of loss and lack, and that the child will necessarily have a primary relationship with one, female person in its infancy. Furthermore, he states that even without a real mother and father the main organising principles for the child's significations will be in terms of the significance of sexual difference. But he does not make this a potentially culturally specific phenomenon — he assumes its timeless universality as one of the major structuring principles of the unconscious.

Feminists, in taking up Lacan's theory, have claimed that it can be made culturally specific; but, with few exceptions, they have not gone on to work this out in detail and have remained wedded to the details of Lacan's theoretical identification of the mother as the object of desire and of the father as being the means for the representation of lack — the 'phallus-penis'. Thus, the potential of Lacan's theory for producing an analysis of the historical specificity of sexed subjectivity is exchanged for analyses which, because they concentrate on expounding the complexities of Lacanian theory rather than asking how we can take it further, often seem to capitulate to the universalism of that theory. The implication is often that subjectivity forged within sexual difference stands outside of any specific social-cultural situation, and that therefore it is unchangeable under any conceivable form of childrearing and social relations, even those that differ radically from any past or present form. It is mainly a question of emphasis — anyone writing about Lacan from a feminist perspective raises the possibility that, under non-patriarchal social relations, subjectivity might be different, but they tend to devote the rest of their analyses to a detailed exposition of Lacan and Althusser in ways which lead one to suppose that they are relatively uninterested in the possibility that different social relations might engender different subjectivities. There are exceptions to this: Adams in her article entitled 'Representation and Sexuality' (1978) asks whether there is anything that can be rescued from psychoanalysis in terms of a theory of how representation and desire might be signified in a non-sexist or non-sex-differentiated society, while she acknowledges that the sexed subject is essential to any theory of psychoanalysis. Brennan *et al.* (1976) go even further in claiming that the dualism of Lacan's mirror-stage may be a function of the alienation in which all human infants are reared in capitalist societies, and of the isolation of the mother-infant relationship. These, surely, are the kinds of questions that we should be asking in an analysis of the relationship between subjectivity and patriarchal social relations.

Another fruitful direction of study is to examine particular historical moments in terms of the relationship between the economic, political and ideological forces in operation, and to ask how this might articulate with the psychic structuring of individuals and groups in the society. There has been interesting work on this in France by Marxist-feminists working within a Lacanian framework. Kristeva's work in semiotics and on women in China is one example of this approach (1977), and Macciocchi's article on women and fascism is another (1979). The problem with all these studies is that they are written in a language which is heavily Lacanian and this makes them extremely inaccessible to the non-specialist reader interested in psychoanalysis, patriarchy and subjectivity. One of the main aims of this section of my chapter has been to make the terminology and enterprise of current psychoanalytic theory somewhat more accessible to feminists who are interested in subjectivity but dismayed and subdued by the language used by Lacan and by many who employ his theory in their analyses.

In the final section of this chapter, I address the problem of what the political significance of a theory of subjectivity might be within the context of Marxist-feminism.

Theory and political practice

There is a considerable degree of disenchantment among some feminists with the work on subjectivity and patriarchy that I have been outlining above. Criticisms are made from three perspectives:

(a) Much of the work on subjectivity and patriarchy serves only to re-emphasise the view that patriarchy is universal and unchangeable, by claiming that the structuring of the unconscious in sexed terms is an inevitable feature of human existence. This is a disturbing and discouraging conclusion for feminists to come to.

(b) Since theories of Marxism and those of feminism are concerned with different theoretical and political objects, it is confusing and incorrect to put them together.

(c) Even where feminists have raised the possibility of the unconscious being structured differently under different forms of social relations, this has by no means led to any substantial modification of the tactics and aims of feminism. The usefulness of such theory for guiding political action is therefore questioned.

In my view, these are closely related questions and this final section is devoted to discussing them.

The conclusion that patriarchy is universal and unchangeable derives from the over-reliance by some feminists on the theorists from whom they draw their analyses. Many of these theorists assume what they are setting out to explain; they posit some universal feature of the human brain or human society which, since it *is* universal, is not amenable to modification under any conceivable form of social relations. Freud assumes, *a priori*, the intrinsic and self-evident value of the penis over the vagina, and so, by implication, does Lacan. Lacan assumes that difference and loss will inevitably be identified with the value-laden difference between the sexes and with the loss of the female caregiver. Many feminists, in adopting the theories of Freud and Lacan, have not confronted the assumption that biological reproduction by the female inevitably results in one, solitary, female caregiver for the child during infancy. Where this has been the case, they have not asked why then the breast does not become a privileged signifier of loss in addition to, or instead of, the penis (as it does in the theories of Klein (1975)). While primary infant care by the biological mother may be a matter of historical fact (and, to some extent, of necessity) in societies where the only method of feeding the infant is on the breast, conditions have changed in many societies. Reproduction, in anything other than the strictly biological sense of gestation and parturition, is not a timeless universal, but is both situated in and co-determining of many other aspects of social relations. Societies differ widely in their marriage and kinship practices as well as in their child-rearing practices, and these practices are accompanied by very different ideologies which may, in turn, be realised in differences in the way that subjectivity is structured. The attempt to link the marriage and kinship practices of different societies to their social organisation of production is a very difficult task, and is the subject of major current controversies in anthropology. Mitchell (*op.cit.*), instead of addressing this problem, turns rather to Lévi-Strauss's analysis of kinship as the exchange of women by men. She equates the taboo on incest between brothers and sisters, which Lévi-Strauss claims is the precondition of kinship, with Freud's theory of the taboo on incest between mother and child — both are meant to be the initiating condition for human culture.[15] But it is precisely the 'over-arching' nature of such statements — their universalism — which makes them inaccessible to any specific historical or social enquiry. On the one hand, as Edholm, Young and Harris (1977) point out, the claim that it is men who exchange women is inadequate as a summary of the complex and different ways in which kinship and marriage are organised in different societies. On the other, if in the face of this, one still wants to claim that it is a 'deep structure' description of what is really going on, then this must be an assumption of the theory rather than an empirical fact. In either case it is a singularly unhelpful starting point for analysis of the relation between the social organisation of production, marriage and kinship patterns, childrearing and subjectivity.

The problem is that anatomical sex and biological reproduction have been, and are still, so central an aspect of our social organisation that it is difficult to distance oneself sufficiently to be able to analyse the *social* categories of 'female' and 'male'. In any discussion which is relevant to an analysis of the sexual division of labour, these categories tend to be taken as unproblematic. However, to take them as unproblematic is to assume that which is the object of study. The same difficulty arises with Engels' (1968 edn.) discussion of the subordination of women. As Brown (1978) has recently pointed out, Engels assumes that a sexual division of labour preceded the seizure by men of the surplus produced in 'primitive communist' societies. Now this *may* be a reasonable assumption, but he gives no reasons for it; and his belief that women's labour originally contributed solely in the home led him to confuse the problem that he was trying to solve — that of the relationship between external economic changes (from hunter-gatherer to accumulating pastoralists) and changes in the power relations of the sexes. It is such assumptions, wether implicit or explicit, which can lead to the position that there is something ahistorical about the 'natures' of women and men, which makes certain aspects of subjectivity and of the sexual division of labour unchangeable in principle, rather than the product of particular biological, economic and political forces.

Recently there has been a good deal of theoretical debate about whether it is in principle possible to combine the theoretical concerns of feminism with a broadly Marxist analysis of social relations. On the one hand Cousins (1978) argues that the inclusion of sexual divisions within the 'discourse' of Marxism is a theoretically improper exercise since Marx's theory of production does not have gender as an analytic category. On the other, Eisenstein and her colleagues in the United States discuss joining together theories of sexual, racial and class divisions as if there were almost no problem at all. The difficulties apparent in an attempt to reconcile such opposed positions arise in part from the fact that there are many different strands to both Marxist and feminist theorising. While it is certainly the case that canonical Marxist theory does not have gender as an analytic category, it has been argued that this is one of a number of gaps in the theory which become apparent when it is used to analyse the present political and industrial situation. However, those who wish to develop a Marxist feminism must clearly go further than simply arguing by analogy from class relations to relations of oppression between the sexes — failure to do this opens up the possibility of a radically separatist politics and an analysis based on untheorised categories of 'male' and 'female'. The difficulty here lies in conceptualising the power relations between the sexes in any way that can be strictly theoretically linked to Marxist theories of the relations of production under captialism and imperialism.

However there are other developments of Marxist theory where it seems quite clear that a theory that fails to take gender into account must be inadequate. The extension of Marxist theory into the areas of ideology and subjectivity,[16] as well as to pre-captialist societies, may not have made use of gender as an analytic category but this is surely a weakness rather than a reason for continuing to exclude it. A theory of ideology that does not deal with the reproduction of sexual oppression throughout all social relations and institutions of the State cannot reflect present-day political realities.

Finally, we have to consider the question of what significance a theory of subjectivity and its relation to ideology might have for the broader concerns of the women's movement. Presumably this depends on how one defines the relation between theory and practice as well as what is 'political' — these continue to be major issues for all Left-wing groups. Looked at one way, one might well argue that theoretical analysis still seems to lead us to the struggles that have been fought by the current women's movement since its inception, such as for more communal childcare or alternatives to the nuclear family. Thus, even where feminists have raised the possibility of the unconscious being structured differently under different forms of social relations, this has by no means led to any substantial modification of the tactics and aims of feminism. Theorising about the formation of subjectivity might therefore look pointless: an unnecessary detour and a waste of energy.

There are a number of tentative answers to such a position. First, work on sexed subjectivity and its relation to ideology can or should provide us with theoretical support for the possibility that the battle against sexist ideology and practice can be fought — that current relations between the sexes are not the inevitable result either of being human or of anatomical difference and the biological role of women in child-bearing which results from it. Secondly, it is important, if we accept any role for theory in political struggles at all, to be able to provide an analysis of sexual oppression which does not depend on any quintessential notion of 'man' or 'woman'. With such a theory one can counter essentialist arguments whether they come from radical separatist or bourgeois thought. Thirdly, the development of a theory of the relation between sexed subjectivity and ideology — which, it must be said, we are very far from achieving — is critical in the fight to resist the notion that the struggle to end sexual oppression can 'wait' on the class struggle, whether this notion is expressed in terms of immediate political priorities or long-term revolutionary change.

However, work on ideology and subjectivity has to avoid becoming a sealed-off theoretical enterprise more concerned with the relation between different 'discourses' than with the political relevance of theory. Despite their potential usefulness, there is a danger of uncritically accepting theories that are ahistorical and whose opacity may disguise inconsistency. This in turn can lead us to theorise sexual divisions in such a way that they cannot be related to the specificities of any actual situation. To the extent that some ways of theorising patriarchal social relations do this they must be rejected.

Notes

1   I am grateful to many people for support and encouragement during the time that it took to write this paper. Apart from various members of the Collective, I should particularly mention Bev Brown, John Churcher,

Karen Clarke, Ruth Frankenberg, Julian Roberts and Cathy Urwin all of whom, at various times, provided extensive comments, rewriting and ideas. They, of course, bear no responsibility for the final product. Ruth Frankenberg is the person who has had to deal most continously with me and the many versions of this paper over the last few years and I am deeply grateful to her for her critical support.

2 *Spare Rib* is a very good source of articles about women's position in societies all over the world. Specifically there is an article in the July issue about women in China. (1979, No.84).

3 See also Riley (1979) for a discussion of this in relation to women's work and nursery provision in Britain during the 1939—45 war.

4 That they were only relatively independent is indicated by fact that most authors writing about Lacan from a Marxist perspective were also members of the so-called 'New Left'. Specifically during the upsurge of interest in Althusserian theory in the 60s and early 70s which was marked by a number of articles in *New Left Review*, Juliet Mitchell was on the editorial board of this journal. Mitchell's (1974) *Psychoanalysis and Feminism* was the first radical reappraisal of psychoanalytic theory from a feminist perspective to be published in English.

5 Indeed Althusser explicitly connects his theory of ideology to Lacan's theory of the Imaginary. Althusser (1971) pp.181—202.

6 I am well aware that by using the terms 'materialism' and 'essentialism', I am raising in a somewhat simplistic fashion very complex epistemological issues which are the subject of much discussion by theorists on the Left at the moment. My excuse is that those reading this paper as an introduction to the field of enquiry will find these terms in any further reading that they do and it was therefore better to confront them, however inadequately, than to ignore them. I have found a starting point for thinking about these terms in the *Theses on Feuerbach* (Selected Works of Marx and Engels, 1968) and in the section on 'The fetishism of the commodity and its secret' in Ch.1 of *Capital, Vol.1* (Marx, 1976).

7 For an introduction to Althusser's theory see Hirst (1976).

8 An exception to this is Sève (1975) who explicitly rejects psychoanalysis in his analysis of the individual/society split. Riley (1978) discusses the work of Sève. It is also worth pointing out that those Marxist authors who have immersed themselves in psychoanalytic theory rarely raise the issue of the politics of the *practice* of psychoanalysis — which is usually only available to the rich and often succeeds only in reinforcing current ideology. There is some discussion of this in Gordon (1977).

9 A good introduction to these writers of the Frankfurt School is provided by Jay (1973). See also Poster (1978).

10 See Freud (1933) Lecture XXXlll on 'Feminity' p.117.

11 Many of the attempts by neo-Freudians to deal more adequately with psychical differences between males and females have lately been mirrored

(often not explicitly) by post-Lacanian theorists who are also feminists. In my view both Montrelay and Irigaray are postulating something intrinsic to the female psyche as opposed to that of the male. Some discussion of Irigaray's work can be found in the journal, *Ideology and Consciousness* (Vol.1) together with an interview with her. *m/f, 1* has a translation of an article by Montrelay and a framework for viewing this is provided by Parveen Adams' article 'Representation and Sexuality' in the same issue.

12 A marvellous reinterpretation of the case of Dora from the point of view of Freud's insertion into the ideology of his time is given in the final pages of Clément and Cixous (1975). To my knowledge this has unfortunately not been translated into English.

13 The distinction here is between the biological instinct (e.g. for food) and the drive which can only be known through its mental representations and aims, and which is therefore involved from the beginning in both emotion and signification.

14 A good introduction to Lacan is provided by Heath (1976). Also Coward and Ellis (1977) do a useful job of situating Lacanian theory within the semiotic tradition.

15 A more detailed working out of Lacanian theory and Lévi-Strauss's theory of exchange from an anthropological point of view is given by Rubin (1975).

16 This is one way of viewing Foucault's work. Adams and Minson (1978) summarise Foucault's position as 'no form of domination without a determinate form of subjectification (*assujetissement*)'. Some of Habermas' work can be regarded as being concerned with a materialist theory of subjectivity (Habermas, 1970).

Further Reading

The footnotes contain much supplementary material — here I provide only some starting points, full details of which may be found in the bibliography. *Marxism, feminism & class*: Eisenstein (1979), Hartmann (1979), Women's Study Group, Birmingham (1978), also the occasional articles in *New Left Review*, *Capital & Class*.

Feminism, ideology & subjectivity: Mitchell (1974), Brennan et al. (1976), other articles in the journals *Working Papers in Sex, Science & Culture* and *Ideology & Conciousness*.

Lacan: for the shortest introductions see *Working Papers in Sex, Science & Culture*; for the most readable, the relevant parts of Wilden (1977); Lemaire (1977) provides a detailed but non-feminist account and there are often (difficult) articles in *Screen*; see also Laplanche & Pontalis (1973) and Coward & Ellis (1977).

Kinship & Subjectivity: Mitchell (1974), Rubin (1975).

M. Barrett (1980) *Women's Oppression Today* has appeared since this book was written. It provides a clear exposition of the major theories within Marxist-feminism. (London: Verso).

Bibliography

Abortion Act (1967). London: HMSO.

Acker, J. (1973) 'Women and social stratification.' *American Journal of Sociology* 78(4):936–45.

Adams, P. (1978) 'Representation and sexuality.' *m/f* 1:65–82.

Adams, P. and Minson, J. (1978) 'The "subject" of feminism.' *m/f* 2:43–61.

Adler, A. (1973) 'Sex.' In J. Baker Miller (ed.), *Psychoanalysis and Women*, pp. 40–50. Harmondsworth: Penguin. (First published 1927.)

Alexander. S. (1976) 'Women's work in nineteenth-century London: a study of the years 1820–50.' In J. Mitchell and A. Oakley (eds), *The Rights and Wrongs of Women*, pp. 59–111. Harmondsworth: Penguin.

Althusser, L. (1971) 'On Freud and Lacan.' In *Lenin and Philosophy, and Other Essays*, pp. 181–202. London: New Left Books.

Alvarez, A. (1974) *The Savage God: A Study of Suicide*, Harmondsworth: Penguin.

Antonis, B. (1975) *The First Pregnancy: Attitudes to Mothering*. Unpublished research. Cambridge: Medical Psychology Unit.

Appleby, J. (1978) 'Modernisation theory and the formation of modern social theories in England and America.' *Comparative Studies in Society and History* 20:259–85.

Archer, J. (1976) 'Biological explanations of psychological sex differences.' In B. Lloyd and J. Archer (eds), *Exploring Sex Differences*, pp. 241–66. London: Academic Press.

Ardener, E. (1972) 'Belief and the problem of women.' In J. La Fontaine (ed.), *The Interpretation of Ritual*, pp. 135–58. London: Tavistock.

Ardener, E. (1975) 'The "problem" revisited.' In S. Ardener (ed.), *Perceiving Women*, London: Dent.

Ardener, S., (ed.) (1975) *Perceiving Women*, London: Dent.

Ardener, S., (ed.) (1978) *Defining Females*, London: Croom Helm.

Ariès, P. (1973) *Centuries of Childhood*, Harmondsworth: Penguin.

Badcock, C.R. (1975) *Lévi-Strauss: Structuralism and Sociological Theory*, London: Hutchinson.

Banks, J.A. and Banks, O. (1964) *Feminism and Family Planning in Victorian England*, Liverpool: Liverpool University Press.

Barnes, J.A. (1974) 'Genetrix: genitor: nature: culture?' In J. Goody (ed.), *The Character of Kinship*, pp. 61–73. Cambridge: Cambridge University Press.

Barnes, M. and Berke, J. (1973) *Two Accounts of a Journey Through Madness*, Harmondsworth: Penguin.

Barrett, M. and Roberts, H. (1978) 'Doctors and their patients: the social control of women in general practice.' In C. Smart and B. Smart (eds), *Women, Sexuality and Social Control*, pp. 41–52. London: Routledge & Kegan Paul.

Barron, R.D. and Norris, G.M. (1976) 'Sexual divisions and the dual labour market.' In D.L. Barker and S. Allen (eds), *Dependence and Exploitation in Work and Marriage*, pp. 47–69. London: Longman.

Bateson, G. (1972) *Steps to an Ecology of Mind*. New York: Ballantine Publ. Inc.

Beauvoir, S. de (1972) *The Second Sex*, Harmondsworth: Penguin. (First published 1949.)

Bebel, A. (1972) *Women Under Socialism*. New York: Schocken. (Originally published as *Die Frau and der Sozialismus*, Berlin, 1922.)

Becker, G. (1964) *Human Capital: A Theoretical and Empirical Analysis with Special Reference to Education*. New York: National Bureau of Economic Research.

Beechey, V. (1977) 'Some notes on female wage labour in capitalist production.' *Capital and Class* 3:45–66.

Beechey, V. (1978) 'Women and production: a critical analysis of some socio-logical theories of women's work.' In A. Kuhn and A. Wolpe (eds), *Feminism and Materialism*, pp. 155–197. London: Routledge & Kegan Paul.

Bell, R.Q., Weller, G.M. and Waldrop, M.F. (1971) 'Newborn and preschooler: organisation of behaviour and relations between periods.' *Monographs of the Society for Research in Child Development* 36, serial no. 142.

Benjamin, J. (1978) 'Authority and the family revisited; or, a world without fathers?' *New German Critique* 13:35–57. Wisconsin.

Benston, M. (1969) 'The political economy of women's liberation.' *Monthly Review* 21:13–27.

Bernardin de Saint-Pierre, J-H. (1966) *Paul et Virginie*, Paris: Garnier-Flammarion. (First published 1788.)

Berndt, R.M. (1962) *Excess and Restraint Among a New Guinea Mountain People*, Chicago: University of Chicago Press.

278 WOMEN IN SOCIETY

Berry, J.W. (1966) 'Temne and Eskimo perceptual skills.' *International Journal of Psychology* 1:207–29.

Beynon, H. and Blackburn, R.M. (1972) *Perceptions of Work*, Cambridge: Cambridge University Press.

Bibring, G. (1961) 'A study of the psychological processes in pregnancy and the earliest mother-child relationship.' *Psychoanal. Study of the Child* 16:9–24.

Binney, V., Harkell, G. and Nixon, J. 'Refuge provision for battered women.' *Housing* Dec. 1979:6–7.

Birns, B. (1976) 'The emergence and socialisation of sex differences in the earliest years.' *Merrill-Palmer Quarterly* 22(3):229–54.

Blackburn, R.M. and Mann, M. (1979) *The Working Class in the Labour Market*, London: Macmillan.

Bland, L., Brunsdon, C., Hobson, D. and Winship, J. (1978) 'Women "inside and outside" the relations of production.' In Women's Studies Group, Centre for Contemporary Cultural Studies, *Women Take Issue*, pp. 35–78. London: Hutchinson.

Blaxall, M. and Reagan, B., (eds) (1976) *Women and the Work Place: the Implications of Occupational Segregation Signs* 1 (No.3, Pt 2). Chicago: University of Chicago Press.

Bluestone, B. (1977) 'Economic theory and the fate of the poor.' In J. Karabel and A.H. Halsey (eds), *Power and Ideology in Education*, pp. 335–40. New York: Oxford University Press.

Bonachich, E. (1972) 'A theory of ethnic antagonism: the split labour market.' *American Sociological Review* 37(5):547–59.

Bone, M. (1978) 'Recent trends in sterilisation.' *Population Trends* 13:13–16. London: OPEC.

Boocock, S. (1978) 'Historical and sociological research on the family and the life cycle: methodological alternatives.' In J. Demos and S. Boocock (eds), *Turning Points: Historical and Sociological Essays on the Family*, Supplement to the *American Journal of Sociology* 84:S366–S394.

Bosanquet, N. and Doeringer, P. (1973) 'Is there a dual labour market in Great Britain?' *Economic Journal* 83:421–35.

Boserup, E. (1970) *Women's Role in Economic Development*, New York: St Martin's.

Bott, E. (1954) *Family and Social Network*, New York: Free Press.

Bowder, B. (1979) 'Wives who ask for it.' *Community Care*, March 1:

Braverman, H. (1974) *Labor and Monopoly Capital*, New York: Monthly Review Press.

Breen, D. (1975) *The Birth of a First Child: Towards an Understanding of Femininity*, London: Tavistock.

Breen, D. (1978) 'The mother and the hospital.' In S. Lipschitz (ed.), *Tearing the Veil*, pp. 17–35. London: Routledge & Kegan Paul.

Brennan, T., Campioni, M. and Jacka, E. (1976) 'One step forward, two steps back.' *Working Papers in Sex, Science and Culture* 1(1):15−45.

Breugel, I. (1978) 'Bourgeois economics and women's oppression.' *m/f* 1:103−11.

British Association of Social Work (1978) Risk Register. London.

Brome, V. (1979) *Havelock Ellis: a Biography*. London: Routledge & Kegan Paul.

Brown, B. (1977) 'Natural and social division of labour: Engels and the domestic labour debate.' *m/f* 1:25−47.

Brown, G. and Harris, T. (1978) *Social Origins of Depression: A Study of Psychiatric Disorder in Women*. London: Tavistock.

Brown, J.K. (1970) 'A note on the division of labour by sex.' *American Anthropologist* 72:1073−8.

Brown, J.K. (1975) 'Anthropology of women: the natural history stage.' *Reviews in Anthropology* 2:526−32.

Brown, P. and Buchbinder, G., (eds) (1976) *Man and Woman in the New Guinea Highlands*, Washington. D.C.: American Anthropological Association.

Brown, P. (in press) 'How and why are women more polite: some evidence from a Mayan community.' In R. Borker, N. Furman, and S. McConnell-Ginet (eds), *Language and Women's Lives: A Feminist Perspective*, New York: Praeger.

Brown, R. (1965) *Social Psychology*, New York: Macmillan.

Brown, R. (1976) 'Women as employees: some comments on research in industrial sociology.' In D. Barker and S. Allen (eds), *Dependence and Exploitation in Work and Marriage*, pp. 21−46. London: Longman.

Brownmiller, S. (1976) *Against Our Will*, Harmondsworth: Penguin.

Buffery, A. and Gray, J.A. (1972) 'Sex differences in the development of spatial and linguistic skills.' In C. Dunstead and D. Taylor (eds), *Gender Differences: Their Ontogeny and Significance*, London: Churchill Livingstone.

Bullough, V.L. (1976) *Sexual Variance in Society and History*. New York: Wiley.

Bullough V.L. and Voght, M. (1973) 'Homosexuality and its confusion with the "secret sin" in pre-Freudian America.' *Journal of the History of Medicine* XXVII (2):143−55.

Burguiere, A. (1976) 'From Malthus to Max Weber: marriage and the spirit of enterprise.' In R. Forster and O. Ranum (eds), *Family and Society: Selections from the Annales: Economies, Societies, Civilisations*, pp. 237−50. Baltimore, Md.: Johns Hopkins University Press.

Burke, P. (1978) *Popular Culture in Early Modern Europe*, London: Maurice Temple Smith.

Burman, S., (ed.) (1979) *Fit Work for Women*, London: Croom Helm.

Burrow, J.W. (1966) *Evolution and Society: A Study in Victorian Social Theory*, Cambridge: Cambridge University Press.

Busfield, J. (1974) 'Ideologies and reproduction.' In M. Richard (ed.), *Integration of the Child into a Social World*, pp. 11–36. Cambridge: Cambridge University Press.

Cadogan, W. (1748) *An Essay Upon Nursing, and the Management of Children*, London: The Foundling Hospital.

Calhoun, C.J. (1978) 'History, anthropology, and the study of communities: some problems in Macfarlane's proposal.' *Social History* 3:363–73.

Cambridge Community Health Council (1979). *Report of Survey of Maternity Services*. Cambridge, England.

Campbell, J.F.K. (1964) *Honour, Family and Patronage*, Oxford: Clarendon.

Caplan, P. and Bujra, J.M., (eds) (1978) *Women United, Women Divided*, London: Tavistock.

Carstairs, G.M. (1967) *The Twice-born*, Bloomington, Indiana: Indiana University Press.

Cartwright, A. (1970) *Parents and Family Planning Services*, London: Routledge & Kegan Paul.

Cartwright, A. (1978) *Recent Trends in Family Building and Contraception*, Office of population censuses and surveys. London: HMSO.

Cartwright, A. (1979) *The Dignity of Labour*, Oxford: Oxford University Press.

Chagnon, N. (1977) *Yanomamo: The Fierce People*, New York: Holt, Rinehart & Winston.

Chance, J.E. and Goldstein, A.G. (1971) 'Internal-external control of reinforcement and embedded figures performance.' *Perception and Psychophysics* 9:33–4.

Chard, T. and Richards, M. (1977) *Benefits and Hazards of the New Obstetrics*, Spastics International Medical Publications. London: Heinemann.

Chasseguet-Smirgel, J. (1981) *Female Sexuality*, London: Virago Press.

Chesler, P. (1972) *Women and Madness*, New York: Doubleday.

Chetwynd, J. and Hartnett, O., (eds) (1978) *The Sex Role System: Psychological and Sociological Perspectives*, London: Routledge & Kegan Paul.

Chiplin, B. and Sloane, P. (1976) *Sex Discrimination in the Labour Market*, London: Macmillan.

Chisholm, J., Woodson, R.H., Da Costa Woodson, E.M. (1978) 'Maternal blood pressure in pregnancy and newborn irritability.' *Early Human Development* 2(2):171–8.

Chodorow, N. (1974) 'Family structure and feminine personality.' In M.

Rosaldo and L. Lamphere (eds), *Woman, Culture and Society*, pp. 43–66. Stanford, Cal.: Stanford University Press.

Chodorow, N. (1978) *The Reproduction of Mothering*, Berkeley, Cal.: University of California Press.

Clement, C. and Cixous, H. (1975) *La jeune née*, Paris: 10/18.

Cohen, S. *et al.* (1978) *The Law and Sexuality: How to Cope with the Law if You're not 100% Conventionally Heterosexual*, Manchester: Grass Roots Books.

Collier, A. (1977) *R.D. Laing*, Hassocks: Harvester.

Coltheart, M. (1975) 'Sex and learning differences.' *New Behaviour* 1 May: 54–7.

Comer, L. (1978) 'Childcare.' *Humpty Dumpty*, Radical Psychology Magazine No. 9.

Comfort, A. (1968) *The Anxiety Makers*, London: Panther.

The Compact Edition of the Oxford English Dictionary (1971). 2 vols. Oxford: Clarendon Press.

Cooper, D. (1972) *The Death of the Family*, Harmondsworth: Penguin.

Coser, R.L. (1978) 'The principle of patriarchy: the case of The Magic Flute.' *Signs* 4(2):337–48.

Counter Information Services (1976) *Women Under Attack*, London: Counter Information Services.

Cousins, M. (1978) 'Material arguments and feminism.' *m/f* 2:62–70.

Coward, R. (1978) ' "Sexual liberation" and the family.' *m/f* 1:7–24.

Coward, R. and Ellis, J. (1977) *Language and Materialism*, London: Routledge & Kegan Paul.

Coward, R., Lipshitz, S., and Cowie, E. (1976) 'Psychoanalysis and patriarchal structures.' In *Papers on Patriarchy Conference*, pp. 6–20. London: Women's Publishing Collective.

Crawford, C. (1977) The historiography of mental 'illness': a case for the social history of madness. M.Sc. Dissertation, University of Sussex.

Crocker, L.G. (1963) *Nature and Culture: Ethical Thought in the French Enlightenment*, Baltimore: Johns Hopkins University Press.

Cromer, L. (1978) 'Childcare.' In *Humpty Dumpty*, Radical Psychology Magazine, No. 9.

Cunnison, S. (1966) *Wages and Work Allocation*, London: Tavistock.

Curley, R.T. (1973) *Elders, Shades and Women*, Berkeley, Cal.: University of California Press.

Cutler, T. (1978) 'The romance of labour.' *Economy and Society* 7(1):74–95.

Dangerfield, G. (1970) *The Strange Death of Liberal England*, London: Paladin.

Darwin, C. (1871) *Descent of Man*. I, iii. p. 100. London: Murray.

Davidoff, L., L'Esperance, J., and Newby, H. (1976) 'Landscape with figures: home and community in English society.' In J. Mitchell and A. Oakley (eds), *The Rights and Wrongs of Women*, pp. 139–75. Harmondsworth: Penguin.

Davis, E.G. (1973) *The First Sex*, Harmondsworth: Penguin.

Davis, N.Z. (1975) *Society and Culture in Early Modern France*, London: Duckworth.

Day, S. (1980) 'The social construction of depression in women.' Unpublished paper. Cambridge: Medical Psychology Unit.

Deer, L.A. (1977) 'Italian anatomical waxes in the Wellcome Collection: the missing link.' *Revista di Storia delle Scienze Mediche e Naturali* 20:281–98.

Delamont, S. and Duffin, L., (eds) (1970) *The Nineteenth-century Woman: Her Cultural and Physical World*, London: Croom Helm.

Delmar, R. (1976) 'Looking again at Engels' *Origin of the Family, Private Property and the State.*' In J. Mitchell and A. Oakley (eds), *The Rights and Wrongs of Women*, pp. 271–87. Harmondsworth: Penguin.

Demos, J. and Boocock, S., (eds) (1978) *Turning Points: Historical and Sociological Essays on the Family.* Supplement to *American Journal of Sociology* 84. Chicago: University of Chicago Press.

Department of Employment (1974) *Women and Work*, Manpower Paper No. 9. London: HMSO.

Derbyshire, P. (1979) 'The regime of sex.' *Gay Left* 8:29–30.

Deutsch, H. (1947) *The Psychology of Women*, vols 1 & 2. London: Research Books Ltd.

Deyon, P. (1975) *Le temps des prisons. Essai sur l'histoire de la delinquance et les origines du systéme penitentiaire*, Paris: Editions Universitaires.

Dinnerstein, D. (1978) *The Rocking of the Cradle and the Ruling of the World*, London: Souvenir Press.

Dobash, R.E., and Dobash, R.P. (1977–8) 'Wives: the "appropriate" victims of marital violence.' *Victimology* 2:426–42.

Dobash, R.E., and Dobash, R.P. (1979a) 'If you prick me do I not bleed?' *Community Care*, 3 May, 26–28.

Dobash, R.E., and Dobash, R.P. (1980) *Violence Against Wives: A Case Against the Patriarchy*, New York: Free Press.

Doeringer, P.B., and Piore, M.J. (1971) *Internal Labor Markets and Manpower Analysis*, Massachusetts: D.C. Heath.

The Domestic Violence (Matrimonial Proceedings) Act (1976). London: HMSO.

Donajgrodzki, A.P., (ed.) (1977) *Social Control in Nineteenth-century Britain*, London: Croom Helm.

Douglas, M. (1966) *Purity and Danger*, London: Routledge & Kegan Paul.

Donnison, J. (1977) *Midwives and Medical Men: A History of Inter-professional Rivalries and Women's Rights*, London: Heinemann.

Donzelot, J. (1977) *La police des familles*, Paris: Les editions de Minuit.

Draper, E. (1972) *Birth Control in the Modern World: The Role of the Individual in Population Control*, London: Pelican.

Draper, P. (1975) '!Kung women: contrasts in sexual egalitarianism in foraging and sedentary contexts.' In R.R. Reiter (ed.), *Toward an Anthropology of Women*, pp. 77–109. New York: Monthly Review Press.

Dubin, R. (1956) 'Industrial workers' worlds: a study of the "central life interests" of industrial workers.' *Social Problems* 3: 131–42.

Duffin, L. (1978) 'The conspicuous consumptive: woman as an invalid.' In S. Delamont and L. Duffin (eds), *The Nineteenth-century Woman: Her Cultural and Physical World*, pp. 26–56. London: Croom Helm.

Duhet, P-M. (1971) *Les femmes et la révolution 1789–1794*, Paris: Gallimard Julliard.

Dyhouse, C. (1978) 'Working-class mothers and infant mortality in England, 1895–1914.' *Journal of Social History* 12:248–67.

Edholm, F., Harris, O., and Young, K. (1977) 'Conceptualizing women.' *Critique of Anthropology, Women's Issue*, vols 9 and 10 :101–30.

Ehrenreich, B., and English, D. (1979) *For Her Own Good: 150 Years of the Experts' Advice to Women*, London: Pluto Press.

Eisenstein, Z.H. (1979) 'Developing a theory of capitalist patriarchy and socialist feminism.' In Z.H. Eisenstein (ed.), *Capitalist Patriarchy and Socialist Feminism*, pp. 5–40. New York and London: Monthly Review Press.

Ellenberger, H. (1970) *The Discovery of the Unconscious*, London: Allen Lane.

Ellis, H. (1897) *Sexual Inversion (Studies in the Psychology of Sex, vol. 1)*. London: A.F. Davis & Co.

Engels, F. (1968a) *The Origin of the Family, Private Property, and the State*. In *Selected Works of Marx and Engels*, pp. 449–583. London: Lawrence & Wishart.

Engels, F. (1968b) *Socialism, Utopian and Scientific* (1880). In *Selected Works of Marx and Engels*, pp. 375–428. London: Lawrence & Wishart.

Engels, F. (1971) *The Condition of the Working Class in England*, Trans. and ed. by W.O. Henderson and W.H. Chaloner. Oxford: Oxford University Press.

Ennew, J. (1978) 'The patriarchal puzzle.' Review of *Critique of Anthropology: Women's Issue* vol. 3(9/10). *m/f* 2:71–84.

Equal Opportunities Commission (1977) *Women and Low Incomes*, November. London: HMSO.

Equal Opportunities Commission (1978) *Second Annual Report 1977*, London: HMSO.

Erikson, E. (1965) 'Inner and outer space: reflections on womanhood.' In R.J. Lifton (ed.), *The Woman in America*, Boston: Houghton Mifflin.

Fagin, L. (n.d.) 'Depression in working-class women.' *Medicine in Society* 3(1):6−8.

Fairbairns, Zoë (1979) *Benefits*. London: Virago.

Fairchilds, C. (1978) 'Female sexual attitudes and the rise of illegitimacy: a case study.' *Journal of Interdisciplinary History* 7:627−67.

Fairweather, H. (1976) 'Sex differences in cognition.' *Cognition* 4:231−80.

Farrell, C. (1978) *My Mother Said. . . . The Way Young People Learned about Sex and Birth Control*, London: Routledge & Kegan Paul.

Fee, E. (1974) 'The sexual politics of Victorian social anthropology.' In M. Hartmann and L.W. Banner (eds), *Clio's Consciousness Raised*, New York: Harper & Row.

Figlio, K. (1978) 'Chlorosis and chronic disease in nineteenth-century Britain: the social constitution of somatic illness in a capitalist society.' *Social History* 3(2):167−97.

Figlio, K. and Jordanova, L. (1979) Review of Andrew Scull, 'Decarceration.' *Radical Science Journal* 8:99−104.

Fine, B. (1975) *Marx's Capital*, London: Macmillan.

Firestone, S, (1971) *The Dialectic of Sex*, London: Jonathan Cape. (Reprinted 1979 London: Women's Press.)

Fogarty, M., Rapoport, R. and Rapoport, R. (1977) *Sex, Career and Family*, London: Allen & Unwin.

Foucault, M. (1965) *Madness and Civilization: A History of Insanity in the Age of Reason*, New York: Mentor Books. (Published in UK by Tavistock, London, 1966.)

Foucault, M. (1975) *Discipline and Punish: The Birth of the Prison*, London: Allen Lane.

Foucault, M. (1976) *Mental Illness and Psychology*, New York: Harper & Row. (First published in French in 1954.)

Foucault, M., (ed) (1978) *I, Pierre Rivière, having slaughtered my mother, my sister and my brother*, (Trans. from French) Harmondsworth: Penguin.

Foucault, M. (1979) *History of Sexuality*, vol. 1. London: Allen Lane.

Freud, S. (1913) *Totem and Taboo*, Standard Edition, Vol. XII. London: Hogarth.

Freud, S. (1920) 'The Psychogenesis of a Case of Female Homosexuality.' *International Journal of Psycho-Analysis* I(ii): 125−49.

Freud, S. (1933) *New Introductory Lectures on Psychoanalysis*, Standard Edition, Vol. XXII. London: Hogarth.

Freud, S. (1935) 'Instincts and their vicissitudes.' In *Collected Papers*, Vol. IV. London: Hogarth.

Freud, S. (1977) *On Sexuality*, Harmondsworth: Penguin. (First published 1905).

Freud, S. and Breuer, J. (1974) *Studies on Hysteria*, Harmondsworth: Penguin. (First published 1895.)

Friedl, E. (1967) 'The position of women: appearance and reality.' *Anthropological Quarterly* 40:97—108.

Friedl, E. (1975) *Women and Men: An Anthropologist's View*, New York: Holt, Rinehart & Winston.

Frisch, H. (1977) 'Sex stereotypes in adult-infant play.' *Child Development* 48:1671—5.

Garai, J. and Sheinfeld, A.(1968) 'Sex differences in mental and behavioural traits.' *Genetic Psych. Monograph* 77:169—269.

Gardiner, J. (1975) 'Women's domestic labour.' *New Left Review* 89:47—58.

Gardiner, J., Himmelweit, S. and Mackintosh, M. (1976) *On the Political Economy of Women*, CSE pamphlet no. 2. London.

Garnsey, E. (1978) 'Women's work and theories of class stratification.' *Sociology* 12(2):223—43.

Gavron, H. (1966) *The Captive Wife: Conflicts of Housebound Mothers*, Harmondsworth: Penguin.

Gay Left. Gay Left Collective, London, 1975.

Gay Liberation Front (1971) *GLF Manifesto*, London.

Gayford, J.J. (1975) 'Wife-battering: a preliminary survey of 100 cases.' *British Medical Journal* 1:194—7.

Gayford, J.J. (1976) 'Ten types of battered wives.' *The Welfare Officer* 1 (Jan.): 5—9.

Giddens, A. (1973) *The Class Structure of the Advanced Societies*, London: Hutchinson.

Gillison, G. (1980) 'Images of the female in Gimi myths.' In C. MacCormack and M. Strathern (eds), *Nature, Culture and Gender*, Cambridge: Cambridge University Press.

Gilman, C.P. (1981) *The Yellow Wallpaper*, London: Virago Press. (Originally published in *The New England Magazine*, January 1892.)

Glacken, C. (1967) *Traces on the Rhodian Shore: Nature and Culture in Western Thought from Ancient Times to the End of the Eighteenth Century*, Berkeley, Cal.: University of California Press.

Glass, D. (1953) *Introduction to Malthus*, London: Watts.

Goffman, E. (1961) *Asylums: Essays on the Social Situation of Mental Patients and Other Inmates*, Garden City, N.Y.: Doubleday.

Goffman, E. (1968) *Stigma: Notes on the Management of Spoiled Identity*, Harmondsworth: Penguin.

Goffman, E. (1979) *Gender Advertisements*, London: Macmillan.

Goldthorpe, J.H., Lockwood, D., Bechhofer, E. and Platt, J. (1969) *The Affluent Worker in the Class Structure*, Cambridge: Cambridge University Press.

Gomm, R. (1976) 'Breast — best or bestial?' *Midwife, Health Visitor, and Community Nurse* 12(10):317—21.

Goodale, J.C. (1971) *Tiwi Wives: A Study of the Women of Melville Island, North Australia*, Seattle and London: University of Washington Press.

Goodale, J.C. (1980) 'Gender, sexuality, and marriage: a Kaulong model of nature and culture.' In C. MacCormack and M. Strathern (eds), *Nature, Culture and Gender*, Cambridge: Cambridge University Press.

Goody, E.N. (1970) 'Legitimate and illegitimate aggression in a West African state.' In M. Douglas (ed.), *Witchcraft Confessions and Accusations*, pp. 207–44. London: Tavistock.

Goody, J., (ed.) (1971) *The Developmental Cycle in Domestic Groups*, Cambridge Papers in Social Anthropology, No. 1. Cambridge: Cambridge University Press.

Goody, J. (1977) *The Domestication of the Savage Mind*, Cambridge: Cambridge University Press.

Gordon, C. (1977) 'The unconscious of psychoanalysis: Robert Castel's *Le psychanalyse: l'ordre psychanalytique et le pouvoir*.' *Ideology and Consciousness* 2:109–27.

Gordon, D.M. (1972) *Theories of Poverty and Underemployment*, Massachusetts: D.C. Heath.

Gordon, L. (1977) *Woman's Body, Woman's Right: A Social History of Birth Control in America*, Harmondsworth: Penguin.

Graham, H. (1978) 'Problems in ante-natal care.' Paper presented to Child Poverty Action Group, and Dept. of Health and Social Security, April 1979. London.

Gray, J. and Buffery, A. (1971) 'Sex differences in emotional and cognitive behaviour in mammals including man: adaptive and neural bases.' *Acta Psychologia* 35:89–111.

Green, S. (1971) *The Curious History of Contraception*, London: Ebury Press.

Greenwood, V. and Young, J. (1976) *Abortion in Demand*, London: Pluto Press.

Grob, G. (1973) *Mental Institutions in America: Social Policy to 1875*, New York: Free Press.

Groddeck, G. (1949) *The Book of the It*, London: Vision Press. (First published in German 1923.)

Habermas, J. (1970) 'Towards a theory of communicative competence.' In H.P. Dreitzel (ed.), *Recent Sociology* 2: pp. 115–148, London: Macmillan.

Haire, N., (ed.) (1930) *Sexual Reform Congress of World League for Sexual Reform*, London: Kegan Paul, Trench, Trubner & Co.

Haller, J. and Haller, R. (1974) *The Physician and Sexuality in Victorian America*, Urbana, Ill.: University of Illinois Press.

Hanmer, J. (1977) 'Community action, women's aid and the Women's Liberation Movement.' In M. Mayo (ed.) *Women in the Community*, London: Routledge & Kegan Paul.

Hareven, T. (1976) 'Modernisation and family history: perspectives on social change.' *Signs* 2:190−206.

Harne, L. (1978) 'Depo-provera in use.' *Spare Rib* 69:28.

Harper, E.B. (1969) 'Fear and the status of women.' *South-western Journal of Anthropology* 25:81−95.

Harris, O. (1980) 'The Laymis of the Central Bolivian Highlands.' In C. MacCormack and M. Strathern (eds), *Nature, Culture and Gender*, Cambridge: Cambridge University Press.

Harrison, B. (1978) *Separate Spheres: Opposition to Women's Suffrage in Britain*, London: Croom Helm.

Harrison, F. (1977) *The Dark Angel: Aspects of Victorian Sexuality*, London: Sheldon Press.

Hartmann, H. (1976) 'Capitalism, patriarchy, and job segregation by sex.' *Signs* 1 (No. 3, Pt. 2):137−67.

Hartmann, H.I. (1979) 'The unhappy marriage of Marxism and feminism: towards a more progressive union.' *Capital and Class* 8:1−33.

Hartnett, O. (1978) 'Sex-role stereotyping at work.' In J. Chetwynd and O. Hartnett (eds), *The Sex Role System*, pp. 76−92. London: Routledge & Kegan Paul.

Heath, S. (1976) ' "Anata Mo.".' *Screen* 17(4):49−66.

Hegel, G.W.F. (1966) *The Phenomenology of Mind*, translated with introduction and notes by J.B. Baillie, 2nd edn. London: George Allen & Unwin.

Hegel, G.W.F. (1952) *The Philosophy of Right*, translated with notes by T.M. Knox. Oxford: Oxford University Press.

Hershman, P. (1977) 'Virgin and mother.' In I.M. Lewis (ed.), *Symbols and Sentiments*, pp. 269−92. London: Academic Press.

Hewitt, M. (1958) *Wives and Mothers in Victorian Industry*, London: Rocklift.

Himes, N.E. (1970) *The Medical History of Contraception*, New York: Schocken. (First published 1936.)

Himmelweit, S. and Mohun, S. (1977) 'Domestic labour and capital.' *Cambridge Journal of Economics* 1(1):15−31.

Hirst, P.O. (1976) 'Althusser's theory of ideology.' *Economy and Society* 5(4): 385−412.

History of Childhood Quarterly: The Journal of Psychohistory, New York, (from 1973).

Hocquenghem, G. (1978) *Homosexual Desire*, London: Allison & Busby.

Hodges, A. and Hutter, D. (1974) *With Downcast Gays*, London: Pink Triangle Press.

Hodges, J. and Hussain, A. (1979) Review article: 'Jacques Donzelot, La Police des Familles.' *Ideology and Consciousness* 5:87−123.

Holt, A. (trans.) (1977) *Selected Writings of Alexandra Kollontai*, London:

Motive Books, Allison & Busby.

Horkheimer, M. (1972) 'Authority and the family.' In *Critical Theory*, pp. 47–128. New York: Herder & Herder.

Horney, K. (1933) 'The denial of the vagina.' *International Journal of Psychoanalysis* 14:57–70.

Horney, K. (1967) *Feminine Psychology*, New York: W.W. Norton.

The Housing (Homeless Persons) Act (1977). London: HMSO.

Hufton, O. (1971) 'Women in revolution 1789–1796. *Past and Present* 53:90–108.

Hufton, O. (1974) *The Poor of Eighteenth-century France*, Oxford: Oxford University Press.

Hufton, O. (1975–6) 'Women and the family economy in eighteenth-century France.' *French Historical Studies* 9:1–22.

Humphries, J. (1977) 'Class struggle and the persistence of the working-class family.' *Cambridge Journal of Economics* 1: 241–58. London: Academic Press.

Humpty Dumpty (1978). Radical Psychology Magazine, No. 9. Issue on childcare.

Hurstfield, J. (1978) *The Part-time Trap*, Low Pay Unit Pamphlet 9, December. London.

Hutt, C. (1972) *Males and Females*, Harmondsworth: Penguin.

Hyde, H.M. (1972) *The Other Love: A Historical and Contemporary Survey of Homosexuality in Britain*, London: Heinemann.

Ignatieff, M. (1978) *A Just Measure of Pain: The Penitentiary in the Industrial Revolution 1750–1850*, London: Macmillan.

Illich, I. (1975) *Medical Nemesis*. Harmondsworth: Penguin.

Illich, I. (1977) *Limits to Medicine. Medical Nemesis: The Medical Expropriation of Health*, Harmondsworth: Penguin.

Jay, M. (1973) *The Dialectical Imagination*, London: Heinemann.

Jeffrey, L. and Pahl, J. (1979) 'Battered women and the police.' Paper presented to the 1979 Conference of the British Sociological Association.

Jephcott, P., Seear, N. and Smith, J.H. (1962) *Married Women Working*, London: Allen & Unwin.

Johnson, R. (1970) 'Educational policy and social control in early Victorian England.' *Past and Present* 49:96–119.

Jordanova, L.J. (1979) 'Earth science and environmental medicine: the synthesis of the late Enlightenment.' In L.J. Jordanova and R. Porter (eds), *Images of the Earth: Essays in the History of the Environmental Sciences*, pp. 119–46. Chalfont, St Giles: British Society for the History of Science.

Jordanova, L.J. (1980) 'Romantic science? Michelet, morals, and nature.' *British Journal for the History of Science* 13(1):44–50.

Jordanova, L.J. (1980) 'Natural facts: an historical perspective on science and sexuality.' In C. MacCormack and M. Strathern (eds), *Nature, Culture and Gender*, pp. 42–69. Cambridge: Cambridge University Press.

Kaberry, P.M. (1939) *Aboriginal Women: Sacred and Profane*, Philadelphia: Blakiston.

Kaberry, P.M. (1952) *Women of the Grassfields*, London: HMSO, Colonial Research Publication 14.

Kelly, L. (1976) The personal is political – using domestic violence as a case study. PhD dissertation, University of East Anglia.

Kenealy, A. (1920) *Feminism and Sex Extinction*. London: T. Fisher Unwin.

Kinsey, A.C., Pomeroy, W.B., Martin, C.E. and Gebhard, P.H. (1953) *Sexual Behavior in the Human Female*, Philadelphia: W.B. Saunders.

Kitzinger, S. (1978) *Women as Mothers*, London: Fontana.

Klein, M. (1975) *The Writings of Melanie Klein*. London: Hogarth Press.

Klein, V. (1965) *Britain's Married Women Workers*, London: Routledge & Kegan Paul.

Knibiehler, Y. (1976) 'Les medecins et la "nature feminine" au temps du Code Civil.' *Annales: Economies, Sociétés, Civilisations* 31(4):824–45.

Knight, P. (1977a) 'Women and abortion in Victorian and Edwardian England.' *History Workshop Journal* 4:57–69.

Knight, P. (1977b) 'I ain't going to have none – I know summat.' *Spare Rib* 64:37–39.

Kolodny, A. (1975) *The Lay of the Land: Metaphor as Experience and History in American Life and Letters*, Chapel Hill: The University of North Carolina Press.

Kollontai, A. (1977) *Selected Writings of Alexandra Kollontai*, Alix Holt (ed.) London: Allison & Busby.

Komarovsky, M. (1940) *The Unemployed Man and his Family*, New York: Institute of Social Research.

Krafft-Ebing, R. von (1939) *Psychopathia Sexualis*, English edition. London: Heinemann Medical Books.

Kristeva, J. (1977) *About Chinese Women*, London: Marion Boyars.

Kroeber, A.L. and Kluckhohn, C. (1952) *Culture: A Critical Review of Concepts and Definitions*, New York: Random House.

Kuhn, A. and Wolpe, A., (eds) (1978) *Feminism and Materialism: Women and Modes of Production*, London: Routledge & Kegan Paul.

Labov, W. (1972) *Sociolinguistic Patterns*, chapters 8 and 9. Philadelphia: University of Pennsylvania Press.

Lasch, C. (1980) 'Life in the therapeutic state.' *New York Review of Books*. 12.6.1980.

Lafitte, F. (1958) 'Homosexuality and the law. The Wolfenden Report in historical perspective.' *British Journal of Delinquency* 1958/9:8–19.

LaFontaine, J.S., (ed.) (1978) *Sex and Age as Principles of Social Differen-*

tiation, ASA Monograph 17. London: Academic Press.

Laing, R.D. and Esterson, A. (1970) *Sanity, Madness and the Family: Families of Schizophrenics*, Harmondsworth: Penguin.

Lamphere, L. (1977) 'Review essay: anthropology.' *Signs* 2(3): 612–27.

Lancet editorial (1974) 'The pill off prescription.' *Lancet* 2:933–4.

Land, H. (1976) 'Women: supporters or supported?' In D. Barker and S. Allen (eds), *Sexual Divisions and Society: Process and Change*, pp. 108–32. London: Tavistock.

Laplanche, J. and Pontalis, J-B. (1973) *The Language of Psychoanalysis*, London: Hogarth.

Lasch, C. (1977) *Haven in a Heartless World: The Family Besieged*, New York: Basic Books.

Laslett, P. (1965) *The World We Have Lost*, London: Methuen.

Lauritsen, J. and Thorstad, D, (1974) *The Early Homosexual Rights Movement (1864–1935)*, New York: Times Change Press.

Leach, E.R. (1970) *Lévi-Strauss*, London: Fontana/Collins.

Leach, E.R. (1978) ' "Cultura", and "Natura-cultura".' In *Enciclopedia Finandi*, Italy.

Leach, P. (1979) *Who Cares? A New Deal for Mothers and Their Small Children*, Harmondsworth: Penguin.

Leeson, J. and Gray, J. (1978) *Women and Medicine*, London: Tavistock.

Lehrman, D.S. (1970) 'Semantic and conceptual issues in the nature-nurture problem.' In L.R. Aronson, E. Tobach, D.S. Lehrman and J.S. Rosenblatt (eds), *The Development and Evolution of Behaviour*, San Francisco: Freeman.

Lemaire, A. (1977) *Jacques Lacan*, London: Routledge & Kegan Paul.

Lenin, V.I. (1972) 'The working class and neo-Malthusianism', 'To Inessa Armand', and Appendix, 'My recollections of Lenin' by Clara Zetkin. In *On the Emancipation of Women*, prepared by the Soviet Women's Committee. Moscow: Progress Publishers.

LePlay, F. (1855) *Les ouvriers Européens*, Paris: L'Imprimerie Imperiale.

Lesbian Left (1977) A collection of papers by women in Lesbian Left. For the National Women's Liberation Conference London.

Lévi-Strauss, C. (1969) *The Elementary Structures of Kinship*, London: Eyre & Spottiswood. (First published 1949.)

Lévi-Strauss, C. (1977) *Structural Anthropology*, vol. 2. London: Allen Lane. (First published 1973.)

Lewis, I.M. (1966) 'Spirit possession and deprivation cults.' *Man*, n.s. 1:307–29.

Lewis, I.M. (1970) 'A structural approach to witchcraft and spirit possession.' In M. Douglas (ed.), *Witchcraft Confessions and Accusations*, pp. 293–310. ASA Monograph 9, London: Tavistock.

Lewis, I.M. (1971) *Ecstatic Religion*, Harmondsworth: Penguin.

Lewis, I.M. and Wilson, P.J. (1967) 'Spirits and the sex war.' Correspondence in *Man*. n.s. 2:626–9.

Lidz, T. (1968) *The Person: His Development Throughout the Life Cycle*, New York: Basic Books.

Liebowitz, L. (1975) 'Changing views of women in society.' *Reviews in Anthropology* 2:532–6.

Linford Rees, W.L. (1976) *A Short Textbook of Psychiatry*, 2nd edition. London: Hodder & Stoughton.

Lipshitz, S. (1978) 'Women and psychiatry.' In J. Chetwynd and O. Hartnett (eds), *The Sex Role System*, pp.93–108. London: Routledge & Kegan Paul.

Lipshitz, S., (ed.) (1978) *Tearing the Veil: Essays in Femininity*, London: Routledge & Kegan Paul.

Litman, G. (1978) 'Clinical aspects of sex-role stereotyping.' In J. Chetwynd and O. Hartnett (eds), *The Sex Role System*, pp. 109–26. London: Routledge & Kegan Paul.

Llewelyn-Davies, M. (1978) 'Two contexts of solidarity among pastoral Masai women.' In P. Caplan and J. Bujra (eds), *Women United, Women Divided*, pp. 206–37. London: Tavistock.

Llewelyn-Davies, M. (n.d.) 'Women, warriors and patriarchs.' Unpublished paper.

Llewelyn-Davies, M., (ed.) (1978) *Maternity: Letters from Working Women*, London: Virago Press.

Lloyd, B. and Archer, J. (1976) *Exploring Sex Differences*, London: Academic Press.

Loux, F. (1978) *Le jeune enfant et son corps dans la medecine traditionnelle*, Paris: Flammarion.

Luker, K. (1975) *Taking Chances: Abortion and the Decision not to Contracept*, Berkeley, Cal.: University of California Press.

Lupton, T. (1963) *On the Shop Floor*, London: Pergamon Press.

m/f: a feminist journal, London: 1978.

Macaulay, R. (1978) 'The myth of female superiority in language.' *Journal of Child Language* 5:353–63.

Macchiocchi, M-A. (1979) 'Female sexuality in Fascist ideology.' *Feminist Review* 1(1):67–82.

Maccoby, E.E. and Jacklin, C.N. (1975) *The Psychology of Sex Differences*, London: Oxford University Press.

MacCormack, Carol Hoffer (1972) 'Mende and Sherbro women in high office.' *Canadian Journal of African Studies* 6:151–64.

MacCormack, Carol Hoffer (1974) 'Madam Yoko: ruler of the Kpa Mende confederacy.' In M. Rosaldo and L. Lamphere (eds), *Women, Culture and Society*, Stanford: Stanford University Press.

MacCormack, Carol Hoffer (1975) 'Bundu: political implications of female solidarity in a secret society.' In D. Raphael (ed.), *Being Female: Reproduction, Power and Change*, pp. 155–63. The Hague: Mouton.

MacCormack, Carol Hoffer (1979) 'Health, fertility and childbirth in the Moyamba District, Sierra Leone.' In C. MacCormack (ed.), *Comparative Studies of Fertility and Childbirth*, London: Academic Press.

MacCormack, Carol (1980) 'Nature. gender, and society.' In C. MacCormack and M. Strathern (eds), *Nature, Culture and Gender*, Cambridge: Cambridge University Press.

MacCormack, Carol, and Strathern, M., (eds) (1980) *Nature Culture and Gender*, New York: Cambridge University Press.

Macfarlane, A. (1977a) 'History, anthropology and the study of communities.' *Social History* 5:631–52.

Macfarlane, A. (1977b) *Reconstructing Historical Communities*, Cambridge: Cambridge University Press.

Macfarlane, A. (1978) *The Origins of English Individualism: The Family, Property and Social Transition*, Oxford: Basil Blackwell.

Macintyre, S. (1974) 'Who wants babies? – The social construction of instincts.' Paper presented at the British Sociological Association Conference on Sexual Division and Society.

McIntosh, M. (1968) 'The homosexual role.' *Social Problems* 16(2)' 182–92.

McLaren, A. (1977) 'Women's work and the regulation of family size: the question of abortion in the nineteenth century.' *History Workshop Journal* 4:70–81.

McLaren, A. (1978) *Birth Control in Nineteenth-century England*, London: Croom Helm.

Madden, J.F. (1973) *The Economics of Sex Discrimination*, Lexington, Mass.: Lexington Books.

Maher, V. (1974) *Women and Property in Morocco*, Cambridge: Cambridge University Press.

Makan, M. (1954) *A Village in Anatolia*, New York: Valentine Mitchell & Co.

Malcolm, J. (1978) 'The one-way mirror.' *The New Yorker* 15 May: 39–114.

Mandel, E. (1975) *Late Capitalism*, London: New Left Books.

Mandelbaum, D.G. (1972) *Society in India*, vol. 1. Berkeley, Cal.: University of California Press.

Marcus, S. (1969) *The Other Victorians*, London: Corgi.

Marcuse, H. (1972) *Eros and Civilisation*, London: Sphere.

Martin, D. (1977) *Battered Wives*, New York: Pocket Books.

Martin, M.K. and Voorhies, B. (1975) *Female of the Species*, New York: Columbia University Press.

Marwick, A. (1977) *Women at War 1914–18*, London: Fontana and the Imperial War Museum.

Marx, K. (1968) 'Theses on Feuerbach.' In K. Marx and F. Engels, *Selected Works*, (1 volume), pp. 28–30. London: Lawrence & Wishart.

Marx, K. (1970) *Critique of Hegel's Philosophy of Right*, Cambridge Studies in the History and Theory of Politics. Cambridge: Cambridge University Press. (First published in 1843.)

Marx, K. (1976) *Capital*, vol. 1. Harmondsworth: Penguin.

Marx, K. and Engels, F. (1968) *Manifesto of the Communist Party*. In *Selected Works of Marx and Engels*, pp. 31–63. London: Lawrence & Wishart.

Mason, T. (1976) 'Women in Nazi Germany.' *History Workshop Journal* 1: 74–113, and 2: 5–32.

Mathieu, N-C. (1978) 'Man-culture and woman-nature?' *Women's Studies International Quarterly* 1:55–65. (First published in 1973.)

Matriarchy Study Group (1977) *Goddess Shrew*, London: Matriarchy Study Group.

Matriarchy Study Group (n.d.) *Menstrual Taboos*, London: Matriarchy Study Group.

Matthiasson, C.J. (ed.) (1974) *Many Sisters: Women in Cross-cultural Perspective*, New York: Free Press.

Mause, L., de (ed.) (1976) *The History of Childhood*, London: Souvenir Press.

Maynard, M. (1979) 'Social work responses to domestic violence.' Paper given at the Women's Research and Resources Centre Summer School, Bradford.

Mayo, M., (ed.) (1977) *Women in the Community*, London: Routledge & Kegan Paul.

Mead, M. (1935) *Sex and Temperament in Three Primitive Societies*, New York: William Morrow & Mentor.

Medick, H. (1976) 'The proto-industrial family economy: the structural function of household and family during the transition from peasant society to industrial capitalism.' *Social History* 3:291–315.

Meek, R., (ed.) (1953) *Marx and Engels on Malthus*, London: Lawrence & Wishart.

Meggitt, M.S. (1964) 'Male-female relationships in the Highlands of Australian New Guinea.' In J.B. Watson (ed.), *New Guinea: The Central Highlands. American Anthropologist* 66 (4, pt. 4):204–24.

Michelet, J. (1860) *La Femme*, Paris: Hachette.

Middleton, C. (1974) 'Sexual inequality and stratification theory.' In F. Parkin (ed.), *The Social Analysis of Class Structure*, pp. 179–203. London: Tavistock.

Milkman, R. (1976) 'Women's work and the economic crisis: some lessons of the Great Depression. *The Review of Radical Political Economy* 8(1):73–97.

Miller, J. (1978) *The Body in Question*. London: Jonathan Cape.

Miller, J.B. (1978) *Towards a New Psychology of Women*, Harmondsworth: Penguin.

Millett, K. (1977) *Sexual Politics*, London: Virago Press.

Mincer, J. and Polachek, S. (1974) 'Family investments in human capital: earnings of women.' *Journal of Political Economy* 82:S76–S108.

Minge-Kalman, W. (1978) 'The industrial revolution and the European family: the institutionalisation of "childhood" as a market for family labor.' *Comparative Studies in Society and History* 20:454–68.

Minuchin, S. (1974) *Families and Family Therapy*, London: Tavistock.

Mitchell, J. (1974) *Psychoanalysis and Feminism*, London: Allen Lane.

Mitchell, J. and Oakley, A. (eds.) (1976) *The Rights and Wrongs of Women*, Harmondsworth: Penguin.

Mitchell, R. (1975) *Depression*, Harmondsworth: Penguin, in association with *Mind*.

Mogey, J.M. (1957) 'A century of declining paternal authority.' *Journal of Marriage and the Family* 19:234–9.

Moore, T. (1967) 'Language and intelligence: a longitudinal study of the first eight years.' Part 1: Patterns of development in boys and girls. *Human Development* 10:88–106.

Morpeth, R. (in press) 'Midwives in a Punjabi village.' *Quaderni Historici*. Turin, Italy.

Moscucci, O. (1978) 'Femininity and mental illness in nineteenth-century England.' B.A. dissertation, University of Bristol.

Moss, H.A. (1967) 'Sex, age and state as determinants of mother-infant interaction. *Merrill-Palmer Quarterly* 13:19–36.

Mozart, W.A. (1971) *Die Zauberflote and Die Entfuhrung aus dem Serail, with an Introduction by Brigid Brophy*, London: Cassell.

Muller, V. (1977) 'The formation of the state and the oppression of women: some theoretical considerations and a case study in England and Wales.' *Review of Radical Political Economics* 9(3):7–21.

Murphy, J. (1972) *The Education Act 1870: Text and Commentary*, Newton Abbot: David & Charles.

Myrdal, A. and Klein, V. (1956) *Women's Two Roles*, London: Routledge & Kegan Paul.

Myron, N. and Bunch, C., (eds) (1975) *Lesbianism and the Women's Movement*, Baltimore, Md.: Diana Press.

Nair, Kusum (1961) *Blossoms in the Dust*, New York: Praeger.

Nathanson, C. (1975) 'Illness and the feminine role: a theoretical review.' *Social Science and Medicine* 9:57–62.

National Women's Aid Federation (1977) *Battered Women, Refuges and Women's Aid*. Available from NWAF, 374 Gray's Inn Road, London N1.

National Women's Aid Federation (1978) *Seventh National Conference*, Available from NWAF, 374 Gray's Inn Road, London N1.

Needham, R. (1967) 'Right and left in Myoro symbolic classification.' *Africa* 37:425–52.

(Dr) Numa Praetorius (pseud.) (1899) 'Die strafrechtlichen Bestimmungen gegen den gleichgeschechtlichen Verkehr historisch und kritisch dargestellt.' *Jahrbuch für sexuelle Zwischenstufen* I:97–158.

Oakley, A. (1972) *Sex, Gender and Society*, London: M. Temple Smith.

Oakley, A. (1974) *The Sociology of Housework*, London: Martin Robertson.

Oakley, A. (1975) 'The medicalised trap of motherhood.' *New Society*, Dec.: 639–41.

Oakley, A. (1976a) *Housewife*, Harmondsworth: Penguin.

Oakley, A. (1976b) 'The family, marriage, and its relationship to illness.' In D. Tuckett (ed.), *An Introduction to Medical Sociology*, pp. 74–109. London: Tavistock.

Oakley, A. (1979) *Becoming a Mother*, London: Martin Robertson.

Oakley, A. (1980) *Women Confined*, London: Martin Robertson.

Offe, C. (1976) *Industry and Inequality*, London: Edward Arnold.

Orbach, S. (1978) *Fat is a Feminist Issue: The Anti-diet Guide to Permanent Weight Loss*, London: Paddington Press. (London: Hamlyn 1979.)

Oren, L. (1974) 'The welfare of women in laboring families: England, 1860–1950.' In M. Hartman and L. Banner (eds), *Clio's Consciousness Raised*, New York: Harper.

Ortner, S. (1974) 'Is female to male as nature is to culture?' In M. Rosaldo and L. Lamphere (eds), *Women, Culture and Society*, pp. 67–87. Stanford: Stanford University Press.

O'Sullivan, S. (1975) 'Sterilisation.' *Spare Rib* 33:10.

Ottinger, D. and Simmons, J. (1964) 'Behaviour of human neonates and pre-natal maternal anxiety.' *Psychol. Rep.* 14:391–4.

Owen, L. (1978) 'Opportunities knocked.' *Observer* 15 Oct. 1978.

Owen, R, (1835) *Lectures on the Marriages of the Priesthood of the Old Immoral World*. Leeds. n.p.

Pahl, J. (1978) *A Refuge for Battered Women*, London: HMSO.

Parlee, M.B. and Rajagopal, J. (1974) 'Sex differences on the embedded-figures test: a cross-cultural comparison of college students in India and in the United States.' *Perception and Motor Skills* 39:1311–14.

Parry, L.A. (1932) *Criminal Abortion*, London: John Bale, Sons and Daniellson.

Parsons, T. (1951) *The Social System*, London: Routledge & Kegan Paul.

Patterson, G.R., Littman, R.A. and Bricher, W. (1967) 'Assertive behaviour in children: a step toward a theory of aggression.' *Monograph Soc. Res. Ch. Dev.* 32, serial no. 113.

Paulme, D., (ed.) (1971) *Women of Tropical Africa*, Berkeley, Cal.: Unversity of California Press.

Payne, J. (1975) 'Childless families.' Research proposal, MRC Medical Sociology Unit. Aberdeen.

Pearsall, R. (1969) *The Worm in the Bud*, Harmondsworth: Penguin.

Peel, J. and Potts, M. (1970) *Textbook of Contraceptive Practice*, Cambridge: Cambridge University Press.

Peristiany, J.G., (ed.) (1966) *Honour and Shame*, Chicago: University of Chicago Press.

Pethick-Lawrence, E. (1938) *My Part in a Changing World*, London.

Pettigrew, J. (1975) *Robber Noblemen: The Political System of Sikh Jats*, London: Routledge & Kegan Paul.

Phayer, J.M. (1977) *Sexual Liberation and Religion in Nineteenth-century Europe*, London: Croom Helm.

Phillips, A. and Rakusen, J. (1978) *Our Bodies Ourselves: A Health Book by and for Women*, Harmondsworth: Penguin.

Phillips, R. (1976) 'Women and family breakdown in eighteenth-century France: Rouen 1780—1800.' *Social History* 2:197—218.

Piore, M. (1970) 'Manpower policy.' In S. Beer and R. Barringer (eds), *The State and the Poor*, Cambridge, Mass.: Winthrop Publishing.

Pitt-Rivers, J. (1968) 'Honor.' In D. Sills (ed.), *Encyclopedia of the Social Sciences*, vol. 6, pp. 503—11. New York: Macmillan.

Pitt-Rivers, J. (1977) *The Fate of Shechem, or the Politics of Sex*, Cambridge: Cambridge University Press.

Pizzey, E. (1974) *Scream Quietly or the Neighbours will Hear*, Harmondsworth: Penguin.

Ploss, H.H. and Bartels, M and P. (1935) *Woman: An Historical, Gynaecological and Anthropological Compendium*, 3 vols London: Heinemann. (First published in German in 1885.)

Poster, M. (1978) *Critical Theory of the Family*, London: Pluto Press.

Potts, M., Diggory, P. and Peel, J. (1977) *Abortion*, Cambridge: Cambridge University Press.

Power, E. (1975) *Medieval Women*, Cambridge: Cambridge University Press.

Prather, J. and Fidell, L.S. (1975) 'Sex differences in the content and style of medical advertisements.' *Social Science and Medicine* 9:23—6.

Psychohistory Review. Springfield, Ill., 1976-

Quinn, N. (1977) 'Anthropological studies on women's status.' *Annual Review of Anthropology* 6:181—225.

Rae, M. (1978) 'New law for battered women.' *Roof* 15 May 1978.

Rape Crisis Centre Report (1977) London: Rape Crisis Centre.

Raphael, D., (ed.) (1975) *Being Female: Reproduction, Power, and Change*, The Hague: Mouton.

Rapoport, R. and Rapoport, R. (1971) *Dual-career Families*, Harmondsworth: Pelican.

Rapoport, R., *et al.* (1977) *Fathers, Mothers and Others*, London: Routledge of Kegan Paul.

Reed, E. (1975) *Women's Evolution: From Matriarchal Clan to Patriarchal Family*, London: Pathfinder Press.

Reich, W. (1968) *The Function of the Orgasm: Sex-economic Problems of Biological Energy*, London: Panther. (First published in German 1942.)

Reich, W. (1971a) *The Sexual Struggle of Youth*, London: Socialist Reproduction. (First published 1931.)

Reich, W. (1971b) *What is Class Consciousness?*, London: Socialist Reproduction. (First published 1933.)

Reich, W. (1972) *Dialectical Materialism and Psychoanalysis*, London: Socialist Reproduction. (First published 1929.)

Reich, W. (1975) *The Mass Psychology of Fascism*, Harmondsworth: Pelican. (First published 1934.)

Reich, W. (1974) *Sexuality and Class Struggle*, London: New Left Books. (German original 1968.)

Reiter, Reina Rapp (1975) Introduction to R.R. Reiter (ed.), *Toward an Anthropology of Women*, pp. 11–19. New York: Monthly Review Press.

Reiter, Reina Rapp (1977) 'The search for origins: unravelling the threads of gender hierarchy.' *Critique of Anthropology, Women's Issue* vols 9 and 10, pp. 5–24.

Reiter, Reina Rapp (1979) 'Review essay: anthropology.' *Signs* 4(3): 497–513.

Report from the Select Committee on Violence in Marriage, together with the Proceedings of the Committee (1975). Session 1974–5, vol. 2. London: HMSO, H.C. 533–1.

Revolutionary Communist Group (1976) *Women's Oppression under Capitalism*, London: RCG Publications.

Reynolds, V. (1976) *The Biology of Human Action*, San Francisco: Freeman.

Rich, A. (1977) *Of Woman Born*, London: Virago.

Richards, A.I. (1950) 'Some types of family structure among the central Bantu.' In A.R. Radcliffe-Brown and D. Forde (eds), *African Systems of Kinship and Marriage*, pp. 207–51. London: Oxford University Press.

Richards, A.I. (1956) *Chisungu: A Girl's Initiation Ceremony among the Bemba of Northern Rhodesia*, London: Faber & Faber.

Richards, M.P.M. (1976) 'Parents and children and non-accidental injury.' Paper presented at a symposium on child abuse at the Royal Society of Medicine, London.

Richman, N. (1976) 'Depression in mothers of preschool children.' *Journal of Child Psychology and Psychiatry* 17:75–8.

Ritcher, H. (1974) *The Family as Patient: The Origin, Nature and Treatment* of Marital and Family Conflicts, London: Souvenir Press.

Riley, D. (1977) 'What do women want? the question of choice in the conduct of labour.' In T. Chard and M. Richards (eds), *Benefits and Hazards of the New Obstetrics*, pp. 62–71. Spastics International Medical Publications. London: Heinemann.

Riley, D. (1978) 'Developmental psychology, biology and marxism.' *Ideology and Consciousness* 4:73–91.

Riley, D. (1979) 'War in the nursery.' *Feminist Review* 2:82–108.

Roberts, D. (1978) 'The paterfamilias of the Victorian governing classes.' In A. Wohl (ed.), *The Victorian Family*, pp. 59–81 London: Croom Helm.

Robertson, P. (1976) 'Home as a nest: middle-class childhood in nineteenth-century Europe.' In L. de Mause (ed.), *The History of Childhood*, pp. 407–31. London: Souvenir Press.

Rogers, L. (1976) 'Male hormones and behaviour.' In B. Lloyd and J. Archer (eds), *Exploring Sex Differences*, pp. 157–84. London: Academic Press.

Rogers, S.C. (1975) 'Female forms of power and the myth of male dominance: a model of female/male interaction in peasant society.' *American Ethnologist* 2:727–56.

Rogers, S.C. (1978) 'Women's place: a critical review of anthropological theory.' *Comparative Studies in Society and History* 20:123–62.

Rohrlich-Leavitt, R., (ed.) (1975) *Women Cross-culturally: Change and Challenge*, The Hague: Mouton.

Rosaldo, M. (1974) 'Woman, culture and society: a theoretical overview.' In M. Rosaldo and L. Lamphere (eds), *Women Culture and Society*, pp. 17–42. Stanford: Stanford University Press.

Rosaldo, M. and Lamphere, L., (eds) (1974) *Women, Culture and Society*, Stanford: Stanford University Press.

Rosch, E. (1978) 'Human categorisation.' In N. Warren (ed.), *Advances in Cross-cultural Psychology* vol. 1. London: Academic Press.

Rosser, J. (1978) 'Sexual identity on becoming a mother: some cultural contradictions.' British Sociological Association Medical Sociology Conference, York.

Rothman, D. (1971) *The Discovery of the Asylum: Social Order and Disorder in the New Republic*, Boston: Little Brown.

Routh, C.H.F. (1878) Medical Press Circular. Quoted in J. Peel, and M. Potts, *Textbook of Contraceptive Practice*, (1970) pp. 5–6. Cambridge: Cambridge University Press.

Rowbotham, S. (1977) *A New World for Women: Stella Browne, Socialist-feminist*, London: Pluto Press.

Rowbotham, S. and Weeks, J. (1977) *Socialism and the New Life*, London: Pluto Press.

Rubery, J. (1978) 'Structured labour markets, worker organisation and low pay.' *Cambridge Journal of Economics* 2:17–36.

Rubin, G. (1975) 'The traffic in women: notes on the "political economy" of sex.' In R. R. Reiter (ed.), *Towards an Anthropology of Women*, pp. 157–210. New York: Monthly Review Press.

Rutter, M. (1972) *Maternal Deprivation Reassessed*, Harmondsworth: Penguin.

Sacks, K. (1974) 'Engels revisited: women, the organisation of production, and private property.' In M. Rosaldo and L. Lamphere (eds), *Women, Culture and Society*, pp. 207–22. Stanford: Stanford University Press.

Sacks, K. (1976) 'State bias and women's status.' *American Anthropologist* 78:565–9.

Sahlins, M. (1976) *Culture and Practical Reason*, Chicago: University of Chicago Press.

Sahlins, M. (1977) *The Use and Abuse of Biology: An Anthropological Critique of Sociobiology*, London: Tavistock.

Sanday, P.R. (1973) 'Toward a theory of the status of women.' *American Anthropologist* 75:1682–1700.

Sanday, P.R. (1974) 'Female status in the public domain.' In M. Rosaldo and L. Lamphere (eds), *Women, Culture and Society*, pp. 189–206. Stanford: Stanford University Press.

Sandell, S. and Shapiro, H. (1977) 'The theory of human capital and earnings of women: women's earnings re-examined.' *Journal of Human Resources* 13:103–17.

Sandler, M., (ed.) (1978) *Mental Illness in Pregnancy and the Puerperium*, Oxford: Oxford University Press.

Sanger, M. (1919) 'Why not birth control in America?' *Birth Control Review*, May, 10–12. Quoted in L. Gordon, *Woman's Body, Woman's Right: A Social History of Birth Control in America*, 1977, Harmondsworth: Penguin.

Sayers, J. (1980) 'Psychological sex differences.' In Brighton Women and Science Collective (eds), *Alice Through the Microscope*, pp. 42–61, London: Virago.

Schaffer, R. (1976) *Mothering*, London: Fontana.

Scheffler, H.W. (1966) 'Structuralism in anthropology.' In *Structuralism*, special edition of *Yale French Studies* October

Schlegel, A. (1972) *Male Dominance and Female Autonomy: Domestic Authority in Matrilineal Societies*, New Haven: Human Relations Area Files Press.

Schlesinger, R., (ed.) (1949) *Changing Attitudes in Soviet Russia: The Family in the USSR*, London: Routledge & Kegan Paul.

Schreiner, O. (1977) *Woman and Labour*, with introduction by Jane Graves. London: Virago.

Scott, H. (1976) *Women and Socialism*, London: Motive Books, Allison & Busby.

Scott, J. (1977) Review of Edward Shorter, *The Making of the Modern Family*, *Signs* 2:692−6.

Scott, J. and Tilly, L. (1975) 'Women's work and the family in nineteenth-century Europe.' *Comparative Studies in Society and History* 17:36−64.

Scull, A. (1977) *Decarceration. Community Treatment and the Deviant − a Radical View*, Englewood Cliffs, N.J.: Prentice-Hall.

Seccombe, W. (1974) 'The housewife and her labour under capitalism.' *New Left Review* 83:3−24.

Sève, L. (1975) *Marxism and the Theory of Human Personality*, London: Lawrence & Wishart.

Sharma, U. (1978) 'Segregation and its consequences in India.' In P. Caplan and J. Bujra (eds), *Women United, Women Divided*, pp. 259−82. London: Tavistock.

Sheilds, S. (1978) 'Sex differences and nineteenth-century scientists.' *New Scientist*, December.

Shorter, E. (1975) *The Making of the Modern Family*, New York: Basic Books.

Shorter, E. (1977) 'Women's diseases before 1900.' Unpublished paper.

Siegler, M. and Osmond, H. (1974) *Models of Medicine, Models of Madness*, New York: Macmillan.

Sillitoe, A. (1973) *Britain in Figures: A Handbook of Social Statistics*, 2nd edition. Harmondsworth: Penguin.

Singh Bedi, Sohinder (1971) *Folklore of Punjab*, India: National Book Trust.

Skultans, V., (ed.) (1975) *Madness and Morals: Ideas on Insanity in the Nineteenth Century*, London: Routledge & Kegan Paul.

Smart, C. and Smart, B. (1978) *Women, Sexuality and Social Control*, London: Routledge & Kegan Paul.

Smith, C. and Lloyd, B. (1978) 'Maternal behaviour and perceived sex of infant revisited.' *Child Development* 49:1263−5.

Smith, M. and Kane, P. (1975) *The Pill off Prescription*, London: Birth Control Trust.

Smith, P. (1979) 'Speech markers and sex.' In H. Giles and K. Scherer (eds), *Social Markers in Speech*, Cambridge: Cambridge University Press.

Smith-Rosenberg, C. (1972) 'The hysterical woman: sex roles and role conflict in nineteenth-century America.' *Social Research* 39: 652−78.

Snell, M. (1979) 'The Equal Pay and Sex Discrimination Acts: their impact in the workplace.' *Feminist Review* 1:37−57.

Spencer, R.F. (1968) 'Spouse-exchange among the North Alaskan Eskimo.' In P. Bohannan and J. Middleton (eds), *Marriage, Family and Residence*, pp. 131−44. Garden City, N.Y.: The Natural History Press.

Srinavas, M.N. (1952) *Religion and Society among the Coorgs of South India*, Oxford: Oxford University Press.

Stärcke, S. (1921) 'The castration complex.' *International Journal of Psychoanalysis* 2:179–201.

Stedman Jones, G. (1976) *Outcast London*, Harmondsworth: Penguin.

Stedman Jones, G. (1977) 'Class expression versus social control?' *History Workshop Journal* 4:162–70.

Steinmetz, S.K. (1978) 'The battered husband syndrome.' *Victimology: an International Journal* 2(3–4):499–509.

Stengel, E. (1970) *Suicide and Attempted Suicide*, Harmondsworth: Penguin.

Stevenson, M. (1978) 'Wage differences between men and women: economic theories.' In A. Stromberg and S. Harkness (eds), *Women Working*, Palo Alto, Cal.: Mayfield.

Stewart-Park, A. and Cassidy, J. (1977) *We're Here: Conversations with Lesbian Women*, London: Quartet.

Stimson, G. (1975a) 'The message of psychotropic drug ads.' *Journal of Communication* 25(3): 153–60.

Stimson, G. (1975b) 'Women in a doctored world.' *New Society*, 1 May: vol. 32, no. 656, pp. 256–7.

Stone, L. (1977) *The Family, Sex and Marriage in England, 1500–1800*, London: Weidenfeld & Nicolson. (Shortened version published by Penguin in 1979.)

Strathern, M. (1972) *Women in Between: Female Roles in a Male World, Mount Hagen, New Guinea*, New York: Seminar Press.

Strathern, M. (1976) 'An anthropological perspective.' In B. Lloyd and J. Archer (eds), *Exploring Sex Differences*, London: Academic Press.

Strathern, M. (1978) 'The achievement of sex: paradoxes in Hagen gender-thinking.' In E. Schwimmer (ed.), *The Yearbook of Symbolic Anthropology*, London: Hurst.

Strathern, M. (1980) 'No nature, no culture: the Hagen case.' In C. MacCormack and M. Strathern (eds), *Nature, Culture and Gender*, Cambridge: Cambridge University Press.

Strathern, M. (in press) 'Self-interest and the social good: some implications of Hagen gender imagery.' In S. Ortner and H. Whitehead (eds), *Sexual Meanings*. Cambridge: CUP.

Stross, B. (1978) 'Tzeltal conceptions of power.' In R.D. Fogelson and R.N. Adams (eds), *The Anthropology of Power* pp. 271–86. New York: Academic Press.

Stycos, J.M. (1962) 'A critique of the traditional planned parenthood approach in underdeveloped areas.' In C.V. Kiser (ed.), *Research in Family Planning*, pp. 477–501. Princeton, NJ: Princeton University Press.

Sullerot, E. (1971) *Women, Society and Change*, New York: McGraw-Hill.

Suter, L. and Miller, H.P. (1973) 'Income differences between men and career women.' *American Journal of Sociology* 78:962—74.

Sutherland, G. (1971) *Elementary Education in the Nineteenth Century*, London: Historical Association.

Sutton, J. (1979) *Women's Aid: State Intervention and Collaboration*, unpublished paper, Department of Social Work, University of Bradford.

Swan, A., Binnington, L. and Potter Lee, N. (1978) 'A woman's perspective.' Paper presented at the International Conference on Child Abuse and Neglect. London: September 1978.

Szasz, T. (1963) *Law, Liberty and Psychiatry*, New York: Macmillan.

Szasz, T. (1965) *Psychiatric Justice*, New York: Macmillan.

Szasz, T. (1970a) *The Manufacture of Madness: A Comparative Study of the Inquisition and the Mental Health Movement*, New York and London: Harper & Row.

Szasz, T. (1970b) *Ideology and Insanity*, Harmondsworth: Penguin.

Szasz, T. (1972) *The Myth of Mental Illness*, London: Paladin.

Taylor, B. (1978) 'The woman-power: religious heresy and feminism in early English socialism.' In S. Lipshitz (ed.), *Tearing the Veil*, pp. 119—44. London: Routledge & Kegan Paul.

Thom, M. (1979) 'Psychoanalysis and Ethnography.' *Cambridge Anthropology*, 4(i):49—74 (Part I) and 4(ii):45—77 (Part II).

Thomas, K. (1977) 'The changing family.' *The Times Literary Supplement*, 21 October 1977: 1226—7.

Thompson, C. (1973) 'Penis envy in women' (1943), pp. 52—57; 'Some effects of the derogatory attitude toward female sexuality' (1950), pp. 58—68; 'Cultural pressures in the psychology of women' (1942), pp. 69—84. All in J.Baker Miller (ed.), *Psychoanalysis and Women*, Harmondsworth: Penguin.

Thompson, E. (1967) 'Time, work-discipline, and industrial capitalism.' *Past and Present* 38:56—97.

Tidswell, H.H. (1906) 'Abortifacients and the decreasing birthrate.' *British Medical Journal*, I, p. 1080.

Tiffany, S.W. (1978) 'Models and the social anthropology of women: a preliminary assessment.' *Man*, n.s. 13:34—51.

Tiger, L. (1969) *Men in Groups*, London: Nelson.

Tilly, L. and Scott, J. (1978) *Women, Work and Family*, New York: Holt, Rinehart & Winston.

Trotsky, L. (1972) *The Revolution Betrayed*, Trans. Max Eastmann. New York: Pathfinder Press. (Originally published 1937.)

Trotsky, L. (1973) 'From the old family to the new,' *Pravda* (1923), and 'To build socialism means to emancipate women and protect mothers,' *Za Novi Byt* (Dec. 1925). Translated in *Women and the Family*, New York: Pathfinder Press.

Trudgill, P. (1975) 'Sex, covert prestige, and linguistic change in the urban British English of Norwich.' In B. Thorne and N. Henley (eds), *Language and Sex: Difference and Dominance*, pp. 88—104. Rowley, Mass.: Newbury House Publishers.

Tuckett, D., (ed.) (1976) *An Introduction to Medical Sociology*, London: Tavistock.

Tunnadine, L.P.D. (1970) *Contraception and Sexual Life*, London: Tavistock.

Tylor, E.B. (1871) *Researches into the Early History and Development of Mankind*, London.

van Baal, J. (1966) *The Dema: Description and Analysis of the Marind-Anim Culture (South New Guinea)*, The Hague: Martinus Nijhoff.

Veith, I. (1965) *Hysteria: The History of a Disease,* Chicago: University of Chicago Press.

Vogel, L. (1978) 'The contested domain: a note on the family in the transition to capitalism.' *Marxist Perspectives* 1:50—7.

Wainwright, H. (1978) 'Women and the division of labour.' In P. Abrams (ed.), *Work, Urbanism and Inequality*, pp. 160—205. London: Weidenfield & Nicolson.

Ward, B. (1970) 'Temper tantrums in Kau Sai: some speculations upon their effects.' In P. Mayer (ed.), *Socialisation: The Approach from Social Anthropology*, pp. 109—25. London: Tavistock.

Weber, G. (1978) 'Women and theories of degeneration.' Unpublished paper presented to the Cambridge Women in Society seminar series, November 1978.

Weeks, J. (1977a) 'Havelock Ellis and the politics of sex reform.' In S. Rowbotham and J. Weeks, *Socialism and the New Life*, pp. 139—85. London: Pluto Press.

Weeks, J. (1977b) *Coming Out: Homosexual Politics in Britian, From the Nineteenth Century to the Present*, London: Quartet Books.

Weeks, J. (1978) 'Movements of affirmation: sexual meanings and homosexual identities.' Paper presented to to the British Sociological Association Conference, 1978.

Weiner, A. (1976) *Women of Value, Men of Renown*, Austin, Texas: University of Texas Press.

Weir, A. (1977) 'Battered women.' In M. Mayo (ed.), *Women in the Community*, London: Routledge & Kegan Paul.

Weitz, S. (1977) *Sex Roles*, Oxford: Oxford University Press.

Welter, B. (1966) 'The cult of true womanhood: 1820—1860.' *American Quarterly* 18:151—74.

Werbner, R.P., Lewis, I.M. (1968) 'Spirits and the sex war.' Correspondence, in *Man*, n.s. 3:129—31.

West, D.J. (1977) *Homosexuality Re-examined*, London: Duckworth.

Westergaard, J. and Resler, H. (1975) *Class in a Capitalist Society*, Harmondsworth: Penguin.

Wilden, A. (1977) 'Critique of phallocentrism: Daniel Paul Shreber on women's liberation.' In A. Wilden, *System and Structure*, pp. 278–301. London: Tavistock.

Williams, R. (1976a) *Keywords: A Vocabulary of Culture and Society*, Glasgow and London: Fontana/Croom Helm.

Wilson, E. (1976a) 'The existing research into battered women.' National Women's Aid Federation, London: 374, Grays Inn Road, London WCI.

Wilson, E. (1976b) *Women and the Welfare State*, London: Tavistock.

Wilson, E.O. (1975) *Sociobiology: The New Synthesis*, Cambridge, Mass.: Belknap Press of Harvard University Press.

Wilson, P.J. (1967) 'Status ambiguity and spirit possession.' *Man*, n.s. 3:366–78.

Winship, J. (1978) *Women at Work Bibliography*, Birmingham: Centre for Contemporary Cultural Studies. Occasional Paper, no. 54.

Wohl, A., (ed.) (1978) *The Victorian Family*, London: Croom Helm.

Wolf, M. (1974) *Women and the Family in Rural Taiwan*, Stanford: Stanford University Press.

Wolff, C. (1973) *Love between Women*, London: Duckworth.

Wolffson. S. (1949) 'Socialism and the family.' (Extract from paper, Moscow, 1936.) Trans. in.R. Schlesinger. *Changing Attitudes in Soviet Russia: The Family in the USSR*, pp.280–315. London: Routledge & Kegan Paul.

Women Against Population Control Group (1973) 'Fertility: economics and ideology'. P. Halperin, J. Kenrick and B. Segal, 2nd Women's Liberation and Socialism Conference, September 1973. London.

Women Against Population Control Group (1974). 'Bucharest: what kind of victory?' London.

Women's Research and Resources Centre (1977). *Women's Liberation: An Introduction*, London: WRRC, Women's Information, Referral and Enquiry Service, A Woman's Place.

Wortis, R.P. (1971) 'The acceptance of the concept of maternal role by behavioural scientists: its effects on women.' *American Journal of Ortho-psychiatry* 41(5):733–45.

Wright, E.O. and Perrone, L. (1977) 'Marxist class categories and income inequality.' *American Sociological Review* 42:32–55.

Wright, H. (1972) 'Fifty years of family planning.' *Family Planning* 21: 63–7.

Wynn, M. and Wynn, A. (1973) *Some Consequences of Induced Abortion to Children Born Subsequently*, London: Foundation for Education and Research in Childbearing.

Young, K. and Harris, O. (1976) 'The subordination of women in cross-cultural perspective.' In *Papers on Patriarchy Conference*. London 1976, pp.38–52. Women's Publishing Collective, Sussex. (OP)

Young, M. (1952) 'Distribution of income within the family.' *British Journal of Sociology* 3:305–21.

Young, M. and Willmott, P. (1975) *The Symmetrical Family*, Harmondsworth: Penguin.

Yudkin, S. and Holme, A. (1963) *Working Mothers and Their Children*, London: Michael Joseph.

Zaretsky, E. (1976) *Capitalism, the Family and Personal Life*, London: Pluto Press.

Note

The following important titles have appeared since this book was written.

Amsden, A. (ed.) (1980) The Economics of Women and Work, Hammondsworth: Penguin.

Anderson, M. (1980) *Approaches to the History of the Western Family, 1500–1914*, London: Macmillan.

Barrett, M. (1980) *Women's Oppression Today*, London: Verso.

Philips, A. & Taylor, B. (1980) 'Sex and Skill: notes towards a feminist economics', *Feminist Review, 6*, pp 79–88.

Index

Virago

If you would like to know more about Virago books, write to us at Ely House, 37 Dover Street, London W1X 4HS for a full catalogue.

Please send a stamped addressed envelope

00012662470

Book Tokens

Give them
the pleasure of choosing
Book Tokens can be bought
and exchanged at most
bookshops